Praise for

Defiant Joy

"Chesterton's explanation of Christianity makes absolute sense of the world. He reminds us that, free of our comforting delusions, reality is a tragic adventure in which we get to participate."

— DONALD MILLER
Author of the *New York Times* bestsellers *A Million Miles in a Thousand Years* and *Blue Like Jazz*

"Just as Chesterton's critical study of Charles Dickens sparked a revival of interest in Dickens's writings, Kevin Belmonte's elegant biography of G. K. Chesterton is like a full-page, four-color ad enticing one to overspend his book budget filling a shelf with the rollicking wit and reasoned faith with which Chesterton cast a magic spell over his own generation . . . and now ours."

— F. LaGARD SMITH
Compiler of *The Daily Bible*

DEFIANT JOY

The Remarkable Life & Impact of
G. K. CHESTERTON

KEVIN BELMONTE

THOMAS NELSON
Since 1798

NASHVILLE   DALLAS   MEXICO CITY   RIO DE JANEIRO

Published in Nashville, Tennessee, by Thomas Nelson. Thomas Nelson is a registered trademark of Thomas Nelson, Inc.

Thomas Nelson, Inc., titles may be purchased in bulk for educational, business, fund-raising, or sales promotional use. For information, please e-mail SpecialMarkets@ ThomasNelson.com.

A search was completed to determine whether previously published material included in this book required permission to reprint. If there has been an error, a correction will be made on subsequent editions.

Library of Congress Cataloging-in-Publication Data

Belmonte, Kevin Charles.
    Defiant joy : the remarkable life & impact of G.K. Chesterton / by Kevin Belmonte.
        p. cm.
    Includes bibliographical references and index.
    ISBN 978-1-59555-201-3
    1. Chesterton, G. K. (Gilbert Keith), 1874–1936. 2. Chesterton, G. K. (Gilbert Keith), 1874–1936—Appreciation. 3. Authors, English—20th century—Biography. I. Title. II. Title: Remarkable life and impact of G.K. Chesterton.
    PR4453.C4Z534 2011
    828'.91209—dc22
    [B]   2010025075

Printed in the United States of America

11 12 13 14 15 RRD 5 4 3 2 1

To Kelly

Contents

[T]hat joy of living which was . . . so conspicuous a trait [in Chesterton].[1]

—NEW YORK TIMES (1936)

[Chesterton] for a time cast . . . his shadow over a considerable part of the world.[2]

—NEW YORK TIMES (1936)

[Chesterton] was in most respects an unusually kind and generous man.[3]

—NEW YORK TIMES (1987)

Chesterton's writing [is] the only thing that justifies devoting a book to him in the first place. To sort out the good from the bad in his work . . . to characterize his still underrated virtues—his imaginative leaps, his brilliance as an aphorist, the music of his prose at its best . . . [4]

—NEW YORK TIMES (1987)

Mr. Chesterton talks about God because God is the most interesting subject for conversation that there is.[5]

—NEW YORK TIMES (1916)

There have been times when I read a lot of theology. The year I spent in England [after graduation from Harvard] I was very nervous and frightened, standing more or less on the threshold of my adult life and career, if any. One of the ways I assuaged my anxiety was to read a lot of Chesterton and C. S. Lewis.[6]

—JOHN UPDIKE (1986)

Author's Note

I have always admired G. K. Chesterton's gift for the simple declarative sentence. Few knew better than he how to nail one's colors to the mast. So we find him writing in the introduction to his classic study *St. Thomas Aquinas* (1933): "This book makes no pretence to be anything but a popular sketch of a great historical character who ought to be more popular. Its aim will be achieved, if it leads those who have hardly even heard of St. Thomas Aquinas to read about him in better books."

Such is the aspiration of this book: to introduce a life and legacy that should be better known. It does not in any way aspire to be a comprehensive or definitive study.

I would also add that to survey all of Chesterton's important books is a task well beyond the scope of any one volume. But among these writings are works that can lay claim to being widely influential, classics of their kind. Such is the purpose of this study: to survey the best and most influential of Chesterton's works—and to do so within the context of a remarkable life.

Chesterton commands attention in several fields: poetry, apologetics, novels, detective fiction, and literary criticism. Though not among the front rank of twentieth-century poets, he wrote some very fine poems. His epic poem, *The Ballad of the White Horse*, has been fulsomely praised by such trenchant critics and writers as C. S. Lewis, Graham Greene, and Garry Wills.[1]

Chesterton wrote three great apologetic works: *Heretics* (published in 1905), *Orthodoxy* (published in 1908), and *The Everlasting Man* (published in 1925). C. S. Lewis's debt to *The Everlasting Man* was profound: it strongly influenced his return to belief in Christianity, and he habitually recommended it to correspondents curious about matters of faith. Two of Chesterton's novels, *The Napoleon of Notting Hill* and *The Man Who Was Thursday*, are considered classics. T. S. Eliot, Kingsley Amis, and Frederick Buechner are three of the more important writers to accord them special praise.

As the author of the Father Brown mysteries, Chesterton created a sleuth whom many see as a worthy rival to Sherlock Holmes. Dorothy Sayers and P. D. James are among the many who have written with great appreciation for Chesterton's gifts in the genre of detective fiction.

Lastly, as a literary critic, Chesterton's writings on the works of Charles Dickens earned him an enduring reputation as "the greatest of all Dickens critics"—a statement given in *The Oxford Reader's Companion to Dickens*.[2] Clearly, Chesterton was a literary force to be reckoned with.

Those who care to turn these pages will soon learn of my indebtedness to many excellent books. If this book spurs some to delve more deeply into Chesterton's life and writings by way of these earlier works, I will count myself fortunate.

I also have great appreciation for a telling reflection made by Dr. William Oddie in his masterly Oxford University Press study, *Chesterton and the Romance of Orthodoxy* (2009): "Chesterton scholarship is, in a sense, in its infancy. Though Gilbert Keith Chesterton died over seventy years ago, little serious work has been done on the implications of his writings.... His works are even now rarely studied.... Much remains to be done before Chesterton's huge oeuvre can be adequately assessed as a major part of the cultural history of the last century."[3] And so it is hoped that this book might encourage young scholars to enter the rich, largely untilled field of Chesterton studies.

I will close with one further thought, or rather second a statement made by Richard Ingrams that is both accurate and just. "The new reader of Chesterton," Ingrams wrote, "will be surprised by ... how contemporary a figure he is."[4] It was this statement (along with kindred convictions from my own reading) that served as a primary inspiration for my putting pen to paper. Chesterton is in many ways our contemporary, and our need of his wisdom, art, humor, love, and humanity is as great as that of the age in which he lived— perhaps greater.

KEVIN BELMONTE
Woodholme
December 2009

Prologue

Ah, well, I am a great and sublime fool. But then I am God's fool, and all His works must be contemplated with respect.[1]

—MARK TWAIN (1877)

G. K. Chesterton was a host unto himself. A supremely gifted journalist, essayist, literary critic, and novelist, he succeeded at every kind of writing he put his hand to. His many works were marked by "startling formulations"[2] that have led some to call him "the Prince of paradox."[3]

And rightly so. But there are reasons enough to think he would have relished Twain's affirmation that he was "God's fool"—and reasons enough to think he would have said as much of himself.[4]

As it happens, he did—writing in his *Autobiography*: "I daresay that there are a good many fools who can call me a friend and also (a more chastening thought) a good many friends who can call me a fool."[5]

Twain and Chesterton were much alike.[6] Both could navigate a sentence with unerring skill. Both could laugh at themselves, and both were honest enough to say they were God's fools. Both possessed a formidable intellect and literary genius. And Chesterton, a charter member of the International Mark Twain Society, [7] had a keen appreciation for Twain's wit. This gift, Chesterton wrote,

> requires an intellectual athleticism, because it is akin to logic. A wit must have something of the same running, working, and staying power as a mathematician or a metaphysician. Moreover, wit is a fighting thing and a working thing. A man may enjoy humour all by himself; he may see a joke when no one else sees it; he may see the point and avoid it. But wit is a sword; it is meant to make people feel the point as well as see it. All honest people saw the point of Mark Twain's wit. Not a few dishonest people felt it. [8]

When it came to Chesterton, all of these traits were augmented by a deep reverence for truth. But that reverence was also clothed in a high and obstinate regard for those with whom he disagreed. On several occasions, he engaged in epic debates with George Bernard Shaw—as formidable an opponent as then bestrode the intellectual landscape. But their contests were anything but occasions for acrimony. By turns robust and civil, witty and profound—they were affairs in which somehow no quarter was given, but both stepped away from the podium as friends.

Chesterton relished debate and often entered the lists. But when he did, his intent was not to destroy but to build up. Not to unleash a withering frontal assault, but to come alongside a fellow pilgrim and offer a hand in friendship. [9] He wished to contend for the faith winsomely, with an erudition marked by wit and bonhomie. [10]

Among his many enduring achievements, Chesterton was a champion of mere Christianity—that collection of great truths and doctrines, as C. S. Lewis has written, upon which nearly all Christians are agreed.[11] As such, he is justly revered by Catholics and Protestants alike.

Both streams of belief flow into my own heritage of faith. My father attended parochial school and was confirmed within the Catholic Church. My mother was reared in a Baptist setting. Two generations before, my Protestant great-grandfather and his elder brother married Catholic girls and brought them home to Maine. I have often wondered how those young brides fared among the often crusty and judgmental Yankees they met. What I do know is that my great-grandfather and great-grandmother were deeply devoted to each other and to God. In the context of that devotion, they found a way to make it all work. I am heir to their devotion and faith.

Which brings me back to Chesterton. His life and writings are an apologetic of enduring worth to Catholics and Protestants alike. God gave him the grace to make it all work—to commend our common faith in an age marked by deep skepticism and hostility to Christianity. We are heir to the genial fusillade of his apologetic—the winsome, arresting, and utterly original outpouring of his reasons for belief.

In his many books, nearly eighty in all,[12] Chesterton wrote about types, characters, and perspectives readily recognizable to the modern reader. The names of the celebrated contemporaries he wrote about may have faded somewhat from our cultural memory, but the essential elements of the human condition haven't altered, nor have the worldviews Chesterton engaged in the arena of ideas. They are with us still. Chesterton's responses and reflections are as cogent, compelling, and timely now as they were in his day. Truth is like that. For as he said, "What a man can believe depends upon his philosophy, not upon the clock or the century."[13]

Chesterton thoroughly examined symptoms of the tired and lifeless modernity he saw all about him. Amid the cacophony of worldviews that clamored for his attention, he saw nothing so vital and alive as the Christianity he had embraced. And if in writing *Heretics* (published in 1905), he described the maladies that afflicted his age, *Orthodoxy* (published in 1908) was his account of how he had found a timeless cure for them all: at the feet of a risen Christ.

In reading Chesterton's books, the reasons for my own hope have been strengthened and enriched. I have encountered a writer of great prescience who invites us to look in a mirror and discover if we see ourselves. The honest-hearted reader who explores his writings will find treasures that remain ever new. My hope is that this book will in some small way foster that good end. For myself, I feel privileged to have sat at the feet of one of God's great and sublime fools. It has been time well spent.

CHAPTER 1

"My Earliest Path"[1]

I love these little people; and it is not a slight thing when they, who are so fresh from God, love us.

—CHARLES DICKENS, THE OLD CURIOSITY SHOP (1841)

Gilbert Keith Chesterton, one of the twentieth century's most gifted men of letters, was born on 29 May, 1874, at Campden Hill, Kensington—a district of West London, England. It would prove to be a year of portents. For it welcomed not only Chesterton but also Sir Winston Churchill into the world: both men of keen intellect, ample girth, and literary skill.

They met once as young men, in 1902. Churchill was then a newly minted MP; Chesterton was the newest light in the literary firmament of London.[2] Their careers would thereafter diverge markedly, but both had an enduring influence.

Churchill's legacy is, of course, one of the ages. He will, it seems, always have something to say—something we need to carry forward. Chesterton's legacy is much the same: the passing of time only seems to underscore the worth and relevance of so much that he wrote and said. He cast a long shadow, and people have cherished walking amid his shadowlands ever since.

✠

"My people," Chesterton wrote in the opening pages of his *Autobiography*, "belonged to [the] old-fashioned English middle class."[3] His father, Edward, "was the head of a hereditary business of house agents and surveyors, which had already been established for some three generations in Kensington"—people who "were always sufficiently successful; but hardly, in the modern sense, enterprising."[4]

Edward Chesterton, if unambitious in matters of business,[5] was not to be faulted for it. His life was that of a semi-invalid because he was prone to heart trouble.[6] Given to domesticity by inclination as well as necessity, he "filled his own house with his life"[7] and made it the center of what was, by any measure, a colorful existence. His son would later call it an "abnormally happy and even merry existence."[8]

The portrait of Edward Chesterton that emerges in his son's *Autobiography* is that of a man who was kind, contemplative, and intellectually curious—a man of personal integrity[9] and artistic sensibility. He was "serene, humorous and full of hobbies."[10] A garrulous man in the best sense of the word, he was fond of talk on any subject.[11] As his son recalled:

> My father was very universal in his interests and very moderate in his opinions; he was one of the few men I ever knew who really listened to argument; moreover, he was more traditional than many in the liberal age; he loved many old things, and had especially a passion for the French cathedrals and all the Gothic architecture opened up by Ruskin in that time.[12]

So far as politics were concerned, the younger Chesterton's memories of his father's views prompted both a flash of humor and an appreciation for the liberalism of the classic tradition to which his father adhered. "My father," he wrote, "was a Liberal of the school that existed before the rise of Socialism; he took it for granted that all sane people believed in private property."[13]

A gifted watercolor artist, Edward Chesterton also had a deep and abiding love of literature. As his son recalled: "[M]y father knew all his English literature backwards, and [because of this] I knew a great deal of it by heart, long before I could really get it into my head. I knew pages of Shakespeare's blank verse without a notion of the meaning of most of it; which is perhaps the right way to begin to appreciate verse."[14]

If Edward Chesterton fostered a great love of literature in his son, his interest in toy theaters also stirred the dreamy boy's first memories and ideas of beauty.[15]

> The very first thing I can ever remember seeing with my own eyes was a young man walking across a bridge. He had a curly moustache and an attitude of confidence verging on swagger. He carried in his hand a disproportionately large key of a shining yellow metal and wore a large golden or gilded crown. The bridge he was crossing sprang on the one side from the edge of a highly perilous mountain chasm, the peaks of the range rising fantastically in the distance; and at the other end it joined the upper part of the tower of an almost excessively castellated castle. In the castle tower there was one window, out of which a young lady was looking. . . .
>
> To those who may object that such a scene is rare in the home life of house-agents living immediately to the north of Kensington High Street, in the later seventies of the last century, I shall be compelled to admit, not that the scene was unreal,

but that I saw it through a window more wonderful than the
window in the tower; through the proscenium of a toy theatre
constructed by my father.[16]

Speaking of this incident in his *Autobiography*, Chesterton
wrote, "[T]hat one scene glows in my memory like a glimpse of
some incredible paradise; and, for all I know, I shall still remember
it when all other memory is gone out of my mind."[17] He underscored this when he wrote: "Apart from the fact of it being my first
memory, I have several reasons for putting it first . . . [for in it] I
recognise a sort of symbol of all that I happen to like in imagery
and ideas."[18] Lastly, he stated: "I have begun with this fragment of
a fairy play in a toy theatre, because it . . . sums up most clearly the
strongest influences upon my childhood."[19]

Chesterton's response to his father's toy theater recalls C. S.
Lewis's childhood response to the toy garden that his brother,
Warren, built on the top of a biscuit tin:

> Once in those very early days my brother brought into the nursery
> the lid of a biscuit tin which he had covered with moss and gar-
> nished with twigs and flowers so as to make it a toy garden or a toy
> forest. That was the first beauty I ever knew. What [a] real garden
> had failed to do, the toy garden did. It made me aware of nature—
> not, indeed, as a storehouse of forms and colors but as something
> cool, dewy, fresh, exuberant. . . . As long as I live my imagination of
> Paradise will retain something of my brother's toy garden.[20]

Other images of beauty crowded in upon Chesterton's memory as a child. "Among my first memories also," he wrote, "are those
seascapes that were blue flashes to boys of my generation; North

Berwick with the cone of green hill that seemed like the hill absolute."[21] Still another kaleidoscope of memory from these years would later form the basis of his epic poem *The Ballad of the White Horse*:

> One of these glimpses . . . is a memory of a long upper room filled with light (the light that never was on sea or land) and of somebody carving or painting with white paint the deal head of a hobby-horse; the head almost archaic in its simplification. Ever since that day my depths have been stirred by a wooden post painted white; and even more so by any white horse in the street.[22]

Chesterton's mother was no less a figure of affection and formative influence than his father. Marie-Louise Grosjean was of Swiss-Scottish descent. Her mother was descended from the Aberdeen family of Keith, hence the origin of G. K.'s middle name.

Once described as "the cleverest woman in London,"[23] Marie-Louise Chesterton not only possessed a keen intellect, but she had a "ready, and very sharp wit" that her son inherited.[24] Described as "immensely kind,"[25] she was also unconventional in her opinions and lively. She reveled as well in the pleasures of the dinner table, preparing "gargantuan meals" and practicing the kind of hospitality that enjoined her guests to "eat enormously."[26] It was little wonder, then, that her famous son would become so ardently devoted to taverns and inns.

Much about his mother's family and forebears seemed larger-than-life, including one fact that most certainly was: she was one of twenty-three children. Her father's family, the Grosjeans, though long settled in England, had come originally from French

Switzerland.[27] As stated above, her mother's family, the Keiths, were Scottish. Both ancestral lines were steeped in romance, or so at least Chesterton believed them to be:

> My mother's family had a French surname; though the family, as I knew it by experience as well as tradition, was entirely English in speech and social habit. There was a sort of family legend that they were descended from a French private soldier of the Revolutionary Wars, who had been a prisoner in England and remained there; as some certainly did.[28]

The air of legend and martial intrigue Chesterton associated with his French relations was complemented by traits he discerned in his Scottish ancestry. "On the other side," he wrote,

> my mother came of Scottish people, who were Keiths from Aberdeen; and for several reasons, partly because my maternal grandmother long survived her husband and was a very attractive personality, and partly because of a certain vividness in any infusion of Scots blood or patriotism, this northern affiliation appealed strongly to my affections; and made a sort of Scottish romance in my childhood.[29]

✥

And what of the homes in Kensington where Chesterton spent his early years? The first of them, the home at Sheffield Terrace, was a place he scarcely knew. But the family's second home, 11 Warwick Gardens (where his family relocated when he was five), was a place long remembered:

Warwick Gardens . . . stood out from its neighbours. As you turned the corner of the street you had a glimpse of flowers in dark green window boxes and the sheen of paint the colour of West country bricks, that seemed to hold the sunshine. The setting of the home never altered. The walls of the dining room renewed their original shade of bronze green year after year. The mantel-board was perennially wine-colour, and the tiles of the hearth, Edward Chesterton's own design, grew more and more mellow.

Books lined as much of the wall space as was feasible and the shelves reached from floor to ceiling in a phalanx of leather. The furniture was graceful, a slim mahogany dining-table, a small sideboard, generously stocked with admirable bottles, and deep chairs.

The portrait of G. K. as a child smiled from a wall facing the fireplace. Walking with his father in Kensington gardens, the fair and radiant beauty of the boy, the flowing curls of graceful poise, held the eyes of the Italian artist, Bacceni, who did not rest until he had conveyed the vision to canvas. . . .

On party nights wide folding doors stood open and through the vista of a warm yet delicate rose-coloured drawing-room you saw a long and lovely garden, burgeoning with jasmine and syringa, blue and yellow iris, climbing roses and rock plants. The walls were high, and tall trees stood sentinel at the far end.[30]

Amidst such a setting, it comes as no surprise that in Chesterton's first years he enjoyed a "sheltered and happy childhood in a comfortable middle-class home, where his interests in art and literature were encouraged by his parents."[31]

This can be seen in the fact that once Chesterton learned to read, he became "a passionate reader, particularly of fairy-tales." Further, he made his father's hobby of constructing toy theaters his own, and his devotion to them continued unabated for the rest of his life. On the less positive side of the ledger, he showed himself to be an "absent-minded [and] untidy child."[32] However, in this he was aided and abetted by his mother, who was far from a martinet in matters of order and cleanliness. She often appeared with "her clothes thrown on anyhow." If G. K. entered a room with dirty hands or unkempt hair, she seems to have been the kind of parent who took no special notice of it. If he was late for a meal, he wasn't chastened.[33] It is not surprising, therefore, that he never shook free of these traits, nor wanted to. In fact, they would become indistinguishable from the man who was G. K. Chesterton, and two of the more colorful aspects of his legend.

Pleasant as the home at Warwick Gardens was, what with happy eccentricities seasoning the supportive environment Chesterton and his parents knew, one great sorrow overshadowed his childhood. Death forever changed everyone's lives when his elder sister Beatrice, whom the family called "Birdie," died at the age of eight. G. K. was only three years old and just learning to speak, but he would always remember the shadow this tragedy cast over his home.[34] For a time, he became seriously ill, and his parents' grief was compounded by worry over his condition.[35] His recovery relieved that worry, but a collective and searing sense of grief lingered.

Edward Chesterton's grief was so overwhelming that he turned within himself and further burdened the grief his wife and young son felt. He would not allow Marie-Louise to speak Beatrice's name, and turned her portrait to the wall. Marie-Louise had lost her daughter. Now she had lost her husband to grief and had lost any solace he might have given—or could have received from her.[36]

Things were simply painful and confusing for G. K., barely old enough to remember the bright light that his sister had been in their lives. In the years following the birth of his little brother, Cecil (born when G. K. was five), both boys were made to live a life in which any reminder of death was shunned. They were forbidden to attend a funeral or even gaze upon a funeral procession. If one was making its way through their street, they were quickly gathered up and told to stay in one of the back rooms of their home until it had passed.[37]

The silence concerning death soon extended to all matters relating to sickness. Edward Chesterton refused to speak of his serious heart condition and tried to ignore others in the family if they were injured or became sick.[38]

Marie-Louise is known to have spoken of Beatrice's death only once after it occurred—a brief and deeply touching moment when she confided to a friend. "I *was* the mother of three children," she said, "and I had a beautiful girl."[39]

G. K., witnessing his father's grief-stricken behavior, could not help being affected by it. As biographer Michael Ffinch has written,

> Chesterton inherited, or rather imitated, these phobias. A child-hood friend, Annie Firmin, remembered how if his brother, Cecil, gave the slightest sign of choking at dinner, Gilbert would "throw down his spoon and fork and rush from the room. I have seen him do it many times." When, many years later, his father lay on his death-bed "it was only with real pain and difficulty that he summoned sufficient fortitude to see the dying man."[40]

Years later, Chesterton wrote of this crushing experience in his *Autobiography*. "I had a little sister who died when I was a child," he wrote:

> I have little to go on; for she was the only subject about which my father did not talk. It was the one dreadful sorrow of his abnormally happy and even merry existence; and it is strange to think that I never spoke to him about it to the day of his death. I do not remember her dying; but I remember her falling off a rocking-horse. I know, from experience of bereavements only a little later, that children feel with exactitude, without a word of explanation, the emotional tone or tint of a house of mourning. But in this case, the greater catastrophe must somehow have become confused and identified with the smaller one. I always felt it as a tragic memory, as if she had been thrown by a real horse and killed.[41]

And so it was to little Cecil Edward, the newest addition to the family, that G. K. and his father and mother turned as a welcome arrival—a baby who could help them assuage their grief and begin to rebuild their shattered lives.

As one might expect, the two brothers became extremely close. They often went at it hammer and tongs, as most brothers are wont to do. But their mutual affection was unimpaired. Later in life they would often, sometimes famously, spar in argument.[42] But for now, one thing was clear: G. K. had a companion whom he loved and could rollick with.

CHAPTER 2

"From Childhood to Boyhood"[1]

A true friend is forever a friend.
—George MacDonald,
The Marquess of Lossie (1877)

Many aspects of Chesterton's early life are well documented. Surprisingly, however, the time when he started school is not one of them. William Oddie, Chesterton's most authoritative biographer, speculates that since he entered St. Paul's School in Hammersmith in the same class as boys who were one or two years his junior, he must have been about nine years old when his formal schooling commenced at his first school: Colet House, a preparatory school founded in 1881.[2]

This would fix the year for the start of Chesterton's school days at 1882 or 1883, probably the latter. Whatever the precise year was, Colet House does not seem to have been better or worse than many schools. To be sure, the founder of the school, Samuel Bewsher, wielded a cane with frightening regularity. Upon entering the schoolroom, he was in the habit of crashing it down on a desk and exclaiming loudly, "Now, then!" At other points during the day, he made a round of the different classes, during which he would single out a hapless boy for questions about the lesson then being taught. If the answers forthcoming were unsatisfactory, "a few hearty whacks" were administered.[3]

One would think that, in such an atmosphere, the prospects for gaining anything like a meaningful education were dim. However, one of Chesterton's classmates, H. A. Sams, recalled that two masters at Colet House were able instructors and treated the students well: the French master and the instructor in Greek.

> Monsieur Devaux was French master.... One day he took a batch of boys to the Hammersmith Baths. On the way back he told them about the Franco-Prussian War, in which he himself had fought not so many years earlier. Then there was Mr. Birch, who in spite of his sinister name was a kindly martinet with mutton-chop whiskers. He introduced us to Greek and somehow robbed it of its terrors. Thanks to him, most of us, I think, imbibed a liking for that musical language expressed in its clear characters.[4]

And what of Chesterton himself? He described his time at Colet House in his *Autobiography*, though he did not mention the school by name when he did so.

From the first, his recollections of the place showed that his was the mind and temperament of an artist. He was drawn to the shapes of letters and felt a mixture of disdain and hearty disinterest for the fine points of grammar.

> To me the ancient capital letters of the Greek alphabet, the great Theta, a sphere barred across the midst like Saturn, or the great Upsilon, standing up like a tall curved chalice, have still a quite unaccountable charm and mystery, as if they were the characters traced in wide welcome over Eden of the dawn. The ordinary small Greek letters, though I am now much more familiar with them, seem to me quite nasty little things like a swarm of gnats.

As for Greek accents, I triumphantly succeeded, through a long series of school-terms, in avoiding learning them at all; and I never had a higher moment of gratification than when I afterwards discovered that the Greeks never learnt them either. I felt, with a radiant pride, that I was as ignorant as Plato and Thucydides. At least they were unknown to the Greeks who wrote the prose and poetry that was thought worth studying; and were invented by grammarians, I believe, at the time of the Renaissance.[5]

In the pages of his *Autobiography*, Chesterton could never quite resist the urge to digress—indeed, he seems at times to welcome the chance to offer a commentary on the subject at hand in an aside. Such was the case as he closed his recollection of the time when he first came to grips with the vagaries of learning Greek and Latin:

I certainly shall not, in the graceful modern manner, turn round and abuse my schoolmasters because I did not choose to learn what they were quite ready to teach. It may be that in the improved schools of today, the child is so taught that he crows aloud with delight at the sight of a Greek accent. But I fear it is much more probable that the new schools have got rid of the Greek accent by getting rid of the Greek. And upon that point, as it happens, I am largely on the side of my schoolmasters against myself. I am very glad that my persistent efforts not to learn Latin were to a certain extent frustrated; and that I was not entirely successful even in escaping the contamination of the language of Aristotle and Demosthenes. At least I know enough Greek to be able to see the joke, when somebody says (as somebody did the other day) that the study of that language is not suited to an age of democracy.[6]

In contrast, one thing about Chesterton's schoolboy days was a source of unalloyed pleasure: the friendships he forged with several classmates. Chief among them was Edmund Clerihew Bentley. The two became friends just before Chesterton left Colet House.

How they met was a circumstance Chesterton always remembered. "When I first met my best friend in the playground," he wrote,

> I fought with him wildly for three quarters of an hour . . . rushing hither and thither about the field and rolling over and over in the mud. . . . When we desisted from sheer exhaustion, and he happened to quote Dickens or the Bab Ballads, or something I had read, we plunged into a friendly discussion on literature which has gone on, intermittently, from that day to this.[7]

This setting and the circumstances that gave rise to Chesterton's lifelong friendship with Bentley were perhaps only possible in an English prep school attended by two intellectually precocious boys. Many boys fight before becoming friends. But for these boys to reconcile following a knockabout brawl by quoting literature was singular.

However improbable its origin, the friendship that emerged that day endured for the rest of their lives. Over time, they grew very close. Long years later, Bentley described his friend as "a man in whose personal society admiration seldom failed to grow to a far deeper feeling."[8] At Chesterton's death, Bentley captured all their friendship had meant to him in one half-sentence, saying, "with Gilbert Chesterton gone the world can never be the same again."[9]

But all this lay far in the future. During their school days, Bentley and Chesterton were just getting to know each other and were delighted to find they had so much in common. As Bentley recalled, it was "the opening of a conversation that was to last, with the minimum of interruption, for seven or eight years."[10] The two became inseparable, together nearly all the time, and writing to each other when they were not.[11] It was a friendship such as few are privileged to find.

⁂

If Chesterton's great good fortune in forging a friendship with Edmund Bentley was a high point of his early years at school, his performance as a student proved something less.

A good deal less, as it happened. This precocious boy was learning passages of Shakespeare by heart, was profoundly influenced by reading George MacDonald's classic fantasy tale *The Princess and the Goblin*—later writing in the introduction of a MacDonald biography that it "made a difference to my whole existence," and "helped me to see things in a certain way from the start"—but was singularly unimpressive as a student. As one classmate remembered: "He meandered through school like a rudderless bark."[12] The period of his initial studies at St. Paul's School, which he entered in January 1887—following his time at the Colet School—could command only a half-hearted interest, which in turn yielded results that were adequate at best.[13]

But why? One explanation might be that Chesterton was so keenly drawn to his own journey through books he had grown to love at home that he did not wish to have anyone interrupt his travels, and resented the structure that formal studies imposed on him. Hitherto, as encouraged and indulged by his parents, he had been able to range freely among the books of his family's library. One can see how he might have resisted being fenced in.

Then, too, as with many a gifted child, formal studies and conventional methods of instruction may quite simply have bored him. His love of language was constantly being fed by Shakespeare on the one hand; while on the other, his imagination was being stirred to the depths through his reading of George MacDonald—a writer who "could write fairy-tales that made all experience a fairy-tale," and "could give the real sense that every one had the end of an elfin thread that must at last lead them to paradise."[14]

For a boy with an artist's gifts, it must have been quite a comedown to have to leave the company of these writers and chafe under the restraint of formal studies. As stated earlier, he loved the shapes of Greek letters. He could only feel disdain for the drudgery of mastering Greek grammar. His own journeys of the mind meant far more to him.

William Oddie wrote supportively of this view and observed: [Chesterton's] tendency to create for himself a kind of private space, from which he could emerge and to which he could return at will, was not one he ever outgrew. Once he had been seized by a train of thought, the reality of the material world could without warning fade into oblivion.[15]

⌗

Before his days at St. Paul's came to a close, however, Chesterton did emerge from his stance of resistance to formal studies. Two factors seem to have accounted for this. One was the largely benign and relaxed atmosphere created at the school by its distinguished headmaster, F. W. Walker. A brilliant scholar in his own right, he was unconventional in that he did not see it as his duty at St. Paul's to train middle-class students "in the manners and deportment of the gentry." The public school cult of sporting prowess was non-existent, and amid such a setting, where academic achievement was nurtured and students like Chesterton were allowed to develop at their own pace, Chesterton began to do better.[16]

The second and most important factor that fed into Chesterton's positive social and academic development was his involvement with the Junior Debating Club or JDC.[17] This gathering of twelve academically gifted young men (all of whom became fast and lifelong friends) was a transformative time in young G. K.'s life.[18] Chesterton's best friend in the JDC was, of course, Edmund Bentley, later famous as a writer of detective fiction. Among the others Chesterton was close to was Lucian Oldershaw, who won a coveted scholarship to Christ Church, one of Oxford University's largest colleges, and who would later become Chesterton's brother-in-law.[19]

Then there were the Solomon brothers, Lawrence and Maurice. Lawrence was a gifted Latin scholar and later served as senior tutor of University College, London.[20] Maurice had a distinguished career in industry, becoming one of the directors of the General Electric Company.[21] Robert Vernède, a gifted young poet, was tragically killed in World War I. Edward Fordham became a writer of satiric poetry and a highly successful barrister.[22] Frederick Salter was later a principal in the Treasury and Chesterton's solicitor.[23] Other members whose full names are known were Waldo d'Avigdor, Digby d'Avigdor, Hubert Arthur Sams, Francis George Lawder Bertram, and B. N. Langdon-Davies.[24] After his marriage, Waldo d'Avigdor joined the Alliance Insurance Company and emigrated to Canada. His brother Digby became a gas engineer. Hubert Sams joined the Indian Civil Service and served as director of General Indian Postal Services. He was knighted in 1931. Near the end of his life, Francis Bertram was given the rank of commander in the Order of the British Empire. He served as inspector of schools and joined the Air Ministry in 1919. He was later deputy director of the Civil Aviation Board. Bernard Noël Langdon-Davies later became a lecturer and literary consultant.[25]

Taken together, this was a very impressive group of young men, and each of them took the club very seriously—so much so that William Oddie has written that it became "the centre of their lives."[26]

The original intent of the JDC was to meet and discuss Shakespeare, but this idea was soon abandoned in favor of a general debating society. Poems, plays, and papers on all manner of literary topics were written. Soon, associated clubs began to form as well: a chess club, a naturalists' society, and a sketching club. A lending library was formed, for which Lawrence Solomon served as librarian. The JDC became so multifarious and extensive that it "was more like an alternative culture" for its young members. They all grew very close. Friendly, festive, as well as intellectually serious—the whole atmosphere of the JDC ran directly counter to the commonplace tales of bullying and corporal punishment that were so often a part of public school life.[27]

For Chesterton, as his biographer Maisie Ward has written, the JDC became "a symbol of the ideal friendship."[28] Beyond this, William Oddie has written that the JDC was "an intellectual crucible" for Chesterton. "It is not too much to say," Oddie wrote,

that the JDC (and, just as importantly, its magazine, *The Debater*) represented for him the kind of intensive intellectual apprenticeship which is for most people served only at university. A good deal of his time was now spent, either in preparing papers to be read to the weekly Friday afternoon meetings, or in writing poetry and prose of various kinds for the magazine, literary activities to which he gave a degree of dedication only intermittently directed toward his schoolwork.[29]

The papers Chesterton wrote for the JDC are astonishing in their range and subject matter. It is not known for certain how many he wrote, but it is known that he wrote papers on Milton, Gray, Spenser, Cowper, Scott, Shelley, and Byron. The paper on Milton foreshadows his future prowess as a literary critic and is all the more remarkable when one bears in mind that it was written by a schoolboy. One passage reads:

> When ascending "next the seat of God" even the Muse of Milton falters and grows weak, and the same diction that is so grand and terrible in the hate and defiances of Satan seems not yet grand enough for a discussion between the persons of the Trinity. Milton's intellect could get as high as the Devil's, but no higher. . . . The glorious or terrible images which almost every line calls up are such as no reader can forget, but which remain within him, a cycle of mystical and eternal pictures; the uprisen Angel of Darkness reeling over the fiery lake on his spear, or flying far and solitary between heaven and earth, the blaze of the crowned and mailed angel warriors, or the sapphire brook murmuring amid the myrtle woods of Eden.[30]

Some seasoned critics would not be ashamed to own such a piece of prose.

Some men are made for friendship. They have a gift for it and greatly desire it. They flourish in the company of others who are like-minded. This is a description of Chesterton at this time of his life. For a description of all that JDC was, the memories of his friend Hubert Sams form one of the best word pictures to have survived. His recollections bring the JDC to life. "Picture," Sams wrote,

> a dozen healthy, boisterous schoolboys, beginning to leave their boyhood and to bud into young manhood, twelve apostles of Letters, straining at the leash on Friday afternoons and listening for the Head Porter to ring the big bell, which meant Liberty till 9.30 on Monday morning, the joyous release at five o'clock, the brisk walk with a pal or two to the House of our host for the evening, the gathering around a well-laden board, the pleasing consumption of cups of tea and of various sweet and sticky cakes, the chaffing and the joking, the gradual subsidence into a semblance of order, the running facetiae on a too serious paper, the gentle rebuke from our one and only G. K. C., the pleasing feeling that we had a holiday till Monday morning (forgive this repetition) and that . . . there was nothing to mar our happiness; the rush of high spirits following the restraint, if any, imposed by the meeting; the walk home, again with a pal as far as he could go. Picture all this and you will have some idea of the JDC.[31]

CHAPTER 3

A Perfect Storm

When [Chesterton's] religion was at its lowest point, in the difficult Art School days, he never lost it entirely. "I hung on to religion," [he later said,] "by one thin thread of thanks."[1]

—MAISIE WARD (1943)

Much as the JDC meant to Chesterton—and it meant all the world to him at this time of his life—he knew that his involvement with the group was bound to change. For by autumn 1892, he had left St. Paul's School to begin taking art classes at the Slade School of Art and, a bit later in 1893, courses in Latin and English literature at University College, London. The others in JDC could go on together for a while yet, as they, being younger than Chesterton, would not go up to university until the autumn of 1894.

One would have thought this would be an exciting time for Chesterton. He'd been drawing all his life and would now be able to immerse himself fully in the visual arts. He could develop his gift.

Yet it was at the Slade School that he experienced a period of desolation unlike any he would ever know. It was his dark night of the soul.

Two developments seemed to have triggered this. In choosing to go to the Slade School, Chesterton was at an unwelcome distance from virtually all of his friends in the JDC. He and Edmund Bentley maintained a steady correspondence, but this could not begin to compensate for all that the JDC had meant when they were all together at St. Paul's.[2] For a time, he still continued to send contributions to the *Debater*, but the last of these efforts was a poem written in late 1892 or early 1893.[3]

Second, Chesterton was away from his family more than he ever had been before. Whatever their eccentricities were, it was a loving home. His mother indulged him, while his father was proud, supportive, and entertaining. And then, of course, his brother, Cecil, had always been a good friend. They rather constantly wrangled, but beneath the arguments and youthful competitiveness lay a very close bond.[4]

Suddenly, all of these sources of support (the most important in his life) were gone, or greatly diminished. In their place was a school where he knew few people—and where for the first time he was exposed to "current trends in art"[5]—in particular the cultural pessimism and decadence so closely associated with London in the 1890s. As scholar George P. Landow wrote, the assumptions underlying much of the poetry, fiction, and art of this time centered on "an anti-Romantic belief in original sin and in fallen man and nature; the omnipresence of evil and the grotesque"; as well as a "lack of health, balance, and innocence." The mood and tone of this period was a marked pervasive cultural atmosphere of "ennui, incompleteness, a sense of loss, exile and isolation."[6]

Portions of Chesterton's dedicatory poem to Edmund Bentley for the novel *The Man Who Was Thursday* form his most powerful recollection of this time of decadence and how it affected him:

A cloud was on the minds of men, and wailing went the
    weather,
Yea, a sick cloud upon the soul when we were boys together.[7]

Further on in the poem, Chesterton spoke of "doubts that drove us through the night" and the decadents themselves, who "twisted even decent sin to shapes not to be named."[8]

For a sensitive young man whose sense of how things are was being altered with alarming speed, all of these factors combined to form a perfect storm. He was unready for all the changes, and Landow's words above could have been applied with equal justice to Chesterton's feelings. It was he who felt overwhelmed by "a sense of loss, exile and isolation." Decades later, writing in his *Autobiography*, he could still remember it vividly:

There is something truly menacing in the thought of how quickly I could imagine the maddest, when I had never committed the mildest crime . . . there was a time when I had reached that condition of moral anarchy within, in which a man says, in the words of Wilde, that "Atys with the blood-stained knife were better than the thing I am." I have never indeed felt the faintest temptation to the particular madness of Wilde, but I could at this time imagine the worst and wildest disproportions and distortions of more normal passion; the point is that the whole mood was overpowered and oppressed with a sort of congestion of imagination. As Bunyan, in his morbid period, described himself as prompted to utter blasphemies, I had an overpowering impulse to record or draw horrible ideas and images; plunging deeper and deeper as in a blind spiritual suicide.[9]

At this time, Chesterton had begun to fill a notebook with "these horrible drawings." One day two of his friends discovered it. Shocked by what they saw, they asked each other, "Is Chesterton going mad?"[10]

To make matters worse, Chesterton was also dabbling in the occult. He "used the planchette freely" and began to experience strange headaches. After them "came a horrid feeling as if one were trying to get over a bad spree, with what I can best describe as a bad smell in the mind."[11] Wherever he turned, it seemed, he was confronted with things that were alien, strange, and unsettling. All this inner turmoil was unfolding amidst a cultural moment that was itself unsettled. Frederick Buechner has described Chesterton's dilemma in this way:

> The decadence and darkness that horrified him in himself were also all around him in those last few years of the nineteenth century. The beliefs and values that mid-Victorian England had looked upon as eternal were giving place to doubt, skepticism, a loss of inner balance, and all that Matthew Arnold could hear of the faith of his fathers was "its melancholy, long, withdrawing roar." Schopenhauer was in vogue, with his grim philosophy that life was nothing more than an illusory, malignant affair that inveigles humankind into reproducing in order to perpetuate it.[12]

Chesterton himself later summed it all up in one sentence: "I did not very clearly distinguish between dreaming and waking; not only as a mood but as a metaphysical doubt."[13] He was in the midst of an existential crisis.

How Chesterton began to struggle free of his despair was something he could not have predicted. Traditional means of sorting things out were largely absent from his life. Neither he nor his parents were particularly religious. He was, therefore, left to his own devices. It was then that something he perhaps only half understood began to fasten itself upon his thoughts. As he later recalled:

> When I had been for some time in these, the darkest depths of the contemporary pessimism, I had a strong inward impulse to revolt; to dislodge this incubus or throw off this nightmare. But as I was still thinking the thing out by myself, with little help from philosophy and no real help from religion, I invented a rudimentary and makeshift mystical theory of my own.[14]

What was this mystical theory? For Chesterton it centered on notions of existence and nothingness. The contrast between them had begun to spur his thinking. And the more he thought about it, the more he began to see something clearly. "Mere existence," he wrote,

> reduced to its most primary limits, was extraordinary enough to be exciting. Anything was magnificent as compared with nothing. Even if the very daylight were a dream, it was a day-dream; it was not a nightmare. The mere fact that one could wave one's arms and legs about . . . showed that it had not the mere paralysis of a nightmare. Or if it was a nightmare, it was an enjoyable nightmare. In fact, I had wandered to a position not very far from the phrase of my Puritan grandfather, when he said that he would thank God for his creation if he were a lost soul. I hung on to the remains of religion by one thin thread of thanks. I [had discovered a] way of looking at things, with a sort of mystical minimum of gratitude.[15]

In this discovery, Chesterton was aided and abetted by writers who would forever remain among his favorites. He was indebted to them not only as artists but also because they had not heeded the pessimistic spirit of the age. "I was assisted," Chesterton wrote,

> by those few of the fashionable writers who were not pessimists; especially by Walt Whitman, by Browning and by Stevenson; Browning's "God must be glad one loves his world so much," or Stevenson's "belief in the ultimate decency of things." But I do not think it is too much to say that I took it in a way of my own; even if it was a way I could not see clearly or make very clear. What I meant, whether or no I managed to say it, was this; that no man knows how much he is an optimist, even when he calls himself a pessimist, because he has not really measured the depths of his debt to whatever created him and enabled him to call himself anything. At the back of our brains, so to speak, there was a forgotten blaze or burst of astonishment at our own existence. The object of the artistic and spiritual life was to dig for this submerged sunrise of wonder; so that a man sitting in a chair might suddenly understand that he was actually alive, and be happy.[16]

It was this realization, this discovery of the mystical minimum, that restored life and sanity to Chesterton. As Buechner has written, Chesterton "was filled with both an enormous sense of thankfulness, and an enormous need for someone or something to thank, which he expressed in a number of the random pieces that [began to appear in his] notebook."[17] But this notebook, started in the autumn of 1894,[18] was a wholly different repository of his thoughts from the book that had earlier been filled with the morbid and macabre. Chesterton rendered his own thoughts in verse:

> *Here dies another day*
> *During which I have had eyes, ears, hands*
> *And the great world round me;*
> *And with tomorrow begins another.*
> *Why am I allowed two?*[19]

Slowly, at his own pace, Chesterton was moving down the road to faith. Grace entered his vocabulary in a wholly new light, and verse seemed the most fitting way to express what he felt:

> *You say grace before meals*
> *All right.*
> *But I say grace before the play and the opera,*
> *And grace before the concert and pantomime,*
> *And grace before I open a book,*
> *And grace before sketching, painting,*
> *Swimming, fencing, boxing, walking, playing, dancing;*
> *And grace before I dip the pen in the ink.*[20]

Soon, Chesterton's thoughts began to take a turn reminiscent of Pascal's *Pensées.*[21] Persistent questions were now the things that lay close to heart. "Have you ever known," he wrote, "what it is to walk along a road in such a frame of mind that you thought you might meet God at any turn of the path?" He framed the answer to that question in a lovely meditation called "The Prayer of a Man Resting":

> *The twilight closes round me*
> *My head is bowed before the Universe*
> *I thank thee, O Lord, for a child I knew seven years ago*
> *And whom I have never seen since.*

Praised be God for all sides of life, for friends, lovers, art,
literature, knowledge, humour, politics, and for the little red
cloud away there in the west—[22]

Biographer Maisie Ward, the wife of his publisher Frank
Ward, read through Chesterton's notebook and gave these glimpses
of grace to the world. She summarized the transformation of this
time in his life as well as anyone ever has. At school, she wrote,
Chesterton was looking for God, but "at the age of 16 he was, he
tells us in *Orthodoxy*, an Agnostic in the sense of one who is not
sure one way or the other. Largely it was this need for gratitude for
what seemed personal gifts that brought him to belief in a personal
God. Life was personal, it was not a mere drift; it had will in it, it
was more like a story."[23]

By the summer of 1894, Chesterton understood that he was
caught up in that story. And he had begun to know its Author.[24]

CHAPTER 4

And Now for a Career

Life without mystery—a sight of the unseen—simply is not life.[1]
—PAUL DWIGHT MOODY, AUGUST 1929

My joy in having begun my life is very great.
—G. K. CHESTERTON TO E. C. BENTLEY, MAY 1895

In 1895, one year after his emergence from despair, Chesterton received communication from an unexpected quarter: an invitation to write for a magazine called the *Academy*. He had just turned twenty-one, and though he could not have known it, this was a first step toward the career that would dominate the rest of his life: that of a journalist.

He wrote about this new development in a letter to Edmund Bentley. He had written a review of a new book from John Ruskin entitled the *Ruskin Reader*, of which the *Academy*'s editor, Mr. Cotton, had heartily approved. "I [had] sent him my review of Ruskin," Chesterton told Bentley,

and [when I went to see him] he read it before me ... and delivered himself with astonishing rapidity to the following effect: "This is very good: you've got something to say: Oh, yes: this is worth saying: I agree with you about Ruskin and about the Century: this is good: you've no idea: if you saw some stuff: some reviews I get: the fellows are practised but of all the damned fools: you've no idea: they know the trade in a way: but such infernal asses: as send things up: but this is very good: that sentence does run *nicely*: but I like your point: make it a little longer and then send it in: I've got another book for you to review: you know Robert Bridges? Oh very good, very good: here it is: about two columns you know: by the way: keep the [copy of] Ruskin for yourself: you deserve that anyhow."[2]

This, Chesterton's first review, was both cutting and pugnacious.[3] He wasted little time in letting his readers know what his opinions were:

Poor Mr. Ruskin has been trotted out again, to do duty this time as a school "Reader." To this end, passages have been selected from his three great works on Art. The editor is Mr. W. G. Collingwood, who in his somewhat premature *Life of Mr. Ruskin*, proved he had not to the full that understanding sympathy with his subject which every biographer should possess. The present work suffers from the same deficiency. It is inconceivable that either Mr. Ruskin or anyone appreciating him rightly could have "attempted to give the main lines of Mr. Ruskin's teaching . . . in a series of extracts from his great early works." The "main lines" of his teaching are to be found, not in his early works, but concentrated in *Unto this Last*, and more diffused in *Time and Tide* and *Fors Clavigera*; and this is a truth so strongly insisted on by Mr. Ruskin himself that the disregard of it by editors, or others who undertake to expound him, is without

justification. Truly, it is pathetic that a man of Mr. Ruskin's cali-
bre and achievements, after giving his fortune and his life to the
service of others, should in his old age be "exploited" . . . for any
purpose whatever.[4]

A new collection of miscellaneous prose by Robert Bridges (a
future poet laureate) fared little better at Chesterton's hands. He
believed Bridges had not been well served by this new offering, and
was unsparing in his critique, which was published on October 19,
1895. "Except that a man is entitled to his own name," Chesterton
wrote,

> the new Robert Bridges might reasonably be asked to choose
> a well-sounding pseudonym. Seriously we should have felt a
> grievance had we bought this book believing it to be the work of
> the poet. It is an altogether unnecessary book, and as the work of
> a clever man, there is no excuse for its publication. . . . Certainly,
> they ought not to be served up in the elegant binding and print-
> ing that are so creditable to Mr. Lane. Mr. Bridges can do better
> work, and should set about it at once.[5]

Chesterton spent the first part of the summer of 1895 with the
family of his JDC friends Lawrence and Maurice Solomon, and
the second half with his parents. Following this, in September
1895, he began work at Redway's, a small publisher, where he sent
out review copies of books and returned rejected manuscripts. He
stayed at Redway's for a year, at the end of which he secured a job
working for the far more reputable firm of Fisher Unwin.[6]

When Chesterton entered the suite of offices occupied by Fisher Unwin at Paternoster Buildings, London, he entered a place where he would spend the next five years of his working life. During the day, he read unsolicited manuscripts. He spent many of his nights writing.

This was a great step forward professionally, but it was not by any means the most important event of the autumn of 1896. The great event of that year, and of his life, was his first meeting with the woman who would become his wife.[7]

Chesterton's first meeting with Frances Blogg left him as thoroughly smitten as ever a young man was. Taken to her home by his JDC friend Lucian Oldershaw, they entered the house together. Shortly thereafter, he was "plumped down on a sofa" next to Frances. Greetings commenced all round, and at one point she "looked straight at him." When she did, Chesterton said to himself "as plainly as if he had read it in a book":

> If I had anything to do with this girl I should go on my knees to her: if I spoke with her she would never deceive me: if I depended on her she would never deny me; if I loved her she would never play with me: if I trusted her she would never go back on me: if I remembered her she would never forget me, I may never see her again. Goodbye. It was all said in a flash: but it was all said.[8]

He did not know it that night, but it was much the same for her. The two had fallen in love at first sight.

All this was true, but they were initially "so shy of each other that it would be months before they could speak to each other about their feelings openly." When they had done so, it was clear "that there never would be anyone else for either of them."[9]

Within two years they were engaged. Chesterton proposed in the summer of 1898, when the two were standing on a small bridge in the middle of St. James's Park, London.[10]

But a problem presented itself. Chesterton was a gifted young writer, and he was gainfully employed. But was his income at this time sufficient to adequately provide for them both? The answer then, and for the foreseeable future, appeared to be no. And so they would wait.

Their engagement lasted three years. The couple wed on June 28, 1901, at Kensington Parish Church. The service was performed by the Reverend Conrad Noel, and their honeymoon was spent on the Norfolk Broads—a beautiful, wild expanse of navigable rivers, shallow lakes, woodland, fens, and grazing marshes. The Broads had been a favored travel destination for Britons since the late nineteenth century, and the surrounding villages recalled an England of another time.

It was a golden hour, and either during or just after their honeymoon, Chesterton wrote a poem for his bride:

> *Between the perfect marriage day*
> *And that fierce future proud, and furled,*
> *I only stole six days—six days*
> *Enough for God to make the world.*
> *For us is a creation made*
> *New moon by night, new sun by day,*
> *That ancient elm that holds the heavens*

Sprang to its stature yesterday—
Dearest and first of all things free,
Alone as bride and queen and friend,
Brute facts may come and bitter truths,
But here all doubts shall have an end.
Never again with cloudy talk
Shall life be tricked or faith undone,
The world is many and is mad,
But we are sane and we are one.[11]

⌘

Meanwhile, inasmuch as they felt free to marry, Chesterton's career prospects had visibly improved. His career as a full-time journalist had commenced in earnest in December 1899, with "Velasquez and Poussin," a review in the *Bookman* so well written that it seemed as though a wunderkind had appeared out of the blue. He was just twenty-five.

That Velasquez was an Impressionist may be called the main thesis of the book, and in one sense, doubtless, it is true enough. But we must beg leave to draw a strong distinction between Impressionism as understood by Velasquez and Impressionism as understood by some young gentlemen we know. Velasquez subjects all detail to effect. There is something magnificent in the breadth, the courage, we had almost said the scorn, with which he splashes in his great backgrounds, as blank and grey as Mr. Whistler's. He is never a realist in the sense that a realist is another name for a snob, a painter of fur that might be stroked, of satin that might be meant for sale. In his wonderful picture of the Dwarf Antonio, for example, there are no properties round the actor. No carpet peers like an ill-mannered dog between his legs; no bedstead or Dutch clock rears itself behind, as insolently truthful as a candid friend. Not that this painter of dwarfs or idiots thinks anything below him. He would paint a turnip seriously; but never with that blatant materialism that seems to say in every line, "this is a turnip; you have often seen one before." His picture would say, the one lesson of all art, all philosophy, all religion, "this is a turnip. You have never seen one before."[12]

But he was not yet done. The second of the two books Chesterton had been asked to review was about the seventeenth-century French painter Nicolas Poussin. "When paganism was re-throned at the Renaissance," Chesterton wrote,

> it proved itself for the first time a religion by the sign that only its own worshippers could slay it. It has taken them three centuries, but they have thrashed it threadbare. Just as poets invoked Mars and Venus, for every trivial flirtation, so Poussin and his school multiplied nymphs and satyrs with the recurrence of an endless wall-paper, till a bacchanal has become as respectable as a bishop and the god of love is too vulgar for a valentine. . . . This is the root of the strange feeling of sadness evoked by the groups and landscapes of Poussin. We are looking at one of the dead loves of the world. Never were men born so much out of the time as the modern neo-pagans. For this is the second death of the gods—a death after resurrection. And when a ghost dies, it dies eternally.[13]

Here, Chesterton had emerged unmistakably as a superb art critic—one with a fluent, arresting, and distinctive style. "This," as biographer Michael Coren has written, "was cultivated and mature criticism of the highest form."[14]

Letters began to arrive in the offices of the *Bookman* inquiring who this reviewer was, as well they might. For while it was a pity that the *Bookman* had published this dual review unsigned, it did have the unintended effect of generating heightened curiosity about the reviewer's identity. Here was a critic of undeniable talent. People wanted to know who he was.

⌘

The skillfully rendered art criticism present in "Velasquez and Poussin" might well have led those on the watch for a book from Chesterton to think the first book to bear his name would feature considered art criticism such as he gave to the world in *G. F. Watts* (published in 1904) or *William Blake* (published in 1910).

Chesterton chose another tack entirely. He did publish two books prior to his marriage to Frances in late June 1901, but they were not anything like what one would have expected given the skill and promise of "Velasquez and Poussin."

Greybeards at Play, published in October 1900, was a book of nonsense verse. As William Oddie has written, it was not the kind of book with which to launch a literary career.[15] This said, it was a very fine book of its kind. Written and illustrated by Chesterton, it is a thoroughly charming book faithfully following a path blazed by Lewis Carroll and Edward Lear.

And it had one very noteworthy admirer. W. H. Auden, writing on the one hundredth anniversary of Chesterton's birth, stated: "I have no hesitation in saying that it contains some of the best pure nonsense verse in English.... By natural gift, Chesterton was, I think, essentially a comic poet."[16] Readers who purchased *Greybeards at Play* could read this delightful bit of verse, among others:

> *I love to see the little stars*
> *All dancing to one tune*
> *I think quite highly of the Sun,*
> *And kindly of the Moon.*
> *The million forests of the Earth*
> *Come trooping in to tea.*
> *The great Niagara waterfall*
> *Is never shy with me.*
> *I am the tiger's confidant,*
> *And never mention names:*
> *The Lion drops the formal "Sir,"*
> *And lets me call him "James."*[17]

Chesterton's next book, published one month later in November 1900, was also a book of verse—a collection called *The Wild Knight*. Despite some fine moments, it was at best an uneven performance. For while it did contain poems still anthologized today, such as "The Donkey" and "A Christmas Carol," others were rather unremarkable and bore the mark of a young man's first effort. He was still finding his voice. However, these lines from "A Christmas Carol" are among the best of his mystical verse:

> *The Christ-child lay on Mary's lap,*
> *His hair was like a light.*
> *(O weary, weary were the world,*

But here is all alright.)
The Christ-child lay on Mary's breast,
His hair was like a star.
(O stern and cunning are the kings,
But here the true hearts are.)
The Christ-child lay on Mary's heart,
His hair was like a fire.
(O weary, weary is the world,
But here the world's desire.)
The Christ-child stood at Mary's knee,
His hair was like a crown,
And all the flowers looked up at Him,
And all the stars looked down.[18]

Chesterton's friends did what they could to help *The Wild Knight* find an audience. One of the closest, Rex Brimley Johnson, sent a copy to Rudyard Kipling.[19] Kipling's reply was kind and helpful. It was the type of response a young poet should welcome. It read in part:

The Elms, Rottingdean,
Nov. 28th.

Dear Mr. Johnson,

Many thanks for *The Wild Knight*. Of course I knew some of the poems before, notably *The Donkey* which stuck in my mind at the time I read it.

I agree with you that there is any amount of promise in the work—and I think marriage will teach him a good deal too. It will be curious to see how he'll develop in a few years. We all begin with arrainging [sic] and elaborating all the Heavens and

Hells and stars and tragedies we can lay our poetic hands on—
Later we see folk—just common people under the heavens . . .

Yours sincerely,

Rudyard Kipling.

P.S. Merely as a matter of loathsome detail, Chesterton has a bad attack of "aureoles." They are spotted all over the book. I think every one is bound in each book to employ unconsciously some pet word but that was Rossetti's.

Likewise I notice "wan waste" and many "wans" and things that "catch and cling." He is too good not to be jolted out of that.[20]

As 1900 drew to a close, Chesterton could look back on a fine tally of his achievements as a writer. There were two books, five articles in the *Bookman*, fourteen articles in the *Speaker*, as well as two instances of occasional verse on political topics—also run in the *Speaker*. Then 1901 carried forward the momentum he had established. He began writing for the *Daily News*, and his first signed piece for that periodical ran on May 31. It was at this time that the byline G. K. Chesterton first began to appear.[21]

CHAPTER 5

An Artist in Words

*I cannot remember when I first met Chesterton. I was so
much struck by a review of Scott's* Ivanhoe *which he wrote
for the* Daily News . . . *that I wrote to him asking who he
was and where he came from, as he was evidently a new star
in literature.*[1]

—GEORGE BERNARD SHAW (1937)

C hesterton's first real appearance in the literary world of
America took place on September 27, 1902, when a review of
The Defendant, his first book of collected essays,[2] was published in
the *New York Times*.

It was a noteworthy debut. The twentieth century was newly
minted, and the unnamed reviewer for the *Times* was well disposed to offer a critique on something out of the common way.
Chesterton had provided just that, as the opening paragraphs of
this book reveal:

In certain endless uplands, uplands like great flats gone dizzy,
slopes that seem to contradict the idea that there is even such a
thing as a level, and make us all realize that we live on a planet
with a sloping roof, you will come from time to time upon whole

valleys filled with loose rocks and boulders, so big as to be like mountains broken loose. The whole might be an experimental creation shattered and cast away. It is often difficult to believe that such cosmic refuse can have come together except by human means. The mildest and most cockney imagination conceives the place to be the scene of some war of giants. To me it is always associated with one idea, recurrent and at last instinctive. The scene was the scene of the stoning of some prehistoric prophet, a prophet as much more gigantic than after-prophets as the boulders are more gigantic than the pebbles. He spoke some words—words that seemed shameful and tremendous—and the world, in terror, buried him under a wilderness of stones. The place is the monument of an ancient fear.

If we followed the same mood of fancy, it would be more difficult to imagine what awful hint or wild picture of the universe called forth that primal persecution, what secret of sensational thought lies buried under the brutal stones. For in our time the blasphemies are threadbare. Pessimism is now patently, as it always was essentially, more commonplace than piety. Profanity is now more than an affectation—it is a convention. The curse against God is Exercise I. in the primer of minor poetry.[3]

It was a potent opening salvo—one that wasted no time in getting down to the business of showing that here was a young writer to be reckoned with. Just twenty-eight, Chesterton knew his way around a sentence—and in this book, he assayed to do nothing less than take on the spirit of his age.

How he did it, to use a baseball metaphor, came out of left field. Nonsense, farce, and jest would be his allies of fostering a new way of seeing.

Now it has appeared to me unfair that humanity should be engaged perpetually in calling all those things bad which have been good enough to make other things better, in everlastingly kicking down the ladder by which it has climbed. It has appeared to me that progress should be something else besides a continual parricide; therefore I have investigated the dust-heaps of humanity, and found a treasure in all of them. I have found that humanity is not incidentally engaged, but eternally and systematically engaged, in throwing gold into the gutter and diamonds into the sea. I have found that every man is disposed to call the green leaf of the tree a little less green than it is, and the snow of Christmas a little less white than it is; therefore I have imagined that the main business of a man, however humble, is defence.[4]

What followed was a patchwork collection of essays on such unlikely subjects as "A Defence of Nonsense," of "Skeletons," of "Rash Vows," of "Slang," and of "Ugly Things." The reviewer for the *New York Times* dubbed Chesterton's style "fantastic reasoning" and his book a collection of "smart" if "rather nonsensical essays."[5]

As the *Times* reviewer saw it, Chesterton had crafted something rather singular and new—or something, at least, that had been untried for quite some time—for as the reviewer noted:

To be amusing over things that are in themselves not so is like extracting sunbeams from cucumbers. It is not everyone's gift, and [Jonathan] Swift is dead long ago. And when the quality of humor is strained it is as the salt that has lost its savor. But it is generally interesting to be left in doubt whether a man is in jest or in earnest, and here the reader may be pardoned if he puts the author down as an artist in words, and as using them to startle and amaze.[6]

Jonathan Swift was but the first of several literary lights to come into the discussion of Chesterton's book—George Eliot and John Milton were to follow. Here was a book that seemed on several levels to prompt rich and telling reflections. In stating this, the *Times* reviewer was saying that readers would make a mistake if they judged Chesterton's cluster of essays to be no more than a lighthearted farce. He did delight in playing with language, teasing out all the shades of color available on his palette. But as an artist in words, Chesterton was something more than a purveyor of farce, though he could clearly excel in that medium when he chose to. He was most properly seen as a jester—someone who could drive home a deeper or neglected truth through humor and seeming nonsense.

That this was true became manifest two years later, in 1905, when Chesterton declared himself to be a jester, saying: "It is not I, it is not even a particular class of journalists or jesters who make jokes about the matters which are of most awful import; it is the whole human race."[7]

This *Times* reviewer had discerned this, as the following passage reveals:

> When, for instance, [Mr. Chesterton] tells us that, "the great sin of mankind, the sin typified by the fall of Adam, is the tendency, not toward pride, but toward humility," we at once wait in expectation; in which we are not disappointed, for shocks, varying in character, come with satisfying frequency.
>
> "If the chaff-cutter had the making of us we should all be straw," says George Eliot, for we are all apt to see things in the

light of our own temperament, or of our own intellectual interests. Thus Mr. Chesterton in his pursuit of paradox sees that the terms "good" and "bad" "never have been used properly," and that the world is in permanent danger of being misjudged in consequence.[8]

The *Times* reviewer had reservations as well about the parochial tone and content in places throughout *The Defendant*. But what rankled most was Chesterton's penchant for not troubling to quote other writings accurately when he referred to them. As the reviewer noted:

> Over all there is a distinctly local color, and even a cockney air, and, though the essays as essays are no worse for that, they are in consequence less than entirely interesting to general readers. Wilfrid Lawson, Forbes Robertson, Chaplin, Harmsworth, and Whitely are not universal celebrities, and Bradshaw, Clapham Builders, Surbiton, and *Pearson's Weekly* are not sufficiently familiar for printed reference. For this reason the book comes abroad and appeals to us in a very "questionable shape." Lack of correctness in quotations also points a moral. Out of four we have noted from Scripture, not one is accurate, and one allusion is referred to as a "fine Biblical phrase," which we fail to recognize or discover. There is a verse from the "Song of Solomon," (p. 25,) not one division which is right, and its exquisite beauty is thereby defaced.[9]

It was fair enough to note the local color element in Chesterton's book and to argue that this might have small appeal for a general readership. But, after all, this was a very British book from a very

British writer. One could just as well have argued that local color might therefore have a certain kind of charm for Anglophiles among a general readership.

The *Times* reviewer was on more solid ground in criticizing Chesterton for laziness and inaccuracy in his use of quotes from other writings. Here was a sin easily avoided, and one often irritating to readers. As such, it did detract from the overall merits of his book.

But these were relatively small objections. The *Times* reviewer genuinely liked *The Defendant* and concluded his review by saying, "notwithstanding what we discern as faults, we are fully aware of the novelty, freshness, and force of many of Mr. Chesterton's arguments. His sympathy with things that are despised of men and his courage in becoming their champion command our admiration."[10]

Meanwhile, in England itself, Chesterton's book had caused a stir and prompted a flurry of reviews. No less a figure in the world of letters than the redoubtable Sir Arthur Thomas Quiller-Couch found things to his liking in *The Defendant*. He is familiar today to readers of *84 Charing Cross Road* as "Q" and more widely celebrated still as the author of *Studies in Literature* and editor of *The Oxford Book of English Verse*. Writing for the *Bookman* in February 1902, Sir Arthur observed:

> The most characteristic, and perhaps most delightful, quality in Mr. Chesterton's writing is his courageous innocence. . . . The most ordinary occurrences in the world are marvellous in his

eyes, and his optimism proceeds from a blessed contentment with a planet which provides so many daily miracles.... [Yet] he is by no means a philosopher in a basket, but a moralist with a good everyday working code.[11]

Quiller-Couch then recommended the essay "A Defence of Rash Vows" as a good place for the reader to begin sampling the best of Chestertonian fare.

The revolt against vows has been carried in our day even to the extent of a revolt against the typical vow of marriage. It is most amusing to listen to the opponents of marriage on this subject. They appear to imagine that the ideal of constancy was a yoke mysteriously imposed on mankind by the devil, instead of being, as it is, a yoke consistently imposed by all lovers on themselves. They have invented a phrase, a phrase that is a black and white contradiction in two words—"free-love"—as if a lover ever had been, or ever could be, free. It is the nature of love to bind itself, and the institution of marriage merely paid the average man the compliment of taking him at his word.[12]

"Better sense could hardly be uttered," Quiller-Couch observed, "even though some minds refuse the coin of good sense until it has been alloyed sufficiently with dullness. To these Mr. Chesterton should not be commended. They will find him unusual, perhaps flighty. But they may be assured that in his vivacious way he is entirely on their side and fighting for the same Bible, though he translate it into unfamiliar language."[13]

All in all, it was a very fine notice from a venerable figure in the literary establishment. Chesterton might well have been a young man (he was only twenty-seven when Quiller-Couch's review appeared), but the reviews he had received made one thing clear: among the journalists plying their trade on Fleet Street, there dwelt a writer who would bear watching.

CHAPTER 6

Eternal Ideas

It is the glory and good of Art
That Art remains the one way possible
Of speaking truth,—to mouths like mine, at least.
—ROBERT BROWNING, THE RING AND THE BOOK (1869)

By May 1906, Chesterton was thirty-two and "famous enough to be one of the celebrities painted or photographed for exhibitions."[1] George Bernard Shaw once memorably described a photo of him taken by the American expatriate photographer Alvin Langdon Coburn:[2]

Chesterton is "our Quinbus Flestrin," the young Man Mountain, a large abounding gigantically cherubic person who is not only large in body and mind beyond all decency, but seems to be growing larger as you look at him "swellin' wisibly," as Tony Weller puts it. Mr. Coburn has represented him as flowing off the plate in the very act of being photographed and blurring his own outlines in the process. Also he has caught the Chestertonian resemblance to Balzac and unconsciously handled his subject as Rodin handled Balzac. You may call the placing of the head on the plate wrong, the focussing wrong, the exposure wrong if you like, but Chesterton is right and a right impression of Chesterton is what Mr. Coburn was driving at.[3]

Shaw had taken to calling Chesterton "the man-mountain" after Swift's usage in *Gulliver's Travels*. It suited him perfectly. Six foot of genius he certainly was, but he was also six foot of prodigious bulk—an Edwardian Dr. Johnson—and then some.

In other ways he was yet like Gulliver—a kind of cosmic town crier marooned amidst the kingdoms of Lilliput and Brobdingnag—where people perpetually see things the wrong way around. He had been put right and now wished to aid others in their search.

Meanwhile, a new opportunity beckoned that would aid that quest in a way no one could have predicted. For in December 1901,[4] Chesterton received a "small literary proposal"[5] from the distinguished editor John Morley, inviting him to write a critical biography of Robert Browning for Macmillan's acclaimed Men of Letters series. "I need not say," he would remember, "that I accepted the invitation."[6]

Just twenty-seven years old, Chesterton would now join the ranks of Anthony Trollope, Henry James, and Thomas Huxley, who had contributed prior volumes. It was, he would say later, "a crown of what I can only call respectability."[7]

❈

When Chesterton's study of Robert Browning was published in May 1903, it had a highly enviable literary pedigree. As such, it was bound to attract the notice of the *New York Times*, which stated in its June 27 review:

Mr. G. K. Chesterton's new book on Robert Browning in the English Men of Letters series, from which we quoted from striking passages last week, seems to have greatly advanced that original and somewhat daring young writer in the esteem of his contemporaries. His oddity and what a London reviewer calls his "boisterous treatment" of his subject, are not likely, perhaps, to satisfy judicious minds, while he is rather careless in his dates and quotations. But he has a fresh and original mind and abundant sympathy, and his book is surely not irreverent. Clement Shorter welcomes his *Study of Browning* all the more cordially as the work of a young man who was never under the influence of the now defunct Browning Society, and does not remember the wild hero worship which surrounded the poet in his later years.[8]

It was a largely positive review, notwithstanding its reference to Chesterton's penchant for quoting from memory and his almost studied indifference regarding the use of dates. What mattered most was the emergence of a "fresh and original mind" in the world of English letters, and this Chesterton surely was. No one before had ever written about Browning as he had, as in this passage:

Though this world is the only world that we have known, or of which we could even dream, the fact remains that we have named it "a strange world." In other words, we have certainly felt that this world did not explain itself, that something in its complete and patent picture has been omitted. And Browning was right in saying that in a cosmos where incompleteness implies completeness, life implies immortality.[9]

And then there was this passage—a plea to shatter the hoary and misguided veneration that had grown up around Browning:

> Browning grew up, then, with the growing fame of Shelley and Keats, in the atmosphere of literary youth, fierce and beautiful, among new poets who believed in a new world. It is important to remember this, because the real Browning was a quite different person from the grim moralist and metaphysician who is seen through the spectacles of Browning Societies and University Extension Lecturers. Browning was first and foremost a poet, a man made to enjoy all things visible and invisible, a priest of the higher passions.[10]

With such moments of keen analysis and brilliant prose to his credit, one can readily see why the publication of *Robert Browning* was a landmark event in Chesterton's young literary life. Heretofore he had been known solely as a journalist plying his trade on Fleet Street. Now, while still in his twenties, he had, in the words of a reviewer for the British periodical *Vanity Fair*, entered "on a new phase of his career as a writer," and joined "the men of letters, as apart from the journalists."[11]

This is a view seconded by literary scholar Bernard Bergonzi, who noted in his essay for *The New Oxford Dictionary of National Biography* that Chesterton's study contained "acute discussions of Browning's poetry," and revealed him to be "an excellent literary critic."

What is more, the text of *Robert Browning* opened a window on Chesterton's intellectual and spiritual development. Bergonzi stated:

> The book's real interest is the extent to which [Chesterton] identifies with his subject, and the clues it offers to his later development.

When he wrote it he was more than a young man embarking on a successful literary career. He was also engaged in a personal struggle to make sense of the world, a struggle which marked all his writing. He emphatically rejected the pessimism, positivism, and determinism which he saw as marking the late nineteenth century, and turned to those writers who were optimists and in love with life and the world, such as Whitman and Stevenson, and Browning, of whom he wrote, "In discussing anything, he must always fall back upon great speculative and eternal ideas." This may or may not have been true of Browning, but it was entirely true of Chesterton. He saw Browning's love of nature and delight in human diversity as implying and resting on a belief in God.[12]

One passage from Chesterton's discussion of Browning as a literary artist reveals the depth of his gratitude to the poet who had helped him to unriddle some of the numinous mysteries of nature and of life:

> One of the deepest and strangest of all human moods is the mood which will suddenly strike us perhaps in a garden at night, or deep in sloping meadows, the feeling that every flower and leaf has just uttered something stupendously direct and important, and that we have by a prodigy of imbecility not heard or understood it. There is a certain poetic value, and that a genuine one, in this sense of having missed the full meaning of things. There is beauty, not only in wisdom, but in this dazed and dramatic ignorance.[13]

One of the most interesting and important of the reviews that *Robert Browning* received was that written by Henry Murray for the *Sunday Sun* of London. At first glance, the name Henry Murray might not prompt a flicker of recognition. But then, that was not his full name. The Henry Murray who reviewed Chesterton's book was none other than Sir James Augustus Henry Murray, the peerless editor of the *Oxford English Dictionary* made famous by Simon Winchester in his best-selling book *The Meaning of Everything*.

One can imagine the setting in which Murray dipped his pen in the inkwell and began to write his review. He was, perhaps, seated at his desk within the "scriptorium" at 78 Banbury Road, Oxford— that curious building where he performed so many tasks associated with editing the *OED*. Murray could bring great erudition and scholarly acumen to bear on virtually any subject of his choosing. His considered estimate of Chesterton's book on Browning thus carried with it no little indication of how the book might be received in the literary world. Should Murray look with favor upon the book, it could do much to smooth the way for a welcome reception among readers more generally.

Murray commenced his remarks on a positive note. "Mr. Chesterton," he wrote, "has done his work admirably, and has produced a really charming and delightful little volume."[14] Then, following a very useful comparison of Browning and Shakespeare, Murray took up the subject of Browning's "verbal obscurity"—a subject upon which Chesterton had, in Murray's judgment, written with "singular force and lucidity."[15] To illustrate why this was so, he then cited the relevant passage from *Robert Browning*—a passage worth giving here in full as it shows what Chesterton could do when in top form. "A man who is intellectually vain," Chesterton wrote,

> does not make himself incomprehensible, because he is so enormously impressed with the difference between his readers'

intelligence and his own that he talks down to them with elaborate repetition and lucidity. What poet was ever vainer than Byron? What poet was ever so magnificently lucid? But a young man of genius who has a genuine humility in his heart does not elaborately explain his discoveries, because he does not think that they are discoveries. He thinks that the whole street is humming with his ideas, and that the postman and the tailor are poets like himself. Browning's impenetrable poetry was the natural expression of this beautiful optimism. *Sordello* was the most glorious compliment that has ever been paid to the average man.

In the same manner, of course, outward obscurity is in a young author a mark of inward clarity. A man who is vague in his ideas does not speak obscurely, because his own dazed and drifting condition leads him to clutch at phrases like ropes and use the formulae that every one understands. No one ever found Miss Marie Corelli obscure, because she believes only in words. But if a young man really has ideas of his own, he must be obscure at first, because he lives in a world of his own in which there are symbols and correspondences and categories unknown to the rest of the world. Let us take an imaginary example. Suppose that a young poet had developed by himself a peculiar idea that all forms of excitement, including religious excitement, were a kind of evil intoxication, he might say to himself continually that churches were in reality taverns, and this idea would become so fixed in his mind that he would forget that no such association existed in the minds of others. And suppose that in pursuance of this general idea, which is a perfectly clear and intellectual idea, though a very silly one, he were to say that he believed in Puritanism without its theology, and were to repeat this idea also to himself until it became instinctive and familiar, such a man might take up a pen, and under the impression that he was saying something figurative indeed, but quite clear and suggestive, write some such sentence as this, "You will not get the godless Puritan into your white taverns," and no one in the length and breadth of the country could form the remotest notion of what he could mean. So it would have been in any example, for instance, of a man who made some philosophical discovery and did not realise how far the world was from it. If it had been possible for a poet in the sixteenth century to hit upon and learn to regard as obvious the evolutionary theory of Darwin, he might have written down some such line as "the radiant offspring of the ape," and the maddest volumes of mediaeval natural history would have been ransacked for the meaning of the allusion. The more fixed and solid and sensible the idea appeared to him, the more dark and fantastic it would have appeared to the world. Most of us indeed, if we ever say anything valuable, say it when we are giving expression to that part of us which has become as familiar and invisible as the pattern on our wall paper. It is only when an idea has become a matter of course to the thinker that it becomes startling to the world.[16]

At this juncture, Murray paid Chesterton a very handsome compliment: "[This] is a quite admirable statement of the case, and one which I have not yet seen surpassed in critical thought and lucidity of expression."[17]

But, Murray went on to say, "Greatly as I admire Mr. Chesterton's handling of his main theme, I have a crow to pluck with him over his treatment of certain of Browning's figures."[18]

At issue was Chesterton's description of Browning's fictional character Fra Lippo Lippi as "an evil man." To this Murray took good-natured but decided exception. Lippi, Murray wrote, has always seemed to me to be one of the most intensely lovable characters in English fiction. If Mr. Chesterton chooses to take the Puritan standpoint, and to say that Lippo stands condemned as an unchaste and bibulous monk, well and good. I can only reply that, at his date, unchastity and bibulosity—if there be such a word—were common failings of Italian ecclesiastics of all grades, and that Lippo's whole-hearted kindliness, his love of life as life, his delight in the beauty, the splendour, the intimate wonder of the world, should save him from any fear of "the greater damnation."[19]

Chesterton had also transgressed, to Murray's way of seeing things, in that he had classed yet another of Browning's fictional characters, Bishop Blougram, as one of the "evil men." Chesterton compounded the offense by placing Blougram on a level with such truly disreputable characters as Djabel, Prince Hohenstiel-Schwangau, and Mr. Sludge the medium. It was here that Murray took Chesterton to task with as much friendly severity as he had within him—kind-hearted man that he was. This classification of Blougram, Murray wrote,

is to me one of the most mysterious in the entire history of criticism. I don't mind admitting that the Bishop is a snob. He shows that strain very clearly as he pours out the final glass of wine for his silent companion, "Gigadibs, the literary man." I don't say that his views are those of a man of any great loftiness of soul or thought. He is obviously a *bon vivant*, a dilettante, and a trifler, with many grave human interests. But, none the less, Browning has expressed through his lips the best apology for—I had almost written the best defence of—supernatural religion I have

ever seen. I am loth to accuse Mr. Chesterton of either hasti-
ness or shallowness of judgment, but I have known Blougram so
long and so intimately that I almost feel, in defending him, that
I have the privileges to be accorded to the man who defends an
absent friend against unmerited aspersion. The poem seems to
me to have at once a deeper and more obvious meaning than Mr.
Chesterton perceives in it.[20]

Having thus admonished Chesterton, Murray then made a fine
distinction concerning the particularly fine passage that marked
the close of *Robert Browning*. This passage, in Murray's view, had
no relevance (as Chesterton had insisted) to Bishop Blougram, but
it was, Murray wrote, "a passage whose *general* acumen I admire."[21]
Returning one last time to a discussion of "Browning's knaves,"
Chesterton observed:

Every one of these meagre swindlers, while admitting a failure
in all things relative, claims an awful alliance with the Absolute.
To many it will at first sight appear a dangerous doctrine indeed.
But, in truth, it is a most solid and noble and salutary doctrine,
far less dangerous than its opposite. Every one on this earth
should believe, amid whatever madness or moral failure, that his
life and temperament have some object on the earth. Every one
on the earth should believe that he has something to give to the
world which cannot otherwise be given. Every one should, for
the good of men and the saving of his own soul, believe that it is
possible, even if we are the enemies of the human race, to be the
friends of God. The evil wrought by this mystical pride, great as
it often is, is like a straw to the evil wrought by a materialistic
self-abandonment. The crimes of the devil who thinks himself

of immeasurable value are as nothing to the crimes of the devil who thinks himself of no value. With Browning's knaves we have always this eternal interest, that they are real somewhere, and may at any moment begin to speak poetry. We are talking to a peevish and garrulous sneak; we are watching the play of his paltry features, his evasive eyes, and babbling lips. And suddenly the face begins to change and harden, the eyes glare like the eyes of a mask, the whole face of clay becomes a common mouth-piece, and the voice that comes forth is the voice of God, uttering His everlasting soliloquy.[22]

"This," Murray wrote, "is a very fine, eloquent, and thoughtful passage. As applied to Mr. Sludge or to Prince Hohenstiel-Schwangau it could not easily be bettered."[23] But, Murray said, returning again to a tone of admonition,

it does not apply to the Bishop [Blougram], who, meant assuredly neither for a saint nor a hero, is not the poor and con-temptible creature as which Mr. Chesterton would have us see him. Browning may have had Cardinal Wiseman in his mind as he penned the poem—indeed, as Mr. Chesterton reminds us, Wiseman was its original instigator and "true begetter." But Browning was not a portrait painter. He drew, not the actual man, but the man symbolic; and he added traits and expres-sions which absolutely differentiated the picture from the original. I find no "panic-stricken and tottering compromise" in Blougram—on the contrary, I find a very firm and assured faith, not in the religion he fed himself by teaching, not in the creed of Peter and Hildebrand, which bade the street stones to be bread, and they were bread, but in the deep underlying need, so real a need to many hearts, of a faith in faith itself. There is a nuance here which a man of Mr. Chesterton's quick intelligence should not have failed to catch.[24]

With such notices in hand, Chesterton must have been very largely pleased. True, Murray had taken him to task on relatively minor matters of character description. But in the main he had recognized in Chesterton a gifted young critic, and one with a great deal of potential. To have had his first book of literary criticism described as "admirabl[e] . . . really charming and delightful"[25] was a fine way to embark on a new phase of his career as a man of letters. He had every reason to hope for better things.

Many years later, in his posthumously published *Autobiography*, Chesterton looked back on the "flattering invitation"[26] John Morley had tendered to him. It had indeed been a groundbreaking literary venture, but it had also held out an offer to undertake a kind of pilgrimage to make sense of the world:

> [The invitation] had just arrived when I was lunching with Max Beerbohm, and he said to me in a pensive way: "A man ought to write on Browning while he is young." No man knows he is young while he is young. I did not know what Max meant at the time; but I see now that he was right; as he generally is. . . .
>
> I will not say that I wrote a book on Browning; but I wrote a book on love, liberty, poetry, my own views on God and religion (highly undeveloped), and various theories of my own about optimism and pessimism and the hope of the world; a book in which the name of Browning was introduced from time to time, I might almost say with considerable art, or at any rate with some decent appearance of regularity. There were very few

biographical facts in the book, and those were nearly all wrong. But there is something buried somewhere in the book; though I think it is rather my boyhood than Browning's biography.[27]

Chesterton's gratitude here is understandable, and his candor is refreshing. But he is too self-effacing. *Robert Browning* was far more than a book in which he wrestled with the transcendent question of life; it had many fine moments of literary analysis. Browning scholar Iain Finlayson—while acknowledging the book's flaws—has written that Chesterton's study continues to be important "for consistently inspired and constantly inspiring psychological judgments about the poet and his work, which he gets right." Finlayson has concluded that in this regard, Chesterton's book "has never been bettered."[28] High praise indeed.

CHAPTER 7

Varied Types

And in all the forms of art which peculiarly belong to civilisation, [Alexander Pope] was supreme. In one especially he was supreme—the great and civilised art of satire. And in this we have fallen away utterly.

So Chesterton wrote in one of the finest essays from one of his best collections of essays: *Varied Types*—or, as it was known in England, *Twelve Types*.[1]

Varied Types represented a new direction for Chesterton. Where *The Defendant* had been a whimsical, often irreverent romp, the essays in *Varied Types* recalled the criticism he had brought to bear in writing reviews like "Velasquez and Poussin." He scrutinized with an artist's eye and a mind steeped in literature and literary understanding. It is one of Chesterton's best books, and one that rewards rereading.

Varied Types was published in September 1903, by Dodd, Mead and Company of New York. When the book appeared, the *New York Times* took note, as it had begun to do increasingly where Chesterton was concerned, and commissioned a review from John White Chadwick, the distinguished Unitarian clergyman and poet who frequently contributed reviews on literary subjects.

Chadwick's January 2, 1904, review appeared on page one of *Saturday Review of Books*, bearing the subtitle "A New Volume of Piquant Essays by a Young Writer Whose Influence Will Be Felt."[2]

The tone of this review evokes the way in which Chesterton burst onto the literary scene of New York at the turn of the twentieth century. If things were rather staid in the literary world of London, they were in New York as well. In his review for the *Times*, Chadwick was voicing the thought of many that here was a breath of fresh air—someone who could foster a new appreciation for old authors by virtue of a thoroughly unconventional way of looking at things.

It was a prospect reviewers for the *Times* welcomed, as confirmed by a brief notice published on March 7, 1903. The article, titled "Mr. Chesterton's Essays," looked ahead to the publication of *Varied Types*, saying this "new book will contain essays on Charlotte Brontë, William Morris, Byron's optimism, Pope's satire, and Stevenson's literary merit—not to mention Tolstoi's and Savonarola's religious and literary attributes."[3]

What is more, the *Times* predicted that Chesterton's forthcoming book would find a ready audience.

G. K. Chesterton, author of "The Defendant," has come to be talked of in London as an essayist, and he now divides the eulogies of the literary press over there with Herbert Paul. . . . Mr. Chesterton has yet to be introduced to us as an essayist. A volume of his, however, will be issued in April through Dodd, Mead & Co. There is little doubt that he will be read. He has a fondness for shattering long-established estimates and for demolishing accepted theories in literature.[4]

Chesterton's essay on Alexander Pope set the stage for much of what was contained in *Varied Types*. It was elegant, well considered, and erudite in unusual ways. Chesterton knew his subject well and had a keen awareness of the unique genius present in Pope's art. And as with this essay, so it was with the other subjects profiled in *Varied Types*—Chesterton could help the reader see them as though for the first time.

From the start, Chesterton's capacity to be thought-provoking was on full display. For those who thought it was easy to write poetry in the classical couplet form, as Pope had done, he had a ready answer. "There was," he wrote,

> a certain discipline in the old antithetical couplet of Pope and his followers. If it did not permit of the great liberty of wisdom used by the minority of great geniuses, neither did it permit of the great liberty of folly which is used by the majority of small writers. A prophet could not be a poet in those days, perhaps, but at least a fool could not be a poet. If we take, for the sake of example, such a line as Pope's:
>
> *Damn with faint praise, assent with civil leer,*
>
> the test is comparatively simple. A great poet would not have written such a line, perhaps. But a minor poet could not.[5]

But Chesterton's best thoughts about Pope centered on the art of satire. This, Chesterton believed, was very nearly a lost art—certainly one that had been too often corrupted. In writing about Pope's use of satire, Chesterton opened a window on an earlier age and also offered a cautionary digression with resonance for our increasingly graceless age.[6] Civility was a banished virtue in his day;

we are no more fortunate. Chesterton's words are prescient as literary criticism: they are potent also as a cultural critique. "We have had a great revival in our time," he wrote,

> of the cult of violence and hostility. Mr. [W. E.] Henley and his young men have an infinite number of furious epithets with which to overwhelm anyone who differs from them. It is not a placid or untroubled position to be Mr. Henley's enemy, though we know that it is certainly safer than to be his friend. And yet, despite all this, these people produce no satire. Political and social satire is a lost art, like pottery and stained glass. It may be worth while to make some attempt to point out a reason for this. It may seem a singular observation to say that we are not generous enough to write great satire. This, however, is approximately a very accurate way of describing the case.[7]

What was needed to write great satire? Chesterton thought he knew the answer. "To write great satire," he wrote, "to attack a man so that he feels the attack and half acknowledges its justice, it is necessary to have a certain intellectual magnanimity which realises the merits of the opponent as well as his defects."[8]

Instead, in England circa 1903, Chesterton lamented that it was "too much the custom in politics to describe a political opponent as utterly inhuman." He recoiled from this, saying "this kind of invective may often have a great superficial success: it may hit the mood of the moment; it may raise excitement and applause; it may impress millions"—but ultimately, he said, it failed utterly to engage "the real ironies" of an opponent's soul—"the mean compromises, the craven silences, the sullen vanities, the secret brutalities, the unmanly visions of revenge. It is to these that satire should reach if it is to touch the man at whom it is aimed. And to reach these it must pass and salute a whole army of virtues."[9]

And so it was that Chesterton felt that his age had much to learn from "the great English satirists of the seventeenth and eighteenth centuries," for "they had this rough, but firm, grasp of the size and strength, the value and the best points of their adversary." In contrast, the Henleyites were wrongly promoting the idea of satirizing a man by expressing "a violent contempt of him, and by the heat of this to persuade others and himself that the man is contemptible."[10]

As an example of how satire ought to be displayed, Chesterton pointed to Pope's famous satire on the essayist Joseph Addison. "Pope," he wrote,

> was not such a fool as to try to make out that Addison was a fool. He knew that Addison was not a fool, and he knew that Addison knew it. . . . He said what was really wrong with Addison; and in calm and clear and everlasting colours he painted the picture . . .

> > *Bear, like the Turk, no brother near the throne,*
> > *View him with scornful, yet with jealous eyes.*
> > *And hate for arts that caused himself to rise.*
> >
> > . . .
> >
> > *Like Cato give his little Senate laws,*
> > *And sit attentive to his own applause.*
> > *While wits and templars every sentence raise,*
> > *And wonder with a foolish face of praise.*[11]

"This is the kind of thing," Chesterton concluded, "which really goes to the mark at which it aims. It is penetrated with sorrow and a kind of reverence, and it is addressed directly to a man. This is no mock-tournament to gain the applause of the crowd."[12]

⊰⊱

One of the highlights of *Varied Types* was Chesterton's review of H. Bellyse Baildon's book *Robert Louis Stevenson: A Life Study in Criticism* (first published in 1901).[13] Where the essay on Alexander Pope had been serious in tone, this review essay on Stevenson was marked by moments of wit, eloquence, and great insight:

> A recent incident has finally convinced us that Stevenson was, as we suspected, a great man. We knew from recent books that we have noticed, from the scorn of "Ephemera Critica" and Mr. George Moore, that Stevenson had the first essential qualification of a great man: that of being misunderstood by his opponents. But from the book which Messrs. Chatto & Windus have issued, in the same binding as Stevenson's works, *Robert Louis Stevenson*, by Mr. H. Bellyse Baildon, we learn that he has the other essential qualification, that of being misunderstood by his admirers.[14]

Following this wry volley, Chesterton wasted little time in coming to his point. Baildon, he said, could at times be an interesting writer, and he had the great advantage of having known Stevenson while at college. Here and there, some of Baildon's criticisms were "remarkably thoughtful and true." Nevertheless, Chesterton wrote,

> it is a very singular fact, and goes far, as we say, to prove that Stevenson had that unfathomable quality which belongs to the

great, that this admiring student of Stevenson can number and marshal all the master's work and distribute praise and blame with decision and even severity, without ever thinking for a moment of the principles of art and ethics which would have struck us as the very things that Stevenson nearly killed himself to express.[15]

Chesterton particularly objected to those portions of Baildon's study that were "perpetually lecturing Stevenson for his 'pessimism.'" This, Chesterton responded, is

surely a strange charge against a man who has done more than any modern artist to make men ashamed of their shame of life. But [Mr. Baildon] complains that, in *The Master of Ballantrae* and *Dr. Jekyll and Mr. Hyde*, Stevenson gives evil a final victory over good. Now if there was one point that Stevenson more constantly and passionately emphasized than any other it was that we must worship good for its own value and beauty, without any reference whatever to victory or failure in space and time. "Whatever we are intended to do," he said, "we are not intended to succeed." That the stars in their courses fight against virtue, that humanity is in its nature a forlorn hope, this was the very spirit that through the whole of Stevenson's work sounded a trumpet to all the brave.[16]

In no place is Chesterton's great regard for Stevenson more in evidence than in the closing paragraph of his essay. Stevenson had waged a lonely battle against the pessimism of his age, and if Baildon had failed to discern this in his study, Chesterton wished his readers to know that he had not. That conviction called forth some of the best writing in *Varied Types*. "The conception," Chesterton wrote, which unites the whole varied work of Stevenson was that romance, or the vision of the possibilities of things, was far more important than mere occurrences: that one was the soul of our life, the other the body, and that the soul was the precious thing. The germ of all his stories lies in the idea that every landscape or scrap of scenery has a soul: and that soul is a story. Standing before a stunted orchard with a broken stone wall, we may know as a mere fact that no one has been through it but an elderly female cook. But everything exists in the human soul: that orchard grows in our own brain, and there it is the shrine and theatre of some strange chance between a girl and a ragged poet and a mad farmer. Stevenson stands for the conception that ideas are the real incidents: that our fancies are our adventures. To think of a cow with wings is essentially to have met one. And this is the reason for his wide diversities of narrative: he had to make one story as rich as a ruby sunset, another as grey as a hoary monolith: for the story was the soul, or rather the meaning, of the bodily vision. It is quite inappropriate to judge "The Teller of Tales" (as the Samoans called him) by the particular novels he wrote.... These novels were only the two or three of his soul's adventures that he happened to tell. But he died with a thousand stories in his heart.[17]

***

A review essay of Elizabeth Barrett Browning's *Casa Guidi Windows* rounded out the series of essays in *Varied Types*.[18] It afforded Chesterton the opportunity to discuss at length the reasons that he believed she should be remembered. Chief among them was the assertion that she was a great poet, irrespective of condescending notions of gender then prevalent. "The delightful new edition," Chesterton wrote, of Mrs. Browning's *Casa Guidi Windows* which Mr. John Lane has just issued ought certainly to serve as an opportunity for the serious criticism and inevitable admiration to which a great poet is entitled. For Mrs. Browning was a great poet, and not, as is idly and vulgarly supposed, only a great poetess. The word poetess is bad English, and it conveys a particularly bad compliment.[19]

Chesterton was not without criticism of Browning's verse, but when he did criticize, he did so with discernment. One thing he disdained was the kind of parlor-room refinement that so often resulted in lifeless poetry. This was a failing with which Browning could not be faulted. "Nothing," Chesterton wrote,

> is more remarkable about Mrs. Browning's work than the absence of that trite and namby-pamby elegance which the last two centuries demanded from lady writers. Wherever her verse is bad it is bad from some extravagance of imagery, some violence of comparison, some kind of debauch of cleverness. Her nonsense never arises from weakness, but from a confusion of powers. If the phrase explain itself, she is far more a great poet than she is a good one.[20]

Part of Browning's greatness, Chesterton felt, was caught up with what he called "the poetry of self-abandonment." When she wrote this type of verse, he said, "she really abandoned herself with the valour and decision of an anchorite abandoning the world." Still, her efforts in this regard were not always successful, and he cited a case in point. "Such a couplet," he wrote, as

> *Our Euripides, the human,*
> *With his dropping of warm tears,*

gives to most of us a sickly and nauseous sensation. Nothing can be well conceived more ridiculous than Euripides going about dropping tears with a loud splash, and Mrs. Browning coming after him with a thermometer. But the one emphatic point about this idiotic couplet is that Mrs. Hemans would never have written it. She would have written something perfectly dignified, perfectly harmless, perfectly inconsiderable. Mrs. Browning was in a great and serious difficulty. She really meant something. She aimed at a vivid and curious image, and she missed it.[21]

Chesterton moved next to an arresting comparison of Browning and Shakespeare, as unexpected as it is valuable. It revealed Chesterton's unique gift for making striking comparisons. When one suddenly appears, it's as though a rabbit had pulled a magician out of a hat.

So it was in this instance. "All great literary art," Chesterton wrote,

involves the element of risk, and the greatest literary artists have commonly been those who have run the greatest risk of talking nonsense. Almost all great poets rant, from Shakespeare downwards. Mrs. Browning was Elizabethan in her luxuriance and her audacity, and the gigantic scale of her wit. We often feel with her as we feel with Shakespeare, that she would have done better with half as much talent. The great curse of the Elizabethans is upon her, that she cannot leave anything alone, she cannot write a single line without a conceit:

> And the eyes of the peacock fans
> Winked at the alien glory,

she said of the Papal fans in the presence of the Italian tricolour:

> *And a royal blood sends glances up her princely eye to trouble.*
> *And the shadow of a monarch's crown is softened in her hair,*

is her description of a beautiful and aristocratic lady. The notion of peacock feathers winking like so many London urchins is perhaps one of her rather aggressive and outrageous figures of speech. The image of a woman's hair as the softened shadow of a crown is a singularly vivid and perfect one. But both have the same quality of intellectual fancy and intellectual concentration. They are both instances of a sort of ethereal epigram. This is the great and dominant characteristic of Mrs. Browning, that she was significant alike in failure and success.[22]

As one might expect, Robert Browning was discussed in Chesterton's essay, and when he was, Chesterton paid husband and wife a tribute that reveals his indebtedness to them both. They had helped him understand the generosity of people at their best, and the limitations of human nature.

"Mrs. Browning and her husband," he wrote,

> were more liberal than most Liberals. Theirs was the hospitality of the intellect and the hospitality of the heart, which is the best definition of the term. They never fell into the habit of the idle revolutionists of supposing that the past was bad because the future was good, which amounted to asserting that because humanity had never made anything but mistakes it was now quite certain to be right.[23]

Here was the kind of wisdom that writers discover, if they find it at all, only after a lifetime of experience and reflection. The man who penned these words was in his late twenties. Chesterton possessed a wisdom, and a gift, as singular as it was rare.

CHAPTER 8

The Tower
That Strikes the Stars

*The ecstasy lay in the one point he had never noticed about
the railings . . . the fact that they were, like the great majority
of others in London, shaped at the top after the manner of a
spear. As a child, Wayne had half consciously compared
them with the spears in pictures of Lancelot and St. George,
and had grown up under the shadow of the graphic
association. Now, whenever he looked at them, they were
simply the serried weapons that made a hedge of steel round
the sacred homes of Notting Hill.[1]*

—G. K. CHESTERTON (1904)

Many couples can recall days when they, as newlyweds, lived in straitened circumstances. The Chestertons were no different. And it was during such a time that Chesterton's first novel, *The Napoleon of Notting Hill*, had its origin. As Maisie Ward wrote:

The story of the writing of *The Napoleon* was told me in part by
Frances, while part appeared in an interview[2] given by Gilbert, in
which he called it his first important book: I was "broke"—only

ten shillings in my pocket. Leaving my worried wife, I went down Fleet Street, got a shave, and then ordered for myself, at the Cheshire Cheese, an enormous luncheon of my favourite dishes and a bottle of wine. It took my all, but I could then go to my publishers fortified. I told them I wanted to write a book and outlined the story of "Napoleon of Notting Hill." But I must have twenty pounds, I said, before I begin.

"We will send it to you on Monday."

"If you want the book," I replied, "you will have to give it to me today as I am disappearing to write it." They gave it.

Frances meanwhile sat at home thinking, as she told me, hard thoughts of his disappearance with their only remaining coin. And then dramatically he appeared with twenty golden sovereigns and poured them into her lap. Referring to this incident later, Gilbert said, "What a fool a man is, when he comes to the last ditch, not to spend the last farthing to satisfy the inner man before he goes out to fight a battle with wits."[3]

"Mr. Gilbert Chesterton has done a wonderful thing; out of the dull, drab orb of modernity he has struck a new vein of romance."[4] So read the opening sentence of a review by F. G. Bettany in the *Sunday Times* on March 27, 1904. The occasion: the appearance of Chesterton's first novel, *The Napoleon of Notting Hill*—a work T. S. Eliot would later praise for the "high imaginative level" it attained.[5]

If ever a first novel sparkled with originality, this book did. One part farce, one part fantasy, and throughout a cautionary tale—reviewers vied with one another to find adjectives that rightly described what Chesterton had written. Some discerned a work of satire, others a societal lament. In truth, the novel was both a parable and a romance—cast amid a premise familiar to readers of H. G. Wells: an England of the future.[6]

Eighty years in the future to be precise. Only this vision of 1984 could not have been more different from George Orwell's more celebrated novel. Chesterton's England was shrouded in a miasma of soft despotism wherein kings were indifferently plucked from the ranks of civil servants. "Some one in the official class made King," Chesterton had written. "No one cared how: no one cared who. He was merely an official secretary."[7]

Apathy really reigned supreme, and in the person of the newly elected king, Auberon Quin, apathy now combined with an eccentricity that had the power to impose its will. And so the boroughs of London (still Edwardian in appearance with their gas lamps and horse-drawn vehicles) were to be transformed by a revival of medieval traditions.

> "Perhaps," [Quin] said, "perhaps the noblest of all my conceptions. A revival of the arrogance of the old mediaeval cities applied to our glorious suburbs. Clapham with a city guard. Wimbledon with a city wall. Surbiton tolling a bell to raise its citizens. West Hampstead going into battle with its own banner. It shall be done. I, the King, have said it."[8]

Ten years on, heralds and heraldry had transformed London's boroughs. London was now a cluster of medieval city states, each with "heraldic coats of arms . . . colorfully uniformed guards [and] governed by provosts in splendid robes."[9] It was all a joke really, a whim born of a desire for entertainment. But what Quin could not have foreseen was that someone took the joke seriously. That someone was the novel's protagonist, Adam Wayne. Where many endured Quin's reconceived London in grudging silence, and others were beginning to chafe at last under their yoke of lunacy, Wayne, the young provost of Notting Hill, was unlike any of them. He loved medieval mores, traditions, and valor—even if the king who had revived them seemed mad to everyone else. Wayne knew nothing of that and loved these things for what they were at heart. He saw a kind of martial poetry in them—a sense of life's purpose— and was stirred to the depths of his being.

When Wayne and Quin met for the first time, it was a scene not to be forgotten—rendered all the more vividly since it was accompanied by one of seven superb illustrations from W. Graham Robertson interspersed throughout the novel. Standing before his king, resplendent in a rich, red robe, and girt with a sword, Wayne declared:

"I bring homage to my King. I bring him the only thing I have— my sword."

And with a great gesture he flung it down on the ground, and knelt on one knee behind it.

There was a dead silence.

"I beg your pardon," said the King, blankly.

"You speak well, sire," said Adam Wayne, "as you ever speak, when you say that my love is not less than the love of these. Small would it be if it were not more. For I am the heir of your scheme—the child of the great Charter. I stand here for the rights the Charter gave me, and I swear, by your sacred crown, that where I stand, I stand fast."

The eyes of all five men stood out of their heads.

Then Buck said, in his jolly, jarring voice: "Is the whole world mad?"

The King sprang to his feet, and his eyes blazed.

"Yes," he cried, in a voice of exultation, "the whole world is mad, but Adam Wayne and me. It is true as death what I told you long ago, James Barker, seriousness sends men mad. You are mad, because you care for politics, as mad as a man who collects tram tickets. Buck is mad, because he cares for money, as mad as a man who lives on opium. Wilson is mad, because he thinks himself right, as mad as a man who thinks himself God Almighty. The Provost of West Kensington is mad, because he thinks he is respectable, as mad as a man who thinks he is a chicken. All men are mad, but the humourist, who cares for nothing and possesses everything. I thought that there was only one humourist in England. Fools!—dolts!—open your cows' eyes; there are two! In Notting Hill—in that unpromising elevation there has been born an artist! You thought to spoil my joke, and bully me out of it, by becoming more and more modern, more and more practical, more and more bustling and rational. Oh, what a feast it was to answer you by becoming more and more august, more and more gracious, more and more ancient and mellow! But this lad has seen how to bowl me out. He has answered me back, vaunt for vaunt, rhetoric for rhetoric. He has lifted the only shield I cannot break."[10]

Despite all that Quin had wrought in his fanciful transformation of London's boroughs, elements of bureaucratic despotism had not been banished from this new collection of petty kingdoms. When several of London's boroughs banded together to force a new road through Notting Hill—all in the name of progress—Adam Wayne and his beloved Notting Hill resisted. The great powers became increasingly dictatorial. Ultimately, Wayne and Notting Hill's residents had no choice but to fight to defend the sovereignty of their city-state. And so the scene for battle was set: one small realm pitted against the combined might and power of the king and the dominant boroughs. Notting Hill prevailed in the end, attended by consequences no one could have foreseen.

⌗

As the introduction to the Oxford World's Classics edition of this novel states, only Chesterton could have hit upon such a literary conceit in his desire to explore the nature of human loyalties, the deceptions of modernity, and the dangers of the monolithic state.[11] But then *The Napoleon of Notting Hill* afforded the opportunity for Chesterton to combine three things he had loved all his life: fairy tales, medieval culture, and the landscape of Edwardian London. In this instance, his novel was simply a fairy tale writ large—set on a larger canvas—to use a term he knew well as a visual artist.

The *New York Times*, for its part, had closely followed the fortunes of this, Chesterton's first novel. Even as it was being written, the *Times* took note. This in itself was no small indication of the stature Chesterton now enjoyed as a man of letters. The reportage then posted by the *Times* recalls literary New York one hundred years ago. Under the heading of "London News," and via a dispatch sent by "Special Cable," the *Times* stated on Saturday, March 12, 1904:

London, March 11.—There has been much curiosity about the first novel of Gilbert K. Chesterton, the brilliant, if paradoxical, essayist and biographer. Its title, "The Napoleon of Notting Hill," was announced some time ago. Notting Hill is a London neighborhood, lying west of Bayswater and north of Kensington. It is a London habit to poke fun at Notting Hill. John Lane will publish the novel March 22. Mr. Chesterton will transport his reader 100 years into the future and enable him to see curious things in London. It is gravely asserted that the principal character is so drawn that there is no difficulty in discovering that it is based on the personality of Max Beerbohm, the humorist and critic. But people are asking what on earth Max could be doing in Notting Hill. He never visits further west than Lancaster Gate.[12]

Two months later, on May 28, the *Times* review appeared in the *Saturday Review of Books*.[13] Its tone clearly indicated that Chesterton was a literary force to be reckoned with. Allowing that the novel was very English in character, speaking most meaningfully to those with a requisite knowledge of "English politics or peculiarly English habits of thought," the *Times* review discerned in Chesterton one of the "bright young men in England"—a member of "the present rising generation" that was "working harder than any previous rising generation ever worked to alleviate the storied national dullness." In this, the *Times* observed, Chesterton was "at all times and everywhere a jester." This was preceded by a discussion of the literary context in which Chesterton had emerged:

Mr. Chesterton has made his mark as an original, sufficiently clear-sighted, and fair-minded critic of literature and the fine arts, gifted largely with what we are in the habit of calling a sense of humor. Taking one clue, as it seems to us, from his friends, Max Beerbohm and James F. Runciman, and another from his friend George Bernard Shaw, (and all of these owe much to William Schwenck Gilbert,) he has exercised his own bright talent to attract and charm all persons who, habitually reading English books, care enough for literature to keep in touch with current criticism. Thus he has gained wide repute in a very short time.[14]

Moving to the close of its review, the *Times* offered a concise and wryly observed introduction to Chesterton's novel. "It begins with some chaff about the futility of prophecy, one of the favorite games of the human race, 'to which,' says Mr. Chesterton, 'so many of my readers belong.'" The best idea one can get of the book, the review concluded, can be gained by reading the opening paragraphs of chapter 2. This was a just observation, as well as a way to isolate one of the best instances in the novel of Chesterton's high-flown satiric style:

> Very few words are needed to explain why London, a hundred years hence, will be very like it is now, or rather, since I must slip into a prophetic past, why London, when my story opens, was very like it was in those enviable days when I was still alive.
>
> The reason can be stated in one sentence. The people had absolutely lost faith in revolutions. All revolutions are doctrinal such as the French one, or the one that introduced Christianity. For it stands to common sense that you cannot upset all existing things, customs, and compromises, unless you believe in something outside them, something positive and divine. Now, England, during this century, lost all belief in this. It believed in a thing called Evolution. And it said, "All theoretic changes have ended in blood and ennui. If we change, we must change slowly and safely, as the animals do. Nature's revolutions are the only successful ones. There has been no conservative reaction in favour of tails."[15]

And all this in a first novel from a writer not yet thirty years old when his book was published. More novels would follow in time to come, but this was a remarkable debut.

CHAPTER 9

Heretics and First Things

We could use another Chesterton today, I think. In a time when culture and faith have drifted even further apart, we could use his brilliance, his entertaining style, and above all, his generous and joyful spirit. When society becomes polarized, as ours has, it is as if the two sides stand across a great divide and shout at each other. Chesterton had another approach: He walked to the center of a swinging bridge, roared a challenge to any single combat warriors, and then made both sides laugh aloud.[1]

—PHILIP YANCEY (2001)

Why did Chesterton write *Heretics* and *Orthodoxy*? At the start, he did not conceive of two books that would explore opposite sides of the same metaphysical coin. He had only the book that would become *Heretics* in view. One overarching thought impelled him. "In our time," he wrote, "philosophy or religion, our theory, that is, about ultimate things, has been driven out, more or less simultaneously, from two fields which it used to occupy"—literature and politics.[2] This was deeply troubling. And so, with no little sense of urgency, Chesterton took it upon himself to mount a defense of philosophy.[3] He would play the town crier and speak directly to his own historical moment, the England of 1905:

Persistently for the last twenty years the ideals of order or liberty have dwindled in our books; the ambitions of wit and eloquence have dwindled in our parliaments. Literature has purposely become less political; politics have purposely become less literary. General theories of the relation of things have thus been extruded from both; and we are in a position to ask, "What have we gained or lost by this extrusion? Is literature better, is politics better, for having discarded the moralist and the philosopher?"

When everything about a people is for the time growing weak and ineffective, it begins to talk about efficiency. So it is that when a man's body is a wreck he begins, for the first time, to talk about health.[4]

Chesterton was a man of deep discernment. While so many of his contemporaries, for example, saw Mark Twain largely as an amiable and seemingly endless font of good humor, Chesterton detected the somberness that infused so much of his writing. As biographer Ron Powers observed: "Twain insisted that the secret source of humor was not joy, but sorrow. G. K. Chesterton was among [the few] who noticed this sometimes subtle dialectic. . . . Twain was 'always serious to the point of madness,' he observed—'an unfathomably solemn man.'"[5] So, when it came to taking the measure of his own historical moment, Chesterton was eminently qualified.[6]

As he looked about him, Chesterton saw himself in the midst of serious times. "Our affairs," he wrote,

are hopelessly muddled by strong, silent men. And just as this repudiation of big words and big visions has brought forth a race of small men in politics, so it has brought forth a race of small men in the arts. Our modern politicians claim the colossal license of Caesar and the Superman, claim that they are too practical to be pure and too patriotic to be moral; but the upshot of it all is that a mediocrity is Chancellor of the Exchequer. Our new artistic philosophers call for the same moral license, for a freedom to wreck heaven and earth with their energy; but the upshot of it all is that a mediocrity is Poet Laureate.[7]

Still the problem, as Chesterton saw it, went far deeper than any hopeless muddle that might beset public affairs. Many leaders and members of the literati—those with considerable influence in shaping public opinion—had become increasingly careless as to whether they were philosophically right. Words had ceased to mean things they had formerly meant. First things were increasingly disregarded. This baleful trend had transformed the meaning of the words *heresy* and *orthodoxy*. *Heresy*, Chesterton wrote, "not only means no longer being wrong; it practically means being clear-headed and courageous." It had become common for people to say, "I suppose I am very heretical," and look around for applause. Meanwhile the word *orthodoxy* had become anathema. "It not only no longer means being right," Chesterton said, "it practically means being wrong."[8] To illustrate the dangers of this, he introduced one of his stark contrasts. "It is foolish," he wrote,

> for a philosopher to set fire to another philosopher in Smithfield Market because they do not agree in their theory of the universe. That was done very frequently in the last decadence of the Middle Ages, and it failed altogether in its object. But there is one thing that is infinitely more absurd and unpractical than burning a man for his philosophy. This is the habit of saying that his philosophy does not matter. . . .

Mr. Bernard Shaw has put the view in a perfect epigram: "The golden rule is that there is no golden rule." We are more and more to discuss details in art, politics, literature. A man's opinion on tramcars matters; his opinion on Botticelli matters; his opinion on all things does not matter. He may turn over and explore a million objects, but he must not find that strange object, the universe; for if he does he will have a religion, and be lost.[9]

Chesterton lamented the fact that so many leaders among his contemporaries had not been good stewards of the moral and intellectual heritage handed down to them. In spelling out what he meant, he described problems still with us more than one hundred years after he put pen to paper:

When the old Liberals removed the gags from all the heresies, their idea was that religious and philosophical discoveries might thus be made. Their view was that cosmic truth was so important that every one ought to bear independent testimony. The modern idea is that cosmic truth is so unimportant that it cannot matter what any one says. The former freed inquiry as men loose a noble hound; the latter frees inquiry as men fling back into the sea a fish unfit for eating. Never has there been so little discussion about the nature of men as now, when, for the first time, any one can discuss it. The old restriction meant that only the orthodox were allowed to discuss religion. Modern liberty means that nobody is allowed to discuss it.[10]

Bearing all this in mind, Chesterton distilled his reasons for writing *Heretics* to one sentence: "But there are some people, nevertheless—and I am one of them—who think that the most practical and important thing about a man is still his view of the universe."[11] And so he would undertake a detailed survey of the cultural landscape—seeking to unriddle and refute prevalent heresies. It was not too late, he believed, to regain ground that had been lost. He would do what he could to foster that good end.

CHAPTER 10

No Definite Image of Good

The purpose of re-ascending to origins is that we should be able to return, with greater spiritual knowledge, to our own situation. We need to recover the sense of religious fear, so that it may be overcome by religious hope.[1]

—T. S. ELIOT (1939)

[Mr. Chesterton] is not thinking of paradoxes for the sake of paradoxes—as some foolish critics may have invited you to suppose. Not a bit of it. . . . He is rummaging in the rubbish heap of words and concepts to which a slovenly race of thinkers has reduced the working dictionary of the English tongue. He seeks the clear word for the clear idea.[2]

—NEW YORK TIMES (1912)

Just before the close of chapter 1 of *Heretics*, Chesterton displayed his ever-present desire to engage in robust, charitable debate. He spoke of the general idea of his book and his "wish to deal with my most distinguished contemporaries, not personally or in a merely literary manner, but in relation to the real body of doctrine which they teach." He was not, for example, "concerned with

Mr. Rudyard Kipling as a vivid artist or a vigorous personality; I am concerned with him as a Heretic—that is to say, a man whose view of things has the hardihood to differ from mine." Nor was he "concerned with Mr. Bernard Shaw as one of the most brilliant and one of the most honest men alive; I am concerned with him as a Heretic—that is to say, a man whose philosophy is quite solid, quite coherent, and quite wrong."[3]

To illustrate what he meant, Chesterton introduced a parable. "I revert," he began,

> to the doctrinal methods of the thirteenth century, inspired by the general hope of getting something done.
>
> Suppose that a great commotion arises in the street about something, let us say a lamp-post, which many influential persons desire to pull down. A grey-clad monk, who is the spirit of the Middle Ages, is approached upon the matter, and begins to say, in the arid manner of the Schoolmen, "Let us first of all consider, my brethren, the value of Light. If Light be in itself good—"
>
> At this point he is somewhat excusably knocked down. All the people make a rush for the lamp-post, the lamp-post is down in ten minutes, and they go about congratulating each other on their unmediaeval practicality. But as things go on they do not work out so easily. Some people have pulled the lamp-post down because they wanted the electric light; some because they wanted old iron; some because they wanted darkness, because their deeds were evil. Some thought it not enough of a lamp-post, some too much; some acted because they wanted to smash municipal machinery; some because they wanted to smash something. And there is war in the night, no man knowing whom he strikes.

So, gradually and inevitably, to-day, to-morrow, or the next day, there comes back the conviction that the monk was right after all, and that all depends on what is the philosophy of Light. Only what we might have discussed under the gas-lamp, we now must discuss in the dark.[4]

In such a state of affairs, Chesterton sought to guide his readers toward a new gaslamp. But first he had to explain why the old one had come to ruin. There was, he said, a "great gap in modern ethics, [an] absence of vivid pictures of purity and spiritual triumph, which lies at the back of the real objection felt by so many sane men to the realistic literature of the nineteenth century."[5] Writers like Ibsen, Maupassant, and Zola were ostensibly the heralds of this realistic literature—a warts-and-all approach to writing that prided itself on presenting ordinary people as they really were—the good, the bad, and the ugly. They saw themselves, in Chesterton's view, as innovators.

But were they really? Chesterton thought not. "The average conversation of average men throughout the whole of modern civilization in every class or trade is such as Zola would never dream of printing," he wrote. "Nor is the habit of writing thus of these things a new habit."[6] Warming to his task, he continued:

> The tradition of calling a spade a spade starts very early in our literature and comes down very late. But the truth is that the ordinary honest man, whatever vague account he may have given of his feelings, was not either disgusted or even annoyed at the candour of the moderns. What disgusted him, and very justly, was not the presence of a clear realism, but the absence of a clear idealism. Strong and genuine religious sentiment has never had any objection to realism; on the contrary, religion was

the realistic thing, the brutal thing, the thing that called names. This is the great difference between some recent developments of Nonconformity and the great Puritanism of the seventeenth century. It was the whole point of the Puritans that they cared nothing for decency. Modern Nonconformist newspapers distinguish themselves by suppressing precisely those nouns and adjectives which the founders of Nonconformity distinguished themselves by flinging at kings and queens. But if it was a chief claim of religion that it spoke plainly about evil, it was the chief claim of all that it spoke plainly about good.[7]

Chesterton was deeply troubled by "the problem of a human consciousness filled with very definite images of evil, and . . . no definite image of good."[8] If this problem persisted, then

light must be henceforward the dark thing—the thing of which we cannot speak. To us, as to Milton's devils in Pandemonium, it is darkness that is visible. The human race, according to religion, fell once, and in falling gained knowledge of good and of evil. Now we have fallen a second time, and only the knowledge of evil remains to us.[9]

Chesterton warned that "a great silent collapse" had taken place in his time. "All previous ages have sweated and been crucified in an attempt to realize what is really the right life, what was really the good man. A definite part of the modern world has come beyond question to the conclusion that there is no answer to these questions."[10]

Acquiescing in this mind-set was an act of sheer and dangerous folly. For Chesterton, it came down to this: many of his contemporaries were seeking to solace themselves in a series of self-deceptions.

Every one of the popular modern phrases and ideals is a dodge in order to shirk the problem of what is good. We are fond of talking about "liberty"; that, as we talk of it, is a dodge to avoid discussing what is good. We are fond of talking about "progress"; that is a dodge to avoid discussing what is good. We are fond of talking about "education"; that is a dodge to avoid discussing what is good. The modern man says, "Let us leave all these arbitrary standards and embrace liberty."

This is, logically rendered, "Let us not decide what is good, but let it be considered good not to decide it." He says, "Away with your old moral formulae; I am for progress." This, logically stated, means, "Let us not settle what is good; but let us settle whether we are getting more of it." He says, "Neither in religion nor morality, my friend, lie the hopes of the race, but in education." This, clearly expressed, means, "We cannot decide what is good, but let us give it to our children."[11]

Chesterton called such self-deception "solemn folly," and to his mind this kind of thinking was personified in the writings of one of his contemporaries, the Irish novelist, short-story writer, poet, art critic, memoirist, and dramatist George Moore, a man who prided himself on being an iconoclast.[12] As one might expect from a man of such diverse talents, Moore's criticisms of convention had something of a scattergun quality. Chesterton recognized Moore's considerable gifts but saw something of a cautionary tale in his restless iconoclasm. To drive his point home, he offered a witty and satirical critique of Moore's fascination with the next big thing:

Moore began his literary career by writing his personal confessions; nor is there any harm in this if he had not continued them for the remainder of his life. He is a man of genuinely forcible mind and of great command over a kind of rhetorical and fugitive conviction which excites and pleases. He is in a perpetual state of temporary honesty. He has admired all the most admirable modern eccentrics until they could stand it no longer.[13]

Moore's capacity for rhetorical flourish and fugitive conviction may have excited some readers and pleased others, but Chesterton was not so easily impressed—particularly since he detected in Moore an unfortunate disdain for certain paradoxes inherent in the Christian tradition. Chesterton, on the other hand, revered these "mysteries" and thought they attested the truth of Christianity. Such points of disagreement provided considerable grist for his intellectual mill. "The truth is," he wrote,

that the tradition of Christianity (which is still the only coherent ethic of Europe) rests on two or three paradoxes or mysteries which can easily be impugned in argument and as easily justified in life. One of them, for instance, is the paradox of hope or faith—that the more hopeless is the situation the more hopeful must be the man. [Robert Louis] Stevenson understood this, and consequently Mr. Moore cannot understand Stevenson. Another is the paradox of charity or chivalry that the weaker a thing is the more it should be respected, that the more indefensible a thing is the more it should appeal to us for a certain kind of defence. [William] Thackeray understood this, and therefore Mr. Moore does not understand Thackeray.[14]

Chesterton's greatest point of concern for Moore centered on the sinfulness of pride and its attendant consequences. Chesterton's study of Catholic teaching had taught him much about this. "Pride," he wrote, "is a weakness in the character; it dries up laughter, it dries up wonder, it dries up chivalry and energy."[15] Pride can foster a solemn kind of folly.[16] It had led to a self-absorption in Moore that drove him to be a continual seeker with no point of rest—a pugnacious man who stoutly defended convictions that shifted, seemingly, from one day to the next.[17]

"A man who thinks a great deal about himself," Chesterton continued, "will try to be many-sided, attempt a theatrical excellence at all points, will try to be an encyclopaedia of culture, and his own real personality will be lost in that false universalism. Thinking about himself will lead to trying to be the universe; trying to be the universe will lead to ceasing to be anything."[18] Here Chesterton invoked a contrast with Robert Louis Stevenson—a writer, Chesterton concluded, who had "at least found a final philosophy of some sort to live by. . . . Mr. Moore is always walking the world looking for a new one."[19]

⁜

When Chesterton was on form, as he so often was in *Heretics*, he could pen a single phrase that cut sham, pretense, or deception to the quick. Many people regard him primarily as a mystery writer or Christian apologist. But he could at times don the mantle of a social critic. When he did, he was formidable and unsparing.

Chapter 13 of *Heretics* was largely concerned with fallacies relating to ethnicity and nationalism that were prevalent in Chesterton's day. In some respects, this chapter seems rather dated and arcane. One could be forgiven for skimming through much of it with only a passing interest.

But one sentence in the opening paragraph stands out above all the others. "An enormous amount of modern ingenuity," Chesterton wrote, "is expended on finding defences for the indefensible conduct of the powerful."[20] Then followed a stinging indictment of England's treatment of Ireland—a country that had for centuries been oppressed and longed for freedom to chart its own national destiny. Chesterton succinctly rejected current English policy. To him it was a "perfectly patent fact" that England, for all its wealth, power, and supposed enlightenment, was "making a ludicrous mess of the government of a [supposedly] poorer nation like the Irish."[21]

This was the contemporary setting Chesterton addressed. But moving beyond it, there is timelessness in his indictment of the myriad ways "modern ingenuity is expended on finding defences for the indefensible conduct of the powerful."[22] We live in an age of spin and scandal, parsing and corruption. The powerful issue seemingly contrite non-apologies and then go on much as they did before. Chesterton lived in such a time as well, though of course the *dramatis personae* were different.

It is in such a setting, regardless of historical moment, that his words carry the most power. One crucial thought comes through in what he wrote: "Be discerning." Respect authority, yes; be thankful for time-honored institutions that have served your nation well; honor those who have served justly and faithfully in public life. But never forget words like those uttered by Lord Acton—"Power tends to corrupt; absolute power corrupts absolutely"—or the sobering insight of Abigail Adams: "Remember, all Men would be tyrants if they could." Parties change; political figures rise and fall; conventional wisdom is one moment in the ascendant and, in another, is treated with utter derision. Governments, churches, institutions of whatever stripe—all are liable to abuse and oppression no less than individuals. Chesterton understood that human nature does not change. He wrote from the same Christian perspective that Acton and Adams did. Like theirs, his words have a claim on our remembrance.

⋇

Chesterton also wrote with great insight about what might be called the literature of snobbishness. In this aspect of their literary criticism, Chesterton and C. S. Lewis were much alike. Lewis, in concert with Owen Barfield, had famously coined the term "chronological snobbery," which for Lewis referred to "the uncritical acceptance of the intellectual climate common to our own age and the assumption that whatever has gone out of date is on that account discredited."[23] Barfield, for his part, defined chronological snobbery as the belief that "intellectually, humanity languished for countless generations in the most childish errors on all sorts of crucial subjects, until it was redeemed by some simple scientific dictum of the last century."[24] Both Lewis and Barfield strongly rejected the "argument that the thinking, art, or science of an earlier time is *inherently* inferior when compared to that of the present."[25] Chesterton heartily asserted the same thing, saying:

> An imbecile habit has arisen in modern controversy of saying that such and such a creed can be held in one age but cannot be held in another. Some dogma, we are told, was credible in the twelfth century, but is not credible in the twentieth. You might as well say that a certain philosophy can be believed on Mondays, but cannot be believed on Tuesdays. You might as well say of a view of the cosmos that it was suitable to half-past three, but not

suitable to half-past four. What a man can believe depends upon his philosophy, not upon the clock or the century.[26]

And so it should not come as a surprise that Chesterton had little love for this literature of snobbishness. And in chapter 15 of *Heretics* we find a passage that foreshadows the writings of Lewis. "The pedantic decisions," Chesterton wrote, "and definable readjustments of man may be found in scrolls and statute books and scriptures; but men's basic assumptions and everlasting energies are to be found in penny dreadfuls and halfpenny novelettes. Thus a man, like many men of real culture in our day, might learn from good literature nothing except the power to appreciate good literature. But from bad literature he might learn to govern empires and look over the map of mankind."[27]

Such a passage richly illustrates why rummaging through the pages of *Heretics* is as rewarding a pastime as one might hope to find. Some sections of the book, as one might expect, relate quite directly to the historical moment in which they were written, but scattered among these portions of the book are paragraphs chock-full of wisdom, wit, and profundity. Such is the case with the following paragraph, again from chapter 15. It dispenses with more foolish notions that have attached themselves to what is "good form" in literature:

> Our wits understand talk, but not what Dr. Johnson called a good talk. In order to have, like Dr. Johnson, a good talk, it is emphatically necessary to be, like Dr. Johnson, a good man—to have friendship and honour and an abysmal tenderness. Above all, it is necessary to be openly and indecently humane, to confess with fulness all the primary pities and fears of Adam. Johnson was a clear-headed humorous man, and therefore he did not mind talking seriously about religion.[28]

The overarching theme of *Heretics* was that the culture in which Chesterton was reared had slipped its traditional moorings. Precise moral ideals had ceased to hold sway among many thought leaders in Britain—and in Western culture more generally. This threatened to undo the societal gains of prior generations. "Never perhaps," he wrote,

> since the beginning of the world has there been an age that had less right to use the word "progress" than we. In the Catholic twelfth century, in the philosophic eighteenth century, the direction may have been a good or a bad one, men may have differed more or less about how far they went, and in what direction, but about the direction they did in the main agree, and consequently they had the genuine sensation of progress.
>
> But it is precisely about the direction that we disagree. Whether the future excellence lies in more law or less law, in more liberty or less liberty; whether property will be finally concentrated or finally cut up; whether sexual passion will reach its sanest in an almost virgin intellectualism or in a full animal freedom; whether we should love everybody with Tolstoy, or spare nobody with Nietzsche;—these are the things about which we are actually fighting most. It is not merely true that the age which has settled least what is progress is this "progressive" age. It is, moreover, true that the people who have settled least what is progress are the most "progressive" people in it.[29]

Chesterton saw many of his contemporaries running headlong to who-knows-where. Since they had "no definite image of good," he worried that they just might get there.

CHAPTER 11

Mr. Dickens's Champion

*Dear G. K. C. As I am a supersaturated Dickensite, I
pounced on your book and read it, as Wegg read Gibbon and
other authors, right slap through.*[1]

—GEORGE BERNARD SHAW (1906)

C hesterton may be said to have written two great literary studies. *Robert Browning*, published by Macmillan in 1903, was
the first. The second, published by Dodd, Mead and Company in
1906, was *Charles Dickens: A Critical Study*. These books represent
the twin pillars of Chesterton's literary criticism. He was never in
better form.

In the years since both studies appeared in print, readers and
critics alike have singled out one or the other as the better of the
two. Some have seen equal merit in both. But if a choice had to be
made between the two, many would choose *Charles Dickens*.

Chief among the reasons for this would be the ripple effect
that Chesterton's book had immediately following its publication.
Seldom does one book, in and of itself, spark a revival of interest in
a writer. But that is precisely what Chesterton's study of Dickens
did. It was both a critical success and a catalyst—a rare feat for
any work of literary criticism. William Oddie, in his authoritative

Oxford University Press study of Chesterton, has written that *Charles Dickens* "led to a popular revival of interest in Dickens' writings, and to the publication of the Everyman edition of his works from 1907 to 1911, with individual introductions to every novel by Chesterton himself (collected in 1911 in *Appreciations and Criticisms of the Works of Charles Dickens*)."[2]

The revival of interest in Dickens sparked by Chesterton's book has never waned. Indeed the complexities of Dickens's literary achievement—the nuances of his literary style, his genius for the comic, the myriad ways that his books hold up a kind of mirror to social conditions, and the profound human sympathy that infuses his writings—all these and many more aspects of Dickens's life and writings continue to be explored. Once seen solely as a popular Victorian novelist, Dickens is now widely viewed as an artist of the first order, and a great novelist by any measure.

At the same time, Chesterton's preeminence among Dickens critics is secure. As Paul Schlicke wrote in *The Oxford Reader's Companion to Dickens*, "The greatest of all Dickens critics, G. K. Chesterton, emerged just after the turn of the century, in a number of writings, most notably in *Charles Dickens* (1906) and in introductions to the Everyman edition of the novels."[3]

Why is Chesterton special as a Dickensian critic? For a start, his "exuberant style" was a powerful complement to his exploration of "Dickens's supreme comic artistry and fecundity, and his glorification of the common man."[4] At the same time, commentators have underscored Chesterton's responsiveness to the humor and humanity of Dickens.[5]

There were other strengths as well. Chesterton's use of paradox, as one might expect, was much in evidence in *Charles Dickens*. But while it was undoubtedly a useful device, it could be a double-edged sword. What was a strength could prove a weakness. As Paul Schlicke observed: "Chesterton's exhilarating (and sometimes maddening) reliance on paradox sheds light on innumerable complexities of Dickens's art." At the same time, Michael Slater wrote that while "Chesterton brilliantly succeeds in conveying the unique flavour of Dickens's art and offers many penetrating insights into the workings of his imagination," there are within his study "occasional lapses into questionable assertions or a facile jokiness."[6]

Still, whatever shortcomings there were in Chesterton's study, they were relatively minor—and far outweighed by the book's virtues—as many first-rate critics were quick to assert. In May 1929, T. S. Eliot told Chesterton by letter, "Your study of Dickens was always a delight to me."[7] Two years earlier, in a published essay on "Wilkie Collins and Dickens," Eliot stated: "There is no better critic of Dickens living."[8]

Charles Dickens: A Critical Study was a book marked by great intuitive insights into Dickens's works—set forth with verve, humor, and arresting imagery. Chesterton could be at once entertaining and profoundly instructive—a rare feat among critics, and one that prefigured moments of C. S. Lewis's wide-ranging literary criticism in his *Preface to Paradise Lost*.[9] In a discussion of Dickens as a mythologist, into which reflections on the modern literature of his time come into play, Chesterton made cogent points by of all things drawing connections to "penny dreadfuls," "the thousand and one tales of Dick Deadshot," and "the thousand and one tales of Robin Hood."[10] Also drawn into the discussion are Shakespeare, elements of Greek mythology, Punch, and stories of Father Christmas—the combined effect warranting the application of words written by Alan Jacobs about C. S. Lewis to Chesterton: here "is a critic of . . . considerable range." Jacobs's observation about "the naturalness with which" Lewis did what he did also applies to Chesterton. And to turn one last phrase from Jacobs to good purpose, Lewis and Chesterton are "laborers in the same vineyard" as critics.[11] They are, in fact, kindred spirits. This can clearly be seen in Chesterton's extended reflections, which are as follows:

> The moderns, in a word, describe life in short stories because they are possessed with the sentiment that life itself is an uncommonly short story, and perhaps not a true one. But in this elder literature, even in the comic literature (indeed, especially in the comic literature), the reverse is true. The characters are felt to be fixed things of which we have fleeting glimpses; that is, they are felt to be divine. Uncle Toby is talking for ever, as the elves are dancing for ever. We feel that whenever we hammer on the house of Falstaff, Falstaff will be at home. We feel it as a Pagan would feel that, if a cry broke the silence after ages of unbelief, Apollo would still be listening in his temple. These writers may tell short stories, but we feel they are only parts of a long story. And herein lies the peculiar significance, the peculiar sacredness even, of penny dreadfuls and the common printed matter made for our errand-boys. Here in dim and desperate forms, under the ban of our base culture, stormed at by silly magistrates, sneered at by silly schoolmasters,—here is the old popular literature still popular; here is the unmistakable voluminousness, the thousand and one tales of Dick Deadshot, like the thousand and one tales of Robin Hood. Here is the splendid and static boy, the boy who remains a boy through a thousand volumes and a thousand years. Here in mean alleys and dim shops, shadowed and shamed by the police, mankind is still driving its dark trade in heroes. And elsewhere, and in all other ages, in braver fashion,

under cleaner skies the same eternal tale-telling goes on, and the whole mortal world is a factory of immortals.

Dickens was a mythologist rather than a novelist; he was the last of the mythologists, and perhaps the greatest. He did not always manage to make his characters men, but he always managed, at the least, to make them gods. They are creatures like Punch or Father Christmas. They live statically, in a perpetual summer of being themselves.[12]

It is also significant that Chesterton adopted this novel approach to his critique of Dickens in 1906, some thirty-five years before Lewis penned his own innovative critique of Milton in *A Preface to Paradise Lost*. (Lewis's book grew out of a series of talks he gave as part of the Ballard Matthews Lectures he delivered at the University College of North Wales in 1941.)

Many have heretofore seen Lewis as the originator of this type of free-ranging criticism, or at least the most celebrated practitioner of it. Chesterton rightly deserves credit for breaking ground in soil Lewis later tilled so fruitfully.

One wonders as well whether Lewis was influenced in his adoption of such a free-ranging style of criticism by Chesterton. It is widely known that he read Chesterton's works and that Chesterton was a great influence in Lewis's return to belief in Christianity. But even if a direct line of influence cannot be drawn from Chesterton to Lewis in this regard, the affinities between their approaches to criticism are striking.

Interesting as the affinities between Chesterton and Lewis are as critics, this is not the only connection between Chesterton and the Inklings—the celebrated group of literary friends that included J. R. R. Tolkien, Charles Williams, and Lewis. In fact, Chesterton's connection to Tolkien also centers in reflections Chesterton offered in his study of Dickens.

Chesterton's description of Dickens as a mythologist suggests a possible affinity with Tolkien, who was a mythmaker in the highest sense of the art. But we are not left in the realm of conjecture here. In one of his most famous essays, "On Fairy Stories," Tolkien himself described portions of Chesterton's study of Dickens that met with his approval. "We need recovery," Tolkien observed.

We should look at green again, and be startled anew (but not blinded) by blue and yellow and red. We should meet the centaur and the dragon, and then perhaps suddenly behold, like the ancient shepherds, dogs, and horses—and wolves. This recovery fairy-stories help us to make. . . .

Recovery (which includes return and renewal of health) is a re-gaining—regaining of a clear view. I do not say "seeing things as they are" and involve myself with the philosophers, though I might venture to say "seeing things as we are (or were) meant to see them"—as things apart from ourselves. We need, in any case, to clean our windows; so that the things seen clearly may be freed from the drab blur of triteness or familiarity—from possessiveness. . . . This triteness is really the penalty of "appropriation": the things that are trite, or (in a bad sense) familiar, are the things that we have appropriated, legally or mentally. We say we know them. They have become like the things which once attracted us by their glitter, or their colour, or their shape, and we laid hands on them, and then locked them in our hoard, acquired them, and acquiring ceased to look at them.

Of course, fairy-stories are not the only means of recovery, or prophylactic against loss. Humility is enough. And there is (especially for the humble) Mooreeffoc, or Chestertonian Fantasy. Mooreeffoc is a fantastic word, but it could be seen written up in every town in this land. It is Coffee-room, viewed from the inside through a glass door, as it was seen by Dickens on a dark London day; and it was used by Chesterton to denote the queerness of things that have become trite, when they are seen suddenly from a new angle. That kind of "fantasy" most people would allow to be wholesome enough; and it can never lack for material.[13]

Aside from what Tolkien wrote above, he shared another point of common ground with Chesterton—one identified by Inklings scholar Peter Kreeft.[14] "The fairy-tale philosopher," Chesterton wrote,

is glad that the leaf is green precisely because it might have been scarlet. He feels as if it had turned green an instant before he looked at it. He is pleased that snow is white on the strictly reasonable ground that it might have been black. Every colour has in it a bold quality as of choice; the red of garden roses is not only decisive but dramatic, like suddenly spilt blood.[15]

This passage, from Chesterton's book *Orthodoxy*, is very like Tolkien's phrase "We should look at green again, and be startled anew."[16] Indeed, it is hard not to think that Tolkien's phrase owes something to Chesterton. As we have seen, Tolkien read and later commented upon passages from *Charles Dickens: A Critical Study*. As someone who had already undertaken a close reading of a famous work by Chesterton and who was also a devoted son of the Catholic Church, it seems unlikely that Tolkien would never have read *Orthodoxy*—the apologia penned by the most celebrated

Catholic writer of Tolkien's early life. Whether or not he did, what is clear is that Tolkien and Chesterton had much in common. Chesterton and Tolkien were also fellow laborers in the same portion of a fruitful vineyard.

However, Tolkien did dissent from Chesterton in one important respect. Though he recognized and praised "Chestertonian Fantasy"—as described above—he felt that such literature had its limitations. "Chestertonian Fantasy," Tolkien wrote,

> has, I think, only a limited power; for the reason that recovery of freshness of vision is its only virtue. The word Mooreeffoc may cause you suddenly to realize that England is an utterly alien land, lost either in some remote past age glimpsed by history, or in some strange dim future to be reached only by a time-machine; to see the amazing oddity and interest of its inhabitants and their customs and feeding-habits; but it cannot do more than that: act as a time-telescope focused on one spot. Creative fantasy, because it is mainly trying to do something else (make something new), may open your hoard and let all the locked things fly away like cage-birds.[17]

Tolkien, as a practitioner of "creative fantasy" and as the author of *The Lord of the Rings*, had entered a realm on another order of magnitude entirely from the "Mooreeffoc" fantasy Chesterton detected in Dickens. Still, he saw virtue in what Chesterton had written about, and that is a significant point of connection between the two writers. Both men had conceived a great appreciation for the "recovery fairy-stories help us to make."[18] Both men sought to foster this appreciation among others through their writings. In this respect both men were allies—and noteworthy apologists for fairy stories.

⌗

Beyond connections to Lewis and Tolkien, the reception that *Charles Dickens: A Critical Study* met with in America is important. It was reviewed twice in the *New York Times*, the first review published on September 29, 1906.

On the positive side of the ledger, the *Times* reviewer offered qualified praise. He judged that Chesterton's study "contains here and there some very good things."[19] The reviewer also stated that Chesterton's book rivaled if not surpassed his earlier study, *Robert Browning.* "Mr. Chesterton's *Charles Dickens: A Critical Study*," the reviewer stated,

> is an eminently readable book. It is not devoid of padding, and there are some whole chapters that may be skipped by one who reads for entertainment and not for knowledge. But who reads Chesterton for knowledge—unless it be for knowledge of Chesterton's curious mind? The "impressionistic" critic's highest aim, as we knew of old, is to recount the "adventures of his soul among masterworks." The adventures of Mr. Chesterton's soul among the masterworks of Charles Dickens are as amusing as the adventures of the same soul in the poetry of Browning. It is an adventurous soul, a picaresque soul, and it finds interesting and exciting adventures wherever it goes.[20]

The *Times* reviewer next drew a distinction between any claims Chesterton's book might have to be regarded as a biography (a claim, as it happened, that Chesterton never made) and recognition it sought as a work of criticism. "As biography," the reviewer stated, "Mr. Chesterton's book is quite superfluous, and, we may add, quite inadequate. As criticism it will hugely delight folks who find enjoyment in literary fireworks."[21]

The *Times* reviewer made a misstep, however, in stating that Chesterton's book was "builded on the false idea that at just this moment Dickens needs a champion among his own people."[22] The fact was that Dickens had never stood in such need of a skilled champion as he did when Chesterton commenced his works of criticism. Dickensian scholar Michael Slater, after saying that "Chesterton brilliantly succeeds in conveying the unique flavour of Dickens's art and offers many penetrating insights into the workings of his imagination,"[23] went on to characterize the precise nature of the services Chesterton had rendered for Dickens:

> Between 1907 and 1909 [Chesterton] wrote individual prefaces for each of Dickens's books as they were reprinted by J. M. Dent in his Everyman's Library. These prefaces, collected under the title *Appreciations and Criticisms of the Works of Charles Dickens* in 1911 ... contain more detailed comment on individual novels than the 1906 book, and some of Chesterton's most interesting and stimulating discussion of Dickens's work can be found here, such as his fine analysis of the centripetal structure of *Bleak House*. In *The Victorian Age in Literature* (1913) Chesterton featured Dickens prominently, defining his as "that most exquisite of arts ... the art of enjoying everybody," and for the rest of his career he continued to champion Dickens as a supremely great artist in a period when most academic critics regarded his achievement with indifference or downright disdain.[24]

The second review of Chesterton's book for the *New York Times* was published on December 29, 1906. It appears to have been a direct reply by letter to the September 29th review. The author of this letter, Hamilton Carr, proved far more insightful as a reader and more cognizant as well of what the precise nature of Chesterton's achievement was in crafting his book. "Gilbert K. Chesterton's critical study of Charles Dickens and his works," Carr began,

> is undoubtedly a valuable contribution to the great mass of notes explanatory of that renowned novelist and his literary methods, but its greatest charm, it seems to me, lies in the glimpses, sometimes delightfully prolonged, which we get of Chesterton himself. The nature of the subject is such as to demand the public attention, and it provides the initial attraction of the criticism, but Chesterton, with his inimitable art, could have proved quite as entertaining, quite as inexhaustibly funny, in his treatment of any author less famous or of any novels less generally read.
>
> Chesterton has been called the master of paradox, outrivaling in that respect his brilliant contemporary G. Bernard Shaw, and in no other work has he so beautifully lived up to his reputation as in the one under consideration. One is never quite sure that Chesterton's estimates are always serious. In fact, he has taught us to be a bit skeptical, a bit wary of sharp turns which lead nowhere. But he always takes us by the hand, in generous compassion, and leads us back at length to the main road, where, after we have jogged on a while, he plays another trick. It is, however, just that sense of the unexpected, the elusive, the unlooked-for deviations, which so charmingly allures us.
>
> Criticism is raised to the level of art in Chesterton's skillful hands. He avoids the stereotyped as to phrase and treatment and erects a literary structure a bit unusual in design and finish, leaving us to stand to one side and admire the completed

product. We stand, too, a trifle awed, noting eccentricity of out-line and alarming angles, which reveal undreamed of structural possibilities, and stifling the while, by the aid of an obtruding sense of justice, innumerable, undefined, half-born objections.

The outline of the "Critical Study" is not at all novel; the reader is not presented with any startling discoveries; there isn't even the intimate atmosphere which some deem so essential between biographer and subject. What there is, though, transcend-ing all such demands in splendidly ignoring them, is Chesterton, sporting blithely on every page in the performance of extraordi-nary antics. He delights in violent contrast, causing us precipitous mental leaps and leaving us at length only dimly conscious of the sudden transition, but immensely pleased, nevertheless, that we've had the experience. In his serious moods (we like to believe him occasionally serious) one catches illuminating views of the thing we call, comprehensively, human nature. But they are the views which Chesterton has photographed and retouched with his interpretive art, although he labels them with Dickens's name.

Through the book an undercurrent of mirth, held within bounds, for the most part, by a substantial but transparent forma-tion of literary dignity and a sense of the properties, bursts forth to the surface with joyous freedom, here and there, but never so hilariously, never so engagingly, as in the chapter devoted to Dickens's grievance against America. Chesterton sees the humor of Dickens's serious attitude, and treats it all as a little joke on his distinguished countryman. He handles the subject irresistibly.

If this latest book of Chesterton's lives, as it undoubtedly will, its years will not be due to the fact that the literary history of one of England's greatest novelists is therein adequately written, with a profound insight and a nice sense of values, but rather to the mature art of the biographer, which completely envelopes the subject and places it in a specially prepared niche, apart from the innumerable works similar in subject, scope, and design.[25]

Within the literary world, it is a truism that trends emerge and supplant one another almost constantly. Few writers and critics who once stood center stage remain there beyond their lifetimes. Literary reputations wax and wane and are subject to continual debate. Yet amidst such a setting, Chesterton is justly famous for having revived the literary reputation of Charles Dickens.[26]

Chesterton's study of Dickens is his most important work of criticism, and the most influential. When it was published in 1906, the literary fortunes of this preeminent Victorian novelist were at a low ebb. He seemed destined to remain among the rank of those novelists who were prolific and popular but consigned to a second tier of literary artistry. Chesterton's study did more than any single book ever has to alter that perception. More than this, Chesterton's criticisms are still read and appreciated. Scholars reference his reflections as a point of departure for further reflection and debate. He continues to be a part of the literary conversation.

Bearing all this in mind, what Chesterton the critic was able to do for Dickens the writer remains singularly impressive. It was, and will remain, one of his greatest achievements as a man of letters.

CHAPTER 12

Why *Orthodoxy* Matters

It is true, that a little philosophy inclineth man's mind to atheism; but depth in philosophy bringeth men's minds about to religion. For while the mind of man looketh upon second causes scattered, it may sometimes rest in them, and go no further; but when it beholdeth the chain of them, confederate and linked together, it must needs fly to Providence and Deity.[1]

—Francis Bacon (1642)

[John] Updike has repeatedly remarked that a God who is not part of daily human affairs is not very real for him. Barth provided him with a God who infuses himself in all aspects of his Creation, thus enabling Updike to "open to the world again." So Barth, with T. S. Eliot, G. K. Chesterton and Miguel Unamuno, helped him "believe."[2]

—Jack De Bellis, The John Updike Encyclopedia

Philosophy is either eternal or it is not philosophy. . . . A cosmic philosophy is not constructed to fit a man; a cosmic philosophy is constructed to fit a cosmos. A man can no more possess a private religion than he can possess a private sun and moon.[3]

—G. K. Chesterton, Introduction to the Book of Job

Maisie Ward, who knew Chesterton better than most, penned the best brief statement ever written about the purpose of the book that became *Orthodoxy*. It was, she said, "supremely Chesterton's own history of his mind [and] the story of how one man discovered Orthodoxy as the only answer to the riddle of the universe."[4]

And it was a masterpiece, Ward tells us—one no less remarkable in that it was written by a man who was only thirty-four when it was published.[5] Chesterton's book carried with it a gravitas and sureness of touch that belied his years. He was, and always had been, an old soul—but an old soul whose words were touched by joy and a sense of wonder.

As for lengthier statements of the book's intent, we have Chesterton himself to thank. In both the preface and introduction to *Orthodoxy*, he stated very explicitly why he put pen to paper. Straightaway, the reader is immersed in the Chestertonian style: spirited, lucid, and sparkling with originality. Here was a book that charted a wholly different course from any *apologia* that had come before.

"The only possible excuse for this book," Chesterton began,

> is that it is an answer to a challenge. Even a bad shot is dignified when he accepts a duel. When some time ago I published a series of hasty but sincere papers, under the name of *Heretics*, several critics for whose intellect I have a warm respect (I may mention specially Mr. G. S. Street) said that it was all very well for me to tell everybody to affirm his cosmic theory, but that I had carefully avoided supporting my precepts with example. "I will begin to worry about my philosophy," said Mr. Street, "when Mr. Chesterton has given us his." It was perhaps an incautious

suggestion to make to a person only too ready to write books upon the feeblest provocation.[6]

In a preface written after the first edition of his book appeared, Chesterton made a subtle distinction. In so doing, he told his readers what he was *not* trying to do in his book:

> It is the purpose of the writer to attempt an explanation, not of whether the Christian Faith can be believed, but of how he personally has come to believe it. The book is therefore arranged upon the positive principle of a riddle and its answer. It deals first with all the writer's own solitary and sincere speculations and then with all the startling style in which they were all suddenly satisfied by the Christian Theology.[7]

In the years following its publication in September 1908, *Orthodoxy* has touched the lives of millions of people. As an account of one man's journey to faith, its power to move, challenge, and inspire remains undimmed. It was hailed as a masterpiece upon its publication.[8] It continues as such now.

Among the readers for whom *Orthodoxy* has been especially meaningful are Garry Wills and Philip Yancey, two of America's most distinguished and respected writers. The two men hail from different faith traditions within Christendom—Wills is a Catholic and Yancey a Protestant—but both found solace and guidance in Chesterton's writings during a crisis of faith.

Wills and Yancey came to Chesterton's writings and found a healing, or recovery, of their faith—though for different reasons. But then, that was very much in keeping with the enduring appeal of *Orthodoxy*. The richness of Chesterton's book was such that there was enough and to spare to help both seekers. With that thought in view, we turn to the accounts both men have given of what they found in Chesterton. We begin with Philip Yancey.

⁂

On September 3, 2001, an exclusive excerpt from Philip Yancey's latest book, *Soul Survivor*, appeared in the pages of *Christianity Today*. Its subtitle was unlike any that had heretofore entered the genre of Christian literature—*How My Faith Survived the Church*. The title of the excerpt itself was unique, "The 'Ample' Man Who Saved My Faith." Its tagline read: "G. K. Chesterton propounded the Christian faith with great wit—and sheer intellectual force."

What followed was an unflinchingly honest memoir in brief. Reared in a fundamentalist church setting rife with racism and legalism, Yancey entered Bible college and was dismayed to find that the furloughed missionaries who were his teachers knew less about science and philosophy than his teachers in high school did. It was a world where intellectual curiosity tended to be punished rather than rewarded.[9]

One would have thought none of Yancey's experiences at this school could have done anything other than blight his questing and deeply felt faith, yet he found one oasis amid the parched desert of legalism. In an unlikely turn of events, it was at this Bible college that Yancey met with two genial subversives: C. S. Lewis and G. K. Chesterton. As he remembered, "they kindled hope [within me] that somewhere Christians existed who loosed rather than restrained their minds . . . above all, [they were Christians] who experienced life with God as a source of joy and not repression."[10]

Over an extended period of time, Yancey, who at one point had largely lost his faith, experienced a slow and halting return to belief, with Chesterton helping him navigate the stormy and unsettled moments of his pilgrim's progress. In his reading of Lewis and Chesterton, Yancey found that he was not alone. That realization brought solace and a gradual renewal. This time of his life marked a turning point: "I devoured everything I could find by these men.... Their words sustained me as a lifeline of faith.... I realized the power of words ... that could sail across time and an ocean and quietly, gently, work a transformation of healing and hope."[11]

As time passed, Yancey began to pick up the pieces strewn about him from the brokenness in his life. It was then that his debt to Chesterton, and to *Orthodoxy*, became especially great.

So what did Yancey find in the pages of this book with the formidable title? He found a writer—and a pilgrim—living in a world that was then not so very different from the world we live in now. He found a writer of great humanity, humility, and humor—a writer with an incandescent intellect who could part company, cogently and charitably, with non-Christian ways of looking at the world. A fair sample of what Yancey found in the pages of *Orthodoxy* appears in chapter 5, which Chesterton called "The Flag of the World." Here, recounting his own odyssey to belief, Chesterton remembered the time when he instinctively recoiled against the cultural pessimism so pervasive in his youth during the 1890s. Then, gradually, he began to understand how Christianity offered an answer to the seemingly insoluble problem he had been wrestling with. "I had often called myself an optimist," he recalled,

> to avoid the too evident blasphemy of pessimism. But all the
> optimism of the age had been false and disheartening for this

reason, that it had always been trying to prove that we fit in to the world. The Christian optimism is based on the fact that we do *not* fit in to the world. I had tried to be happy by telling myself that man is an animal, like any other which sought its meat from God. But now I really was happy, for I had learnt that man is a monstrosity. I had been right in feeling all things as odd, for I myself was at once worse and better than all things. The optimist's pleasure was prosaic, for it dwelt on the naturalness of everything; the Christian pleasure was poetic, for it dwelt on the unnaturalness of everything in the light of the supernatural. The modern philosopher had told me again and again that I was in the right place, and I had still felt depressed even in acquiescence. But I had heard that I was in the *wrong* place, and my soul sang for joy, like a bird in spring. The knowledge found out and illuminated forgotten chambers in the dark house of infancy. I knew now why grass had always seemed to me as queer as the green beard of a giant, and why I could feel homesick at home.[12]

When *Orthodoxy* was first published, a British publication called *Outlook* gave it a review. "Many of [Mr. Chesterton's] sayings," the review stated, "are a joy to the mind, and his analyses of the differences between Christianity and other religions is a continual pleasure from the force and originality of the imagery."[13]

Sixty years later, the *New York Times* published a review in much the same vein. "[Chesterton's] polemics," it read, "against the fashionable pessimism and decadence of the day . . . crystallized in *Orthodoxy*, one of the great apologias of the 20th century, in which he defends magic, mysticism, good conduct, free will and the belief in a God whose greatest secret may be the mirth in heaven."[14]

These reactions were very similar to those which Yancey felt following his reading of *Orthodoxy*. Chesterton, he wrote, "resuscitated my moribund faith [and] . . . he helped awaken in me a sense of long-suppressed joy."[15]

At another point in Yancey's account, he remembered a passage from Chesterton's study of *St. Francis of Assisi*: "Rossetti makes the remark somewhere, bitterly but with great truth, that the worst moment for the atheist is when he is really thankful and has nobody to thank."[16] These words in turn stirred Yancey's memories of *Orthodoxy*—and he offered a telling summary of one of Chesterton's most important ideas from that book: "A person in search of meaning resembles a sailor who awakens from a deep sleep and discovers treasure strewn about. . . . Fallen humanity is in such a state. Good things on earth—the natural world, beauty, love, joy—still bear traces of their original purpose, but amnesia mars the image of God in us."[17]

Yancey's reading of *Orthodoxy* led him to many of Chesterton's other works. Later, at a time when he was researching various Christian treatments of the problem of pain, Yancey read *The Man Who Was Thursday*, a wildly different kind of book from *Orthodoxy*—despite the fact that they were published within a year of each other. One could be forgiven for thinking that *The Man Who Was Thursday*, a novel that has often been described as a work of fantasy or a metaphysical thriller, would have no bearing on the problem of pain. Yet as a fictionalized account of how one man struggles to find meaning in a world of bleak pessimism, political anarchy, and social upheaval (this was an era, it should be remembered, when assassinations and bombings were common), *The Man Who Was Thursday* afforded Chesterton an opportunity to revisit a time when he had known a dark night of the soul and to recount (however obliquely) how hope returned as sunrise greets a better day. Yancey read about all of this, and it impressed him deeply. "[Like Chesterton,] I too came to believe in the good things of this world—first revealed to me in music, romantic love, and nature—as relics of a wreck, and as bright clues into the nature of a reality shrouded in darkness."[18]

Sometimes we are allowed the grace of returning a debt of gratitude. After Yancey's tribute to Chesterton first appeared in print, he was asked to adapt it to serve as an introduction for a new edition of *Orthodoxy*.[19] He did so, and that introduction has helped commend Chesterton to a wholly new readership. "We read to know we're not alone," it has been said. Philip Yancey remembered that sometimes we read and find joy.

�֍

In July 2002, a review of Garry Wills's book *Why I Am a Catholic* was published in the *New York Times*. The reviewer, Jack Mills, took note of the deeply troubling time in Wills's life—a time when the greatest questions one can ask threatened to be his undoing. "As Jesuit novice," Mills wrote,

> Wills underwent a crisis of faith in reality itself: does anything exist, or are we trapped in a dream? He survived that crisis with the help of a sensitive confessor and the chapter entitled "The Suicide of Thought" in G. K. Chesterton's *Orthodoxy*. A few years later, Wills left the Society of Jesus; but from that moment to this, Chesterton's vision of "the mystical minimum"—gratitude to God for the miracle that anything at all is—seems to have remained for him an intellectual bedrock.[20]

One might have thought, given Wills's intellect and studious temperament, that the writings of Cardinal Newman might have meant much in helping him secure a firm footing upon intellectual bedrock; but such was not the case. "It was Chesterton," he wrote, "not Newman, who came to my rescue in the seminary."[21]

A passage from Chesterton's study of Chaucer, the author of *The Canterbury Tales*, became especially meaningful to Wills as he struggled free of his despair. "There is at the back of all our lives," Chesterton had written, "an abyss of light, more blinding and unfathomable than any abyss of darkness; and it is the abyss of actuality, of existence, of the fact that things truly are, and that we are ourselves incredibly and sometimes almost incredulously real."[22]

This was, as Wills explained, what Chesterton called "the mystical minimum" of being—"a creative act by which God continually draws everything up out of the abyss of nothingness."[23] As Wills began to understand this idea, he saw that God had drawn him, and every other human being, out of that abyss. That realization restored to him a sense of wonder, as great a gift as he ever received. "This approach to God," Wills wrote,

> does not find him back in the past, at the origin of things—we are always at the origin of being, present to us as God's continuing act. It does not find him off in the mental future, at the end of a chain of syllogisms or tenuous mental connections. It begins within, by a wonder at the moment-by-moment continuance of one's own being.[24]

Wills understood all of this based on his reading of *Orthodoxy*. His confessor, Father Joe Fisher, had seen much of life. He had what Wills called "the Chestertonian attitude"—*la joie de vivre*—which showed itself in ways that helped an intellectually troubled young friend find his way. Fisher listened with kindness and counseled with perception and good humor. One of the best points of advice Wills received was to read the writings of Fisher's intellectual and spiritual mentor, Chesterton. "Father Fisher," Wills remembered,

> pointed me to specific passages in *Orthodoxy* that seemed to be describing my condition with an eerie exactitude. Chesterton, I would learn, had gone through a solipsistic, even suicidal, period in his own adolescence. One chapter in *Orthodoxy* is called "The Suicide of Thought." As I read it then, Chesterton's breezy public manner did not hide from my morbidly receptive state the private experience from which he wrote it—an experience he described in his *Autobiography*: "I had thought my way back to thought itself. It is a very dreadful thing to do; for it may lead to thinking that there is nothing but thought.... While dull atheists came and explained that there was nothing but matter, I listened with a sort of calm horror of detachment, suspecting there was nothing but mind."
>
> Chesterton's path out of this mental cul-de-sac followed what he called the "mystical minimum" of being. If there is nothing but one's own dream of a senseless world, the dream itself exists, and that is an inexplicable miracle. The dream of a void is outside the void. Even if it is a vision of evil, the evil can be there only because it has attached itself to something good, to existence. Pure evil, since it would be purely destructive, must (in its purity) annihilate itself. I soon learned that Augustine used a similar argument in his struggle to free himself from Manichaeism.[25]

This notion of the mystical minimum, Wills learned, served Chesterton well. When, for example, Chesterton tried to understand humility as manifested in the life of Saint Francis of Assisi, the mystical minimum pointed the way to understanding. "It was by this deliberate idea of starting from zero," Chesterton wrote, "from the dark nothingness of his own deserts, that he did come to enjoy even earthly things as few people have enjoyed them; and they are in themselves the best working example of the idea. For there is no way in which a man can earn a star or deserve a sunset."[26]

In response to this, Wills wrote that "the personal nature of creation as God's act explains, for Chesterton at least, our instinct to be grateful to things simply for existing, to feel an obligation to the sunrise. Having a conscience means feeling we owe the universe something in return."[27]

This portion of *Why I Am a Catholic* called forth some of Wills's best writing. Reflecting on some of the intellectual difficulties faced by Christian believers one hundred years earlier, he offered a distillation of Chesterton's thought, wedded to one of his finest poems. "The Christians of the nineteenth century," Wills wrote,

> were intimidated by vast reaches of space or time. But if size is the criterion, Chesterton said, then we would all be inferior to the nearest tree. Creation is as wondrous in a tiny thing as in the vast sum of things. The instant is as improbable as the eons.

> "Elder Father, though thine eyes
> Shine with hoary mysteries,
> Canst thou tell what in the heart
> Of a cowslip blossom lies?"
> "Smaller than all lives that be,
> Secret as the deepest sea,
> Stands a little house of seeds,

Like an elfin granary."
"Speller of the stones and weeds,
Skilled in nature's crafts and creed,
Tell me what is in the heart
Of the smallest of the seeds?"
"God Almighty, and with Him
Cherubim and Seraphim,
Filling all eternity—
Adonai Elohim."[28]

Another of Chesterton's writings that explored kindred themes was *The Ballad of the White Horse*. This epic poem has been treasured by many Christian thinkers, C. S. Lewis among them.[29] Among its many literary virtues, the *Ballad* speaks to the great themes caught up in the wonder of creation. In crafting his epic, Chesterton was expressing a debt of gratitude that held particular resonance for Wills, who wrote:

When Chesterton calls the God of creation the "conqueror of chaos in a six-days war," he spoke as a beneficiary of that campaign. Each day in the creation narrative is a victory over nothingness, and we are in on the conquest, each moment that the world continues to exist. In "The Ballad of the White Horse," King Alfred feels indebted to the humble workers of his kingdom because they are images of the God who labors for us all:

And well may God with the serving folk
Cast in His dreadful lot;
Is not He too a servant,
And is not He forgot?

For was not God my gardener
And silent like a slave;
That opened oaks on the uplands
Or thicket in graveyard gave?
And was not God my armorer,
All patient and unpaid,
That sealed my skull as a helmet
And ribs for hauberk made?
Did not a great grey servant
Of all my men and me,
Build this pavilion of the pines,
And herd the fowls and fill the vines,
And labour and pass and leave no signs
Save mercy and mystery?[30]

Fine as Wills's writings on Chesterton are, reviewers have not always understood or appreciated why they form a significant portion of his literary oeuvre. For in addition to the passages found in *Why I Am a Catholic*, Wills also published a book-length study of Chesterton's thought and writings, *Chesterton: Man & Mask*, which appeared in 1961. Wills later prepared a revised edition of this book, with a new introduction, published under the title *Chesterton* by Doubleday in 2001. *Why I Am a Catholic* was published one year later, in 2002, and it was there that Wills addressed some of the criticism he had received for dwelling at such length on Chesterton—a writer many of them had dismissed. "Some reviewers of my books," he wrote,

have complained that I quote Chesterton too much. A friend even told me to lay off the man, since one could trivialize one-self by association with a writer often disparaged as an empty paradox-monger. Despite the admiration for Chesterton expressed by Kafka and Borges, by Eliot and Auden, his huge body of superficial journalism has hidden the core of his thinking. Yet I believe in paying intellectual debts, and one of my largest debts was to him. That is why I served for a time as an advisor to the *Chesterton Newsletter*, and helped direct a dissertation on Chesterton at Northwestern University. Whatever things I disapprove of in Chesterton (and there are many), I still admire what it is not too pretentious to call his theological writings. . . . My Catholic upbringing would have been very different but for him. I now think I can go farther into the mysteries of faith with Augustine for a guide. But Chesterton was the Virgil to Augustine's Beatrice in my own journey up from Inferno.[31]

Among the many debts that readers owe to Wills for his searching and eloquent reflections on Chesterton is the best description yet written of what people will find should they care to turn to the pages of *Orthodoxy*. "Chesterton," Wills wrote, "described his style as the representation of familiar things from unsuspected angles, under new lights of the imagination, that we might see them with innocence of surprise."[32]

CHAPTER 13

A Melodramatic Sort of Moonshine

G. K. C., Gilbert Keith Chesterton, great, greatly articulate Roman convert and liberal, has been dead now for two years. For a unique brand of common-sense enthusiasm, for a singular gift of paradox, for a deep reverence and a high wit, and, most of all, for a free and shamelessly beautiful English prose, he will never be forgotten.[1]

So said Orson Welles on Monday, September 5, 1938, the evening when his radio play adaptation of Chesterton's novel *The Man Who Was Thursday* aired for the first time.

And it was an occasion—an international occasion, as it turned out. Chesterton's acclaimed adaptation, staged by the *Mercury Theatre on the Air*, was broadcast throughout America by CBS on its network of ninety-seven stations (then the largest network in America).[2] It aired simultaneously on the "coast to coast" network of the CBC in Canada—a network that reached some 76 percent of the population.[3]

And Welles's radio play adaptation of Chesterton's novel was in some pretty distinguished company, airing just under two months before his more celebrated broadcast of the dramatization of H. G. Wells's *War of the Worlds*—an epochal event in the history of radio.

During the 1930s, much as families watch television now, they gathered in the millions each evening around the family radio—perhaps a model like the widely popular Philco 90 "cathedral style" radio. Once turned on, it would take a moment for the tubes to warm up. Then, amid the crackle that millions had come to know so well, the voice of their favorite radio announcer or perhaps a bit of music could begin to be heard. Such was the setting on Monday evening September 5, 1938, when listeners heard the CBS announcer say:

> CBS ANNOUNCER: Next Monday night at this same time, the Lux Radio Theater will resume its series of broadcasts over the same stations as last year. The first presentation will be *Spawn of the North*, with George Raft, Fred MacMurray, John Barrymore, Dorothy Lamour, and Akim Tamiroff. Remember the first broadcast, next Monday at 9 p.m., Eastern Daylight Saving Time.
>
> ANNOUNCER: The *Mercury Theater on the Air!*
>
> MUSIC: Theme . . . (continues in the background) . . .
>
> ANNOUNCER: The Columbia Broadcasting System takes pleasure in presenting Orson Welles and the *Mercury Theater on the Air* in the ninth and last of a unique summer series of Monday evening broadcasts; the series which has marked radio's first presentation of a complete theatrical producing company.

Again tonight, the regularly-affiliated stations of the Columbia Broadcasting System are joined for this program by a coast-to-coast network of the Canadian Broadcasting Corporation.

This evening, our play is Mr. Welles's own adaptation of G. K. Chesterton's famous novel, *The Man Who Was Thursday*. But just before it begins, here is the director of the Mercury Theater, the star and producer of these broadcasts, Orson Welles.

WELLES: Good evening, ladies and gentlemen. G. K. C.—Gilbert Keith Chesterton—great, greatly articulate Roman convert and liberal, has been dead now for two years. For a unique brand of common-sense enthusiasm, for a singular gift of paradox, for a deep reverence and a high wit, and, most of all, for a free and shamelessly beautiful English prose, he will never be forgotten.

"It must be wonderful to be famous." According to the story, that's what the young lady said to the fat man—the fabulously fat, the fantastic, the famous fat man—when he took her to lunch at a fashionable restaurant and everybody turned and stared.

"Tell me," she said, "Do people always recognize you? Does everybody always know who you are?"

"Well, my dear," said Mr. Chesterton, "If they don't, they ask."

Mr. Chesterton's *The Man Who Was Thursday* is a little like that. Roughly speaking, it's about anarchists. 'Twas written, remember, in the boom of bomb-throwing, in those radical, irresponsible days of the nihilists. And, roughly speaking, it's a mystery story. It can be guaranteed that you will never, never guess the solution until you get to the end; it is even feared—that you may not guess it then. You may never guess what *The Man Who Was Thursday* is about. But, definitely—if you don't, you'll ask.

Though it could boast a radio drama pedigree and popular commendation from an auteur like Orson Welles, *The Man Who Was Thursday* has always seemed, as Welles pointed out, to rather deftly defy description. Novelist Jonathan Lethem, in his introduction to the Modern Library edition of the novel, offered one of the best brief summaries of the book to appear in print. He freely acknowledged its easy ability to elude description, but he stated that therein lay part of its special appeal. "How do you autopsy a somersault?" Lethem asked. "G. K. Chesterton's *The Man Who Was Thursday* is one of the great stunts ever performed in literary space, one still unfurling anytime you glance at it, as perfectly fresh and eloquent as a Buster Keaton pratfall."[4] Lethem then ventured some literary comparisons to help the modern reader place Chesterton's novel in context. *The Man Who Was Thursday*, he wrote,

> constructs its own absolute and preposterous terms in the manner found most often in certain children's books, *Alice in Wonderland*, or Norton Juster's *The Phantom Tollbooth*, or Russell Hoban's *The Mouse and His Child*. Like those books, it offers the possibility of being about everything and nothing at once, and vanishes at the end with the air of a dream. Like them it begs to be reread.[5]

Lethem's introduction to Chesterton's novel undertakes further artistic comparisons that are at once provocative and helpful in
stimulating literary conversation. Himself a novelist whose books
resist easy placement in literary genres, Lethem maintained that
"there aren't really characters in *Thursday*, not any more than there
are characters in Lewis Carroll or in a drawing by M. C. Escher, or
in John Lennon's 'I Am the Walrus.'" Then follows a fine insight
as to Chesterton's purpose as an author. "The real characters,"
Lethem wrote, "are the ideas. Chesterton's nutty agenda is really
quite simple: to expose moral relativism and parlor nihilism for the
devils he believes them to be."[6]

Lethem is quite right here to focus on Chesterton's implacable
opposition to moral relativism and parlor nihilism, but this opposition was far from a nutty agenda. Chesterton was in dead earnest.
Borrowing stylistically from Poe and anticipating the work of
younger contemporaries like Kafka,[7] Chesterton's purpose was
nothing less than to deal moral relativism and parlor nihilism a
death blow through a novel that was one part farce and one part
metaphysical thriller.[8] There was an undoubted element of jest in
Chesterton's book, as he himself wrote in one of the most revealing
passages from his book *Charles Dickens*—a passage that has a great
deal to do with what Chesterton was trying to accomplish in writing *The Man Who Was Thursday*:

A farcical occultism is the very essence of "The Midsummer
Night's Dream." It is also the right and credible essence of "The
Christmas Carol." Whether we understand it depends upon
whether we can understand that exhilaration is not a physical
accident, but a mystical fact; that exhilaration can be infinite,
like sorrow; that a joke can be so big that it breaks the roof of

the stars. By simply going on being absurd, a thing can become godlike; there is but one step from the ridiculous to the sublime.

Dickens was great because he was immoderately possessed with all this; if we are to understand him at all we must also be moderately possessed with it. We must understand this old limitless hilarity and human confidence.[9]

The Man Who Was Thursday was also, as Frederick Buechner has written, a novel that acknowledged as great a debt for deliverance from despair as any artist has voiced. As stated earlier, during Chesterton's years at art college (1893–94), he endured a searing period of darkness and despair. Amid a welter of confusing and conflicting emotions about his sense of himself and the world, he became deeply depressed. These feelings of desolation were heightened by dabbling in spiritualism and the occult, largely through the use of a ouija board. In his posthumously published *Autobiography*, he described this time of his life as one in which he was "playing with hellfire." He began to experience headaches and what he described as "a bad smell in the mind." All of these experiences conspired together to make him feel as through he were "plunging deeper and deeper in a blind spiritual suicide." Concerned friends began to fear for Chesterton's sanity.[10]

But then he was, as C. S. Lewis famously would be later, surprised by joy. Recoiling with horror from the abyss into which he had stared during his time of despair, he embarked on a quest for truth. As he would later write, "One searches for truth, but it may be that one pursues instinctively the more extraordinary truths."[11]

This search culminated in his embrace of the most extraordinary truth of all—found at the feet of a risen Christ with healing in his wings. He later described how this dawn of truth lightened his darkness:

> Satan was the most celebrated of Alpine guides, when he took Jesus to the top of an exceeding high mountain and showed him all the kingdoms of the earth. But the joy of Satan in standing on a peak is not a joy in largeness, but a joy in beholding smallness, in the fact that all men look like insects at his feet. It is from the valley that things look large; it is from the level that things look high; I am a child of the level and have no need of that celebrated Alpine guide. I will lift up my eyes to the hills, from whence cometh my help.[12]

It is here that Buechner offers a crucial insight: "Having been given back his life and his sanity, [Chesterton] was filled both with an enormous sense of thankfulness and an enormous need for someone or something to thank."[13] Following his embrace of Christianity, Chesterton's art could not help reflecting this overarching reality.[14]

Moving on from Buechner's exploration of Chesterton's novel, one of the most interesting of all literary comparisons offered for *The Man Who Was Thursday* was made by C. S. Lewis. It was no less provocative than anything Jonathan Lethem wrote, nor was it any less adamant that Chesterton's novel should be regarded as a classic. Writing in 1946, Lewis stated:

> Compare [Chesterton in *The Man Who Was Thursday*] with another good writer, Kafka. Is the difference simply that one is "dated" and the other contemporary? Or is it rather that while both give a powerful picture of the loneliness and bewilderment which each one of us encounters in his (apparently) single-handed struggle with the universe, Chesterton, attributing to the universe

a more complicated disguise, and admitting the exhilaration as well as the terror of the struggle, has got in rather more; is more balanced: in that sense, more classical, more permanent?[15]

�֍

Much of what has been said above concerns more recent explorations of *The Man Who Was Thursday*. However, important reviews were written about it upon its release in 1908.

In America, the novel received one favorable review notice that must have been especially gratifying to Chesterton. The *New York Times* review of his book was written by none other than Hildegarde Hawthorne, the granddaughter of Nathaniel Hawthorne, and an accomplished author in her own right.[16] Her review was titled "G. K. Chesterton's Fantastic Novel." Its subtitle declared, "'The Man Who Was Thursday' May Be a Nightmare or a Jest or a Sermon."

The writings of Nathaniel Hawthorne, among them the classic novel *The House of Seven Gables* and stories like "The Minister's Black Veil," had gothic or surrealist elements. So there was something very fitting about Hawthorne's granddaughter taking the measure of *The Man Who Was Thursday*—a book with its own share of the surreal.[17]

And Ms. Hawthorne had a great deal to say about Chesterton's novel, proving herself one of the novel's more trenchant critics, and someone who said some of the best things ever written about the book. "It begins," she wrote,

> with a hint of sarcasm, a touch of wonder, of incongruity, but not more than you yourself run across now and then, here or there, as you pursue the business of living. The gestures made are a bit

extravagant, the sentiments expressed a trifle bizarre, it may be. But, after all, you have seen similar gestures and smiled at like sentiments—perhaps even indulged in them yourself!

Then it grows somewhat more amazing. Odder adventures come more and more thickly; each new character is endowed with stranger attributes. You feel the stress of an almost Homeric struggle. It is too modern to be borne, too ancient to be any longer believed in. But somehow, keeping the thread of Thursday's personality as a guide, you go on, overwhelmed yet intact, through a world where everything begins to be a huge, impossible turmoil—as though the giddy globe were spinning through space at an immense increase of speed.[18]

Hawthorne's observation about Thursday's personality serving as a guide was highly perceptive. There are ways in which *The Man Who Was Thursday* can be seen as borrowing from a work like *The Pilgrim's Progress*. Both tales unfold amidst a dream. Both possess moments of martial valor. Both have elements of the nightmarish or diabolic, as in Christian's fight with Apollyon and Gabriel Syme's flight from Professor Worms:

The sealed and sullen sunset behind the dark dome of St. Paul's had in it smoky and sinister colours—colours of sickly green, dead red or decaying bronze, that were just bright enough to emphasise the solid whiteness of the snow. But right up against these dreary colours rose the black bulk of the cathedral; and upon the top of the cathedral was a random splash and great stain of snow, still clinging as to an Alpine peak. It had fallen accidentally, but just so fallen as to half drape the dome from its very topmost point, and to pick out in perfect silver the great orb and the cross. When Syme saw it he suddenly straightened himself, and made with his sword-stick an involuntary salute.

He knew that that evil figure, his shadow, was creeping quickly or slowly behind him, and he did not care. It seemed a symbol of human faith and valour that while the skies were darkening that high place of the earth was bright. The devils might have captured heaven, but they had not yet captured the cross.[19]

Hawthorne's concluding remarks deserve to be cited in full, for they provide a cogent summary of the novel, interspersed with superb analysis. "Up to a certain point," she wrote, Chesterton's novel

is apparently the tale of men under a spell of adventure and endeavor. Then mystery and allegory take their turn in the scene. Life, huge, shapeless, cruel and loving, killing and saving, full of antitheses, appearing to each one under a different aspect, measuring each man according to the strength of his soul, turns its strange face upon us. Life, whose soul is law, nature, whose expression is law, confront the frantic lawlessness of struggling man—and behold, those very struggles prove to be based on law again. And when at the last you sit on the thrones with the Council of Days, you see the mad, miraculous world dance by, moving to a harmony none the less invincible because only half heard.

Mr. G. K. Chesterton calls this tale, "The Man Who Was Thursday," a nightmare. A satirical skit it is on those tempestuous moderns who take up the cudgels—or rather, the bomb—against society, law, and order, and, with furious speech and frantic paradox, set out, bound by many a secret oath, to restore chaos. Disguised they must be, and what disguise could serve to hide such desperate crimes to the community? One only, and an old one; simply to proclaim themselves the Anarchists they are, and everywhere to shout abroad their fearful sentiments and deadly plans. Heading the general throng of Anarchists is the Council of Seven, nicknamed after the days of the week. Thursday, the poet-hero, who is, moreover, a policeman, manages to attain this council by a set of curious happenings. His subsequent adventures and discoveries make up the nightmare.

And this story is told as Mr. Chesterton tells things, with wit and paradox nudging you into frequent smiles, with felicitous phrase and apt simile—quotable from page to page. It is all a huge joke, a quite absurd and laughable fantasy—or is it a sermon—or is it even an explanation. Read the book and make your choice. In any event you are not likely to lay it down unread, and it is possible you may even go so far as to read a lot of yourself into it. At least you will be certain that if it is an absurd jest, there is yet a something of solemnity hidden in the laughter . . . when you listen to Syme's description of the President, or to the replies of the Six Days to the question addressed them by Sunday, you know he is talking quite seriously and simply of things it is easier to feel than to express.[20]

✠

Sixty years after Hildegarde Hawthorne published her review of *The Man Who Was Thursday*, the British novelist and critic Kingsley Amis published an article that also discussed the novel at length. The article appeared in the October 13, 1968, edition of the *New York Times*. Both complimentary and critical, Amis's observations were testament to the enduring appeal of Chesterton's atypical classic. "Of supposedly serious contemporary writers," Amis began, "Gilbert Keith Chesterton was the first to make a strong and genuine impression on me. 'Contemporary' is perhaps misleading: he and I only overlapped by 14 years, but I had come to value him enough to be dashed and bewildered by his death in 1936."[21]

Hereafter followed a series of reflections that showed how greatly Chesterton had influenced an important writer. Amis's article was as much an expression of a personal debt as it was a critique—and both elements of his piece are of equal value. "One never quite gets over any early attachment," he wrote.

> Even now I see something romantic, almost heroic, about Chesterton, while deploring what in those days I knew nothing of, his self-indulgent polemical writing and the whimsical playing with paradoxes so common in his later fiction. However, at least two of his novels and two or three dozen stories (mostly the justly celebrated Father Brown detective shorts) retain all their appeal.[22]

This was significant, but it was *The Man Who Was Thursday* in particular that captured Amis's youthful imagination. His writing here recalls C. S. Lewis's writing to Charles Williams in 1936 about his discovery of Chesterton.[23] "I was instantly hooked," Amis wrote,

> by the mysterious title, the sinister subtitle—"A Nightmare"—the prefatory poem, with its again sinister hints of a vast conspiracy stealthily taking over men's minds:

> > *A cloud was on the mind of men,*
> > *And wailing went the weather,*

Yea, a sick cloud was upon the soul
When we were boys together.
Science announced nonentity
And art admired decay;
The world was old and ended:
But you and I were gay;
Round us in antic order
Crippled voices came—
Lust that had lost its laughter,
Fear that had lost its shame. . . .
This is a tale of those old fears,
Even of those emptied hells,
And none but you shall understand
The true thing that it tells—
Of what colossal gods of shame
Could cow men and yet crash;
Of what huge devils hid the stars,
Yet fell at a pistol-flash.

This part has an up-to-date ring, but Chesterton, who was born in 1874, was only talking about late-Victorian rationalism and the "decadent" movement of the nineties, favorite targets of his. I thought he was bringing me news of the devil (who often turned up in other stuff I was reading at the time), or warning me that most grown-ups were mad (an equally acceptable idea).[24]

Amis moved next to a discussion of how *The Man Who Was Thursday* might be categorized, or rather, he confessed his inability to hit upon a satisfactory description. "Attempts to fix a label break down," he wrote. Continuing, he reflected:

It is not quite a political bad dream, or a metaphysical adventure, or a cosmic comedy in the form of a spy story, but it has something of all these. Anyway, it is unique, and also, what is not all that much easier to bring about, magnetically readable. We open in a remote quarter of that Edwardian London which Chesterton knew so exactly and lovingly. Outside the immediate center, this cannot have been such a very different place from contemporary London: a conglomeration of linked villages, each with its own look and feel and smell, a continual variousness I have never found in any North American city.[25]

Chesterton, Amis continued, was a master stylist when he fully marshaled his powers of description. Part of the novelist's art is the ability to create a setting and mood that linger in the memory. In *The Man Who Was Thursday*, Chesterton's gift in this regard was on full display. Amis wrote of "the special intensity [Chesterton] always brought to descriptions of times of day and effects of light, reminding us that he started life with ambitions to become a painter."[26]

Next, in a transition that rivaled one of Chesterton's sudden narrative twists, Amis considered the similarities of plot between *The Man Who Was Thursday* and a novel written by the creator of James Bond, Ian Fleming. At first glance, this might seem a bit of a stretch, but Amis made a compelling case. "In pursuance of a sort of bet," Amis wrote,

[Lucian] Gregory takes Syme to dinner in a greasy riverside pub that turns out to serve champagne and lobster mayonnaise. More surprisingly, dinner table and diners presently descend *en bloc* into an underground chamber—shades, or rather anticipations, of Ian Fleming's *Live and Let Die*. For me, at any rate, this is much more than a coincidence. James Bond and Gabriel Syme differ in innumerable ways, but they share a quality of romance, of color and chivalry, almost of myth, that attracts me a lot more deeply than anything about the down-to-earth and up-to-the-minute heroes of writers like Len Deighton and John Le Carré.[27]

Here was where Chesterton the writer began to speak most meaningfully to Amis as a young reader. Decades after his first encounter with Chesterton's novel, he retained a powerful memory of the moment when Gabriel Syme "set out by moonlight, in a heavy cloak and carrying a sword-stick, to take the war to the enemy."[28] Here two sentences in particular seized upon his imagination: "[Syme's] chivalric folly glowed in the night like a great fire. Even the common things he carried with him—the food and the brandy and the loaded pistol—took on exactly that concrete and material poetry which a child feels when he takes a gun upon a journey or a bun with him to bed."[29] Following this, Amis wrote, "I can still feel the gentle shock of reading that sentence for the first time, that flash of realization, not that you fully understand the author, but, far rarer and more memorable, that the author knows all about you."[30]

With the sureness of touch that marks a novelist at the height of his powers, Chesterton could transition effortlessly from scenes of the macabre and sinister to the more traditional motif of a high and holy quest. Amis's concluding remarks reflect his admiration for these qualities in Chesterton, and a final comparison with more recent novels of mystery and suspense. About *The Man Who Was Thursday*, Amis wrote:

The Anarchist Council members turn out to be a set of frightening grotesques, not merely malignant, but with a hint of the spiritual evil that from now on begins more and more to color the tale. The eyes of Saturday are covered by black glasses, as if they were too frightful to see. Monday, the Secretary, has a smile that goes up on one side of his face and down on the other and is wrong. The face of Sunday, the huge President, is so vast that Syme is afraid that at close quarters it will be too big to be possible, and he will have to scream.

When the spectacles and the mask of anarchy are removed, however, Saturday is human enough, a policeman, in fact, from Syme's own special branch, The Last Crusade. (I would love to see that emblazoned on some door in Scotland Yard.) One by one the other Days declare themselves on the side of the law, until only the Secretary stands between police and President. But Monday is Sunday's agent, with the power of turning the world itself against the crusaders. The chase sweeps across a France of sturdy peasants and soldierly patriots and cultured men of wealth (more fun to read about, at least, than most real Frenchmen) transformed one by one, in true nightmare fashion, into fanatical friends of anarchy. Finally the champions of reason and order, and of Christendom, turn at bay. . . .

"The Man Who Was Thursday" is high melodrama and is written in that style. In one of his essays, with characteristically deliberate overemphasis, Chesterton claims that melodrama is much more like life than realism is. Well, I only know that, after a surfeit of supposedly realistic accounts of the workings of espionage organizations, after reading about the 20th gray man in a gray raincoat with a sawn-off Smith and Wesson Centennial Airweight at his hip, I long for The Last Crusade and Gabriel Syme with his cloak and sword-stick, and wish that there were a few more books like this.[31]

⌗

Near the end of his life, Chesterton penned what could be regarded as his last word about his book. It was published in the *Illustrated London News* on June 13, 1936, just one day before his death:

> *The Man Who Was Thursday* . . . was not intended to describe the real world as it was, or as I thought it was. . . . It was intended to describe the world of wild doubt and despair which the pessimists were generally describing at that date; with just a gleam of hope in some double meaning of the doubt, which even the pessimists felt in some fashion.[32]

In the same article, Chesterton had self-deprecatingly called his book "a very melodramatic sort of moonshine." But perhaps there was a larger truth in play in this description. Moonshine has been welcomed by many a weary traveler in the night: it helps them find their way.

CHAPTER 14

Chesterton, Mencken, and Shaw

*Some critics are like chimney-sweepers; they put out the fire
below, and frighten the swallows from their nests above; they
scrape a long time in the chimney, cover themselves with soot,
and bring nothing away but a bag of cinders, and then sing
from the top of the house as if they had built it.[1]*

—HENRY WADSWORTH LONGFELLOW, TABLE TALK (1878)

A mong those who occasionally loosed barbs in Chesterton's
direction was H. L. Mencken—the noted literary critic and
wordsmith. Brilliant, learned, and noted for his acerbic style, Mencken
relished journalistic swordplay as few others did.

Chesterton did not escape the flourish of Mencken's rapier. For
while he admired Chesterton's gifts—among them the "shock of pleasant surprise" and the "sting of devilish and delightful heresy"[2] present
in Chesterton's early books—he came to believe that Chesterton was
too prolific by half and had started to repeat himself. The shock of
pleasant surprise had precipitously diminished. Chesterton had become
for him "a faded charmer."[3] By May 1911, Mencken was writing,

The wine of Chestertonian wit begins to lose its headiness and
flavor, as all wine must when the seller makes endeavor, with the

aid of rain water, to turn a bottle into a butt. . . . [Chesterton's] whole stock was exhausted before he was halfway through his second book—but he kept on and on and on. He is still printing books today, at intervals of six months.[4]

Mencken also seems to have developed a hearty disdain for Chesterton's worldview. But perhaps this was only to be expected, for Mencken was one of the twentieth century's "celebrities of unbelief."[5]

That Chesterton published too frequently and had begun to repeat himself was a fair criticism and one that others had voiced. But then he earned his living by his pen and had publisher demands to satisfy for new product. All things considered, this was a forgivable offense, albeit one that could have been avoided with a bit more editorial and authorial discipline.

One of Mencken's lengthier and more important critiques of Chesterton is found in his review of Chesterton's book *George Bernard Shaw* (published in 1909). Mencken's January 1910 review, "Chesterton's Picture of Shaw," brings together three of the more incandescent minds of the era. Mencken, Chesterton, and Shaw were also three of the most popular writers in the Anglo-American world at this time. For a start, Mencken was not enamored of Chesterton's book inasmuch as it aspired in any way to be a biography. "If you approach Gilbert K. Chesterton's *George Bernard Shaw* as serious biography," Mencken wrote,

> you will find it amazing in the things it contains and irritating beyond measure in the things it doesn't contain; but if you throttle your yearning for facts and look only for entertainment you will fairly wallow in it. The cleverest man in all the world, with the second cleverest as his subject, is here doing his cleverest

writing. The result is a volume as diverting as Nietzsche's *Also Sprach Zarathustra*, and as obviously unauthentic. It belongs, not to history, but to philosophic fable. I have shelved it among my more furious epics, cheek by jowl with *The Estimable Life of the Great Gargantua*, the Book of Revelation, *Fécondité* and *The Story of Mary MacLane*.[6]

All hyperbole aside, this arrow fell short of its mark. Chesterton had no intention of writing a straightforward biography. He called his book a "rough study"—which is to say it was more in the nature of a critique.[7]

Mencken was on slightly firmer ground when he alleged that Chesterton's book belonged in the realm of "philosophic fable." But rather than offering any representative passages that showed why this was so, Mencken settled for damning with faint praise—a rhetorical flourish devoid of any real potency since it offered nothing by way of evidence. "Mr. Chesterton's word picture," he wrote, "of this entirely imaginary colossus [Shaw] spreads itself over some two hundred or more delectable pages, and in the course of drawing it he takes occasion to prove that he, too, is a philosophic Sandow."[8]

This sentence, with its obscure allusions (Eugen Sandow was a late nineteenth-century bodybuilder) was Mencken's way of saying that Chesterton's study was little more than a book-length gladiatorial display intended to show that he was every bit Shaw's equal in the intellectual arena.

But intellectual one-upmanship was not Chesterton's intent, and it was disingenuous to say so. What was much more to the point, and where Mencken was on much surer ground, was to say that Chesterton saw the occasion of a study of Shaw's ideas and art as a forum in which to contrast these things with his own deeply held beliefs about the way things were, or ought to be. This Mencken had readily and rightly discerned. "There are, in fact," he wrote,

> lengthy passages in which Shaw recedes into the background, losing his character as a hero and taking on the shadowy outlines of a mere text. In these passages Mr. Chesterton maintains anew his familiar theses—that the only real truths in the world are to be found in the Nicene Creed, that science is a snare and human reason a delusion, that Hans Christian Andersen was a greater man than Copernicus, that sentiment is more genuine than hydrochloric acid, that all race progress is empty appearance. Of his dialectic manner, it is not necessary to give examples, for every habitual reader of books knows it well, and enjoys it hugely without letting it convince him. He is the world's foremost virtuoso of sophistry and paralogy. Not since St. Augustine have the gods sent us a man who could make the incredible so fascinatingly probable.[9]

In criticizing *George Bernard Shaw* and another of Chesterton's books, *Alarms and Discursions*, Mencken sometimes became enamored of his own rhetorical flourishes. In a word, he was so busy being clever that he ceased to be serious. He charged Chesterton with sophistry but was himself guilty of ad hominem flippancy—too often indulging a kind of scattershot cleverness. He ridiculed Chesterton or his ideas without engaging them—he censured without really considering if Chesterton had said something that was true or valid. Chesterton's ideas, Mencken said, "had been dead so long, they seemed newborn."[10] Chesterton, he suggested, should "renew his stock of ideas—preferably in the moldy tomes of the Thomists, the Scotists and the Ockhamites, where he seems to have got the shopworn stock that he is now trying to sell for the fourteenth time."[11] It might have been good theater to marshal clever ways of saying "your ideas are silly and outmoded," but Mencken never got around to examining the merits or perceived shortcomings of Chesterton's beliefs. If Chesterton was too often spendthrift in publishing so much, Mencken could at times be intellectually lazy. Cleverness, however artfully worded, is no substitute for a serious engagement with an opponent's ideas. It was an old trick, and few played it better than Mencken could.[12]

�֎

But then, as one might have suspected, Chesterton gave as good as he got—though much less caustically—as an article written in June 1930 for the *Illustrated London News* reveals. Here, Chesterton wrote: "I have so warm an admiration for Mr. Mencken as the critic of Puritan pride and stupidity that I regret that he should thus make himself out a back number out of mere irreligious irritation."[13]

So what, precisely, was it that had drawn down Mencken's ire? He had, apparently, taken great exception to ideas being advanced by proponents of what was then called "the New Physics." The specifics of this rather arcane chapter in scientific history aren't of any real importance here. What is important is that Chesterton specifically stated how much he admired Mencken's intellect, and he was quick to point out areas where they agreed. "Mencken," Chesterton wrote, is "a brilliant man of letters."[14] Even where he did criticize, as in the following paragraph, Chesterton did not ridicule:

> The new physicists are not propagandists, but Mr. Mencken, so far from reverencing them ... desperately refuses to respect them even as scientists. And he takes up this extraordinary position

for no reason in the world, except that they will not say exactly what he tells them to say, in the world of morals and metaphysics. But it is rather hard to ask them to drop all their scientific work for fear they should get a little ahead of Mr. Mencken.[15]

The same tone had been present in 1926, four years earlier, when Chesterton wrote another article, called "Mencken on Democracy," for the *Illustrated London News*. Its opening paragraph read:

Mr. H. L. Mencken has written a book called "Democracy," as Mr. Sinclair Lewis wrote a book called "Babbitt," and perhaps the two titles stand for very much the same thing. Both these ingenious writers devote their considerable talents to making game of government by what Whitman would have called The Average Man, but what Babbitt would have called The Regular Guy. But, though they both make a fine protest against provincialism, there is a sense in which their protest is too provincial. The very largeness of America isolates and therefore imprisons them. For it is large things that really limit us, because they prevent us from seeing anything beyond.[16]

Amidst the critique of Mencken, there is a clearly more liberal share of charity than was present in Mencken's criticisms. As David Stewart wrote:

It is difficult, though not impossible, for a critic like Mencken to voice his disdain and unhappiness at "the way things are in the world" without becoming a misanthrope. People whose literary lives and times overlapped in some way with Mencken's—George Bernard Shaw, E. B. White, G. K. Chesterton—each voiced an incisive critique while remaining an ally, rather than an accuser, of his fellow mortals. But Mencken did not achieve such balance.[17]

Chesterton's capacity for charity toward those with whom he disagreed was colorfully captured by one of his occasional opponents in debate, Cosmo Hamilton:

> To hear Chesterton's howl of joy ... to see him double himself up in an agony of laughter at my personal insults, to watch the effects of his sportsmanship on a shocked audience who were won to mirth by his intense and pea-hen-like quarks of joy was a sight and a sound for the gods. ... It was monstrous, gigantic, amazing, deadly, delicious. Nothing like it has ever been done before or will ever be seen, heard and felt like it again.[18]

✠

One might have thought that Bernard Shaw himself would have been less enamored of Chesterton's book about him than Mencken was, but this does not seem to have been the case. Shaw's overall reaction was a mixture of amusement and appreciation. "This book," Shaw began in a high spirited review of Chesterton's book that was reprinted in the *New York Times*,

> is what everybody expected it to be: the best work of literary art I have yet provoked. It is a fascinating portrait study; and I am proud to have been the painter's model. It is in the great tradition of literary portraiture: it gives not only the figure, but the epoch. It makes the figure interesting and memorable by giving it the greatness and spaciousness of an epoch, and it makes it

attractive by giving it the handsomest and friendliest personal qualities of the painter himself.[19]

Shaw did feel that Chesterton had missed the mark in offering a trenchant critique of his views, but the way in which he said so recalls their animated, witty, yet very civil public debates. He thought Chesterton wrong but still thought well of Chesterton. "Generally speaking," Shaw said,

> Mr. Chesterton's portrait of me has the limitations of a portrait, which is, perhaps, fortunate in some respects for the original. As a picture, in the least personal and most phenomenal sense, it is very fine indeed. As an account of my doctrine, it is either frankly deficient and uproariously careless or else recalcitrantly and (I repeat) madly wrong.[20]

Then followed a very genuine tribute to Chesterton: "there is endless matter in G. K. C." It was, fair enough, a play on words that could have been a bit of ribbing about Chesterton's ample girth, but such seems not to have been the case. Shaw's review had run on to considerable length—some 3,019 words in all. At one point, he seems to have realized he was going on a bit. It was here that he said: "But I must stop arbitrarily or my review will be longer than [Chesterton's] book! For there is endless matter in G. K. C."[21]

Shaw capped his "review" with one final bit of fun at Chesterton's expense. It was dispensed with liberal amounts of bonhomie, even if it made a serious point in jest. Shaw had tried to bring Chesterton around to his way of thinking—a rather quixotic endeavor, since there was little chance of it happening. Still, Shaw stood by his views, even as he stood by his friend. "My last word," he wrote, must be that, gifted as [Chesterton] is, he needs a sane Irishman to look after him. For this portrait essay beginning with the insanity of beer for beer's sake does stop short of the final far madder lunacy of absurdity for absurdity's sake.

I have tried to teach Mr. Chesterton that the will that moves us is dogmatic; that our brain is only the very imperfect instrument by which we devise practical means for fulfilling that will; that logic is our attempt to understand it and to reconcile its apparent contradictions with some intelligible theory of its purpose; and that the man who gives to reason and logic the attributes and authority of the will—the Rationalist—is the most hopeless of fools; and that all I have got into his otherwise very wonderful brain, is that whatever is reasonable and logical is false, and whatever is nonsensical is true.[22]

✠

But by far the best thing about Chesterton's book on Shaw is that it contains some of his best moments as a writer. *George Bernard Shaw* may not at times bear much relation to Shaw the person (a fact Shaw himself was quick to point out in his article in *The Nation*—and a fact both friends could laugh about)—but that did not mean the book did not present a ready platform from which Chesterton could take up some of his favorite topics and offer some of his best writing about them. This is the real merit of Chesterton's book: Shaw the biographical subject was in this sense a catalyst for Chesterton the essayist—and a potent one at that.

The book began with one of the greatest opening lines in a work classed as a critical study. "Most people," Chesterton wrote, "either say that they agree with Bernard Shaw or that they do not understand him. I am the only person who understands him, and I do not agree with him."[23] Just a few pages later, Chesterton unsheathed this witticism: "Shaw is like the Venus of Milo; all that there is of him is admirable."[24]

Chesterton's sense of wit was in fine form, but he was no less on form in offering some very fine moments of criticism. His gifts as a prose stylist were also on full display. "A legend has run round the newspapers," he said,

> that Bernard Shaw offered himself as a better writer than Shakespeare. This is false and quite unjust; Bernard Shaw never said anything of the kind. The writer whom he did say was better than Shakespeare was not himself, but Bunyan. And he justified it by attributing to Bunyan a virile acceptance of life as a high and harsh adventure, while in Shakespeare he saw nothing but profligate pessimism, the *vanitas vanitatum* of a disappointed voluptuary. According to this view Shakespeare was always saying, "Out, out, brief candle," because his was only a ballroom candle; while Bunyan was seeking to light such a candle as by God's grace should never be put out.[25]

Philosophical criticism is seldom written accessibly, still less often with wit. But Chesterton could perform this high-wire act with skill, as when he examined the supposed origins of Shaw's worldview. "The temporary decline of theology," Chesterton wrote,

> had involved the neglect of philosophy and all fine thinking; and Bernard Shaw had to find shaky justifications in Schopenhauer for the sons of God shouting for joy. He called it the Will to

Live—a phrase invented by Prussian professors who would like to exist, but can't. Afterwards he asked people to worship the Life-Force; as if one could worship a hyphen.[26]

But wit was not the only arrow in Chesterton's rhetorical quiver. There were unexpected moments of great eloquence and feeling within the pages of his book on Shaw, as in Chesterton's definition of music. "Music," he said, "is mere beauty; it is beauty in the abstract, beauty in solution. It is a shapeless and liquid element of beauty."[27]

Then too, Chesterton had always been deeply distrustful of philosophical notions like Nietzsche's idea of the Superman, and its influence upon Shaw.[28] Writing twenty-four years before Hitler assumed power (heavily influenced by Nietzsche's theories), Chesterton wrote with great prescience that "the superstition of what is called the Superman" was one "which bids fair to be the chief superstition of the dark ages which are possibly in front of us."[29] In the same vein, he warned of the dangers of despotism and totalitarianism. "Powerful men who have powerful passions," he said, "use much of their strength in forging chains for themselves; they alone know how strong the chains need to be."[30]

George Bernard Shaw was also a book rich in metaphor about the dangers of cultural malaise—even within his own profession of journalism. "Modern criticism," he wrote, "like all weak things, is overloaded with words. In a healthy condition of language a man finds it very difficult to say the right thing, but at last says it. In this empire of journalese a man finds it so very easy to say the wrong thing that he never thinks of saying anything else. False or meaningless phrases lie so ready to his hand that it is easier to use them than not to use them. These wrong terms picked up through idleness are retained through habit, and so the man has begun to think wrong almost before he has begun to think at all."[31]

Lastly, Chesterton's abiding concern for the modern mind could be rendered in homely phrases that left a lasting impression, as in this cautionary word: "The modern mind is not a donkey that wants kicking to make it go on. The modern mind is more like a motor-car on a lonely road which two amateur motorists have been just clever enough to take to pieces, but are not quite clever enough to put together again."[32] Chesterton penned his study of Shaw in the hope that his readers, Shaw not least among them, might turn to Christianity as he had: for as he could never forget, nor cease to tell others, his faith had helped him to put his mind back together again.

CHAPTER 15

The Advent of Father Brown

*As a disciple of Poe and a rival of Sir Arthur Conan Doyle,
the ingenious Mr. Gilbert Chesterton has made a by no
means contemptible showing in the series of tales of the
homicidal and criminal which have been collected [in* The
Innocence of Father Brown*].*[1]

—NEW YORK TIMES, DECEMBER 1911

*Father Brown has a sharp clerical brain, a feeling for the turn
of the screw, and an unastounded sense of the human drama.*[2]

—V. S. PRITCHETT

Father Brown, that quintessentially English detective, made his
first appearance in a highly unlikely place: the *Saturday Evening
Post.* "Valentin Follows a Curious Trail" (better known by its later title,
"The Blue Cross") was published in its pages on June 23, 1910, and so
began the career of one of the most famous sleuths in literature.[3] The
opening paragraph of "The Blue Cross" was vintage Chesterton and
presented one of the best opening scenes in all detective fiction:

Between the silver ribbon of morning and the green glittering
ribbon of sea, the boat touched Harwich and let loose a swarm

of folk like flies, among whom the man we must follow was by no means conspicuous—nor wished to be. There was nothing notable about him, except a slight contrast between the holiday gaiety of his clothes and the official gravity of his face. His clothes included a slight pale grey jacket, a white waistcoat, and a silver straw hat with a grey-blue ribbon. His lean face was dark by contrast, and ended in a curt black beard that looked Spanish and suggested an Elizabethan ruff. He was smoking a cigarette with the seriousness of an idler. There was nothing about him to indicate the fact that the grey jacket covered a loaded revolver, that the white waistcoat covered a police card, or that the straw hat covered one of the most powerful intellects in Europe. For this was Valentin himself, the head of the Paris police and the most famous investigator of the world; and he was coming from Brussels to London to make the greatest arrest of the century.[4]

Here, from the outset of this story, were several of the elements people subsequently came to prize about the Father Brown mysteries: an inimitable style, the presence of evocative landscapes, and a vivid, closely observed descriptive technique.

No less singular was the first appearance of Father Brown, the "very short Roman Catholic priest" who made one of the most inauspicious entrances in the history of detective fiction:

Valentin . . . almost laughed. The little priest was so much the essence of those Eastern flats; he had a face as round and dull as a Norfolk dumpling; he had eyes as empty as the North Sea; he had several brown paper parcels, which he was quite incapable of collecting. The Eucharistic Congress had doubtless sucked out of their local stagnation many such creatures, blind and helpless, like moles disinterred. Valentin was a sceptic in the severe style of France, and could have no love for priests. But he could have pity for them, and this one might have provoked pity in anybody. He had a large, shabby umbrella, which constantly fell on the floor. He did not seem to know which was the right end of his return ticket.[5]

No, this first description of Father Brown was not one to inspire confidence. Certainly, Valentin took little notice of the little priest who couldn't seem to get out of his own way. But he would take notice of Father Brown before this tale was through, and so would readers throughout the English-speaking world. For as V. S. Pritchett once observed: "Father Brown ha[d] a sharp clerical brain, a feeling for the turn of the screw, and an unastounded sense of the human drama."[6] This little priest with the nondescript appearance was a crime-solving dynamo.

⊞

Where in the world did such an unlikely sleuth come from? As it happened, Chesterton didn't have to look very far at all for inspiration. His close friend, Father John O'Connor, was the model for Father Brown.

They met in the spring of 1904, when the Chestertons were on holiday in West Yorkshire. O'Connor, based at St. Anne's Church in Keighley, had long wished to meet Chesterton. This was arranged, and the two walked together over a "bit of moorland . . . among the finest in Yorkshire, especially when white clouds race across the blue."[7]

When the walk concluded, the two were fast friends. In the years that followed, the two men became very close, and Frances

Chesterton came to have a great affection for O'Connor as well. Chesterton was often amazed at his friend's insight into human nature and the spiritual wisdom that flowed from his storehouse of experience. Theirs was a friendship marked by an "atmosphere of unique confidence and intimacy."[8] Over the course of many visits, this friendship ripened. As Maisie Ward once observed, "With both Frances and Gilbert it was among the closest of their lives. Their letters to him show it: the long talks, and companionable walks over the moors."[9]

In return, Father O'Connor found a friend whose faith, intellect, and literary gifts he greatly admired. "I thank God," he told Chesterton early on, "for having gifted you with the spirituality which alone makes literature immortal."[10]

Both men long remembered the circumstance that led to the creation of Father Brown. "On their second meeting," Maisie Ward wrote,

> Father O'Connor had startled, indeed almost shattered Gilbert, with certain rather lurid knowledge of human depravity which he had acquired in the course of his priestly experience. At the house to which they were going, two Cambridge undergraduates spoke disparagingly of the "cloistered" habits of the Catholic clergy, saying that to them it seemed that to know and meet evil was a far better thing than the innocence of such ignorance. To Gilbert, still under the shock of a knowledge compared with which "these two Cambridge gentlemen knew about as much of real evil as two babies in the same perambulator," the exquisite irony of this remark suggested a thought. Why not a whole comedy of cross purposes based on the notion of a priest with a knowledge of evil deeper than that of the criminal he is converting?[11]

And so Father Brown was born. But that was one, among many reasons, why Chesterton was indebted to Father O'Connor for the gift of his friendship.

᛭

Sir Arthur Conan Doyle was still living when the first story involving Father Brown was published. But this new piece of detective fiction published in the *Saturday Evening Post* in 1910 differed widely from any tale of Sherlock Holmes. One could even say that this new tale was highly unique. The master detective it introduced was as wont to delve into matters of metaphysics as he was the minutia of forensic analysis. Self-deprecating humor and a searching, sympathetic knowledge of humanity were other distinguishing hallmarks of this story, as they were of all the stories of Father Brown that were to follow from the endlessly inventive pen of G. K. Chesterton. In all, he would write some fifty-two Father Brown stories.[12]

One of the best ways to understand and appreciate the singular nature of Chesterton's achievement in creating the character of Father Brown is to see the little priest for what he was not. No one has written better about seeing Father Brown from this perspective than P. D. James, one of Chesterton's worthy successors as a mystery writer. "Unlike most of the Golden Age heroes of detective fiction," she wrote,

> [Father Brown] works alone. He has no professional supporter
> to do the routine legwork or provide additional police support
> when required, as has Lord Peter Wimsey in Inspector Parker.
> He is not bizarrely eccentric, as is Agatha Christie's Poirot.
> Unlike Sherlock Holmes, he has no Watson to ask questions

which the more simple-minded readers might like to put and whose purpose is to demonstrate the great detective's brilliance and superior intellect. Naturally, given the decades in which he operates, he has no scientific advice available, indeed no official person whose help he can readily enlist in moments of crisis. He solves crimes by a mixture of common sense, observation, and deduction, and by his knowledge of the human heart. After years of hearing confessions, he knows the best and worst of which human beings are capable even though those secrets are locked in his heart. As he says to Flambeau, the master thief whom he outwits in "The Blue Cross" and whom he restores to honesty, "Has it never struck you that a man who does next to nothing but hear men's real sins is not likely to be wholly unaware of human evil?"[13]

These stories met at once with a great and enduring popularity. When they were collected and published for the first time in book form in July 1911, as *The Innocence of Father Brown*, they met with critical acclaim as well. The *New York Times* was foremost among the periodicals of record to praise the book: "Mr. Chesterton," its review stated, "writes extremely good detective stories—detective stories the more fascinating because if there is about them a hint of irony, there is also more than a hint of poetry and a shadow—or, if you will, a glow—of the mystic and the supernatural."[14]

As the *Times* saw it, the stories in *The Innocence of Father Brown* recalled the "mingled pity, benevolence, and nobler rage for right reflected by Robert Louis Stevenson in the quest of the Rajah's diamond"[15]—a comparison that doubtless pleased Chesterton greatly, as Stevenson was one of his literary heroes. And indeed, the *Times* was surely right to detect the influence of Stevenson in Chesterton's tales. Continuing in this vein, the reviewer for the *Times* saw other comparisons worth making as well:

> From this comparison with Stevenson it will appear that Mr. Chesterton is something more than a plot concocter, with a knack of getting at the plot backward—like [Conan] Doyle. Rather he is an artist with something of the art of Poe himself. There are also, of course, the qualities which may be called Chestertonian, the gift of flashing sidelights, a certain trick of seeming to see out of the back of the head.[16]

In 1983, nearly fifty years after the last of the Father Brown stories was published, the *New York Times* published a review of *The Father Brown Omnibus*, a one-volume anthology of all the Father Brown stories, reissued by Dodd, Mead & Co. The review, written by Walter Goodman, maintained that Chesterton's stories still held their own and still possessed the power to beguile and entertain that is the hallmark of classic detective fiction.

At the start of his review, Goodman observed that the Father Brown stories "may be read as a man of faith's response to the 'ratiocinative tales' of Edgar Allen Poe, the scientific huggermugger of Sherlock Holmes and the skeptical drift of the century."[17] He then complimented Chesterton's deft use of aphorism. "Father Brown," Goodman wrote, "attributes his skill at detection to his faith in the logic of God's world: 'I can believe the impossible,' he says, 'but not the improbable.'"[18]

On the less positive side of the ledger, Goodman believed that Chesterton could at times be preachy. Arguing that "Father Brown is convinced that atheists, secularists, humanists, rationalists and their ilk are all susceptible to superstition,"[19] Goodman took exception to a statement by Father Brown that is one of the most famous lines penned by Chesterton: "It's the first effect of not believing in God that you lose your common sense, and can't see things as they are."[20] Chesterton, Goodman concluded, "liked setting Father Brown up against secular minds so that he might best them."[21]

But these were small criticisms in the context of Goodman's review. He saw much to like in *The Father Brown Omnibus*. He detected parallels between Father Brown and Edgar Allan Poe's Inspector Dupin in that Father Brown "notices what is missing from the scene [of a crime]."[22] Another strength in the way that Father Brown was drawn as a character was "his ability to assess, without illusion, what men and women are capable of doing to and for one another. As he remarks while figuring out who poisoned whom in 'The Quick One,' 'You've got to see people as they are.'"[23]

Goodman was also complimentary in saying that almost every Father Brown story "offers pleasure in its asides."[24] In the end, three words may be said to have summarized Goodman's assessment of *The Father Brown Omnibus*. The stories within it, he wrote, are "elegantly turned tales."[25]

In saying this, Goodman was onto something. Referencing Chesterton's craftsmanship as a writer of detective fiction, he put his finger on a consideration often overlooked. At its best, detective fiction is, and always has been, far more than just a popular genre, a form of pulp fiction devoid of genuinely artistic possibilities. Building on this idea, it might seem highly unlikely that the detective story would prove a genre in which Chesterton's greatest gifts as an artist would be on display, but as writers like P. D. James have noted, there is much to be said for this. "Chesterton," she wrote, never wrote an inelegant or clumsy sentence. The Father Brown stories are brilliantly written in a style richly complex, imaginative, vigorous, poetic, and spiced with paradoxes. He was an artist as well as a writer and he sees life with an artist's eye. He wanted his readers to share that poetic vision, to see the romance and numinousness in commonplace things.[26]

James, a highly accomplished writer of detective fiction herself, knew better than most what a preeminent writer of mysteries should look like. Chesterton fit the bill. She was particularly taken by Chesterton's skill "at evoking the effect of changing light on landscape, its power to transmogrify and beguile, so that the seemingly mundane and familiar became pregnant with mystery."[27] One passage from the story "The Song of the Flying Fish" perfectly illustrates what she meant:

> Outside, the last edges of the sunset still clung to the corners of the green square but inside a lamp had already been kindled; and in the mingling of the two lights the coloured globe glowed like some monstrous jewel and the fantastic outlines of the fiery fishes seemed to give it indeed something of the mystery of a talisman; like the strange shapes seen by a seer in the crystal of doom.[28]

The best of the Father Brown stories show Chesterton at his best as a writer: disciplined, employing a painterly prose style, displaying a ready sympathy with those whose lives have been touched by brokenness, and a redemptive thread that is at once profoundly human and arresting. There are passages in these stories of genuine beauty, pathos, and great good humor. The best of these tales bear the touch of a master. And, as P. D. James has written, Chesterton was well in advance of his time. He saw the possibilities of detective fiction as a genre and imbued it with a richness seldom present in the works of other writers.[29] "We read the Father Brown stories," she said, "for a variety of pleasures, including their ingenuity, their wit and intelligence, and for the brilliance of the writing. But they provide more. Chesterton was concerned with the greatest of all problems, the vagaries of the human heart."[30]

In the end, there is far more to the Father Brown stories than meets the eye. The best of them were perhaps the best forum for his artistry as a writer—and they may well embody another trait no less telling or important. Do the Father Brown stories offer the best collective summation of Chesterton's reasons for belief? Does he, in the guise of masterful detective fiction, point the reader to the solution of questions caught up with life's greatest mysteries? It would seem that the answer to that question might well be yes.

CHAPTER 16

The Great Ballad

I tell you naught for your comfort,
Yea, naught for your desire,
Save that the sky grows darker yet
And the sea rises higher
Night shall be thrice night over you,
And heaven an iron cope.
Do you have joy without a cause,
Yea, faith without a hope?[1]

(1911)

C hesterton had been dead for nearly five years when these lines from his epic poem, *The Ballad of the White Horse*, appeared in the *Times* of London under the heading "Sursum Corda" (lift up your hearts). Devastating news had reached England of the fall of the island of Crete to a combined force of German and Italian troops. More than twelve thousand British Commonwealth soldiers were now prisoners of war, and the nation was trying to come to terms with this, one of the darkest moments of World War II.[2]

Chesterton's words struck a chord deep within the British people. Many wrote to the *Times* asking for the source of the quotation. As Joseph Pearce has beautifully stated, "The evocation of a thin yet unbreakable thread of faith in the face of adversity summed up the hopes and fears of England at this time."[3]

Nor would this be the last time words from Chesterton's great ballad stirred the hearts of people throughout Britain. Several months after the *Times* first printed lines from *The Ballad of the White Horse*, Winston Churchill gave the great speech in which he spoke of "the end of the beginning." It was on this occasion that the *Times* again quoted Chesterton's poem, printing a couplet that formed a powerful complement to the prime minister's words:

> "The high tide!" King Alfred cried.
> "The high tide and the turn!"[4]

Had he lived, or had his dear Frances lived to witness these moments, they would have rejoiced that words he had written thirty years before were rallying Britain during a time of peril unlike any that nation had ever known. And they would have recognized the high honor as well of such a close association with the words of Mr. Churchill. Both occasions were moments of poignancy and power— rare moments when poetry stirs something deep within a nation's soul.

But while this was without question the highest kind of praise that could have been accorded Chesterton's poem, it was far from the sole instance when its stirring lines made a deep impression upon people who read it.

C. S. Lewis, according to his biographer and friend George Sayer, knew much of the *Ballad* by heart. He thought it "marvelous stuff" and said to Sayer in 1934: "Don't you like the way Chesterton takes hold of you in that poem, shakes you, and makes you want to cry? . . . Here and there it achieves the heroic, the rarest quality in modern literature."[5] Elsewhere, Lewis described the *Ballad* as "permanent and dateless"[6] and then offered this considered assessment: "Does not the central theme of the *Ballad*—the highly paradoxical message which Alfred receives from the Virgin—embody the feeling, and the only possible feeling, with which in any age almost defeated men take up such arms as are left them and win?"[7]

⁂

The Ballad of the White Horse was a poem unlike any other in the Chesterton canon. It was, as Garry Wills wrote, his "most serious artistic endeavor" as a poet—one that took four years to complete—and an undertaking that called forth his most extended labor and care in composition.[8]

And so, for four years, Chesterton labored over his ballad and revised it. He delayed publication. It was the only time in his career that he took such great pains.[9] This underscores both the importance that this subject held for him and his desire to get it right. All his life, the white horse had been his "private symbol of chivalry." This symbol, and the legends caught up with it, were so much a part of his imaginative life that fragments of the poem came to him in his sleep.[10]

The concept of the poem goes back as far as 1906, a time when Father John O'Connor remembered talking with Chesterton about it while they were walking on the Yorkshire moors. By April 1907, Chesterton was ready to publish a "Fragment from a Ballad Epic of Alfred" in the *Albany Review*.[11]

As he worked, one overarching principle shaped his work. As Maisie Ward recorded, he wrote *The Ballad of the White Horse* "guided by his favourite theory that to realize history we should not delve into the details of research but try only to see the big things."[12] Chesterton himself wrote about this approach at some length:

> People talk about features of interest; but the features never make up a face. . . . They will toil wearily off to the tiniest inscription or darkest picture that is mentioned in a guide book as having some reference to Alfred the Great or William the Conqueror; but they care nothing for the sky that Alfred saw or the hills on which William hunted.[13]

This was an idea that Chesterton refined still more as he readied the final galleys of his book for publication, and when he came to write the prefatory note for it, he stated explicitly that he was not seeking to craft an epic ballad infused with historicity:

> This ballad needs no historical notes, for the simple reason that it does not profess to be historical. All of it that is not frankly fictitious, as in any prose romance about the past, is meant to emphasize tradition rather than history. King Alfred is not a legend in the sense that King Arthur may be a legend; that is, in the sense that he may possibly be a lie. But King Alfred is a legend in this broader and more human sense, that the legends are the most important things about him. . . . I write as one ignorant of everything, except that I have found the legend of a King of Wessex still alive in the land. . . . A tradition [that] connects the ultimate victory of Alfred with the valley in Berkshire called the Vale of the White Horse.[14]

No less important to a right understanding of the origin of *The Ballad of the White Horse* is the centrality "of the Christian idea which had made England great and which he had learnt from Frances." [15] As he wrote his verses dedicatory to her:

> *Wherefore I bring these rhymes to you*
> *Who brought the cross to me,*
> *Since on you flaming without flaw*
> *I saw the sign that Guthrum saw*
> *When he let break his ships of awe*
> *And laid peace on the sea.*[16]

The basic plot of *The Ballad of the White Horse* is a straightforward affair—one derived from legends handed down through history. Christian men, Saxon, Roman, Briton, and Celt, are banded together to mount a desperate defense of their land against the Danes—a defense of the sacred things of faith, in defense of the human things of daily life—a defense even of the old traditions of pagan England.

King Alfred is the leader in this desperate struggle, and words attributed to him were placed by Chesterton on the title page of his book. It was a creed that Chesterton himself had fully embraced. Alfred's ancient words were a call to his life purpose:

> *I say, as do all Christian men,*
> *that it is a divine purpose that rules, and not fate.*[17]

Such a context and collection of legends allowed Chesterton the chance to bring together two things he had long desired to unite: the powerful symbol of chivalry he had always loved with the faith he had come to love.

As for the structure of his epic poem, it was divided into eight books, totaling 2,684 lines. The poem extended more than 182 pages in the first British edition.

And it marked an epoch in Chesterton's career. Writing in 1944, Maisie Ward commented that many people had come to regard *The Ballad of the White Horse* as "the greatest work of his life."[18] Forty years later, Christopher Hollis offered one of the most important scholarly assessments of the *Ballad* when he wrote: "The year 1911 was chiefly notable in Chesterton's life for the appearance of his long poem, *The Ballad of the White Horse*—one of the two or three outstanding ballads in modern English literature. . . . It is certainly one of the first and the most widely quoted of all such English ballads of this century."[19]

And what of contemporary views closer to Chesterton's time? In 1922, the English poet and critic Theodore Maynard edited an anthology called *Our Best Poets*. It was issued by the prestigious house of Henry Holt, the publisher of Robert Frost's poems. In the pages of this book, Maynard said he considered *The Ballad of the White Horse* "the crowning achievement" of Chesterton's career and judged it to be "incomparably the greatest poetic work of this century."[20] Beyond this, Maynard's book did much to commend Chesterton's *Ballad* to a wider audience. *Our Best Poets* was reviewed in the *New York Times*, and that had the ripple effect of bringing the *Ballad* into important literary conversations.

A more measured, but nonetheless very appreciative review appeared in the *New York Times* on February 4, 1912. "Poetry," the reviewer began, "is still being written. If any doubt, let him read Gilbert K. Chesterton's *Ballad of the White Horse*."[21] This book of epic verse, the reviewer went on to say, is based upon the legends told of Alfred the Great, and is (with the exception of some talky-talky monologues on the part of King Alfred) a rattling good poem of religion and war—two excellent things that in their purity usually go together. Here and there stanzas stand out in fairly startling relief, as:

> *But who shall look from Alfred's hood*
> *Or breathe his breath alive?*
> *His century like a small dark cloud*
> *Drifts far; it is an eyeless crowd,*
> *Where the tortured trumpets scream aloud*
> *And the dense arrows drive.*

And, again, this of an illuminated missal:

> *It was wrought in the monk's slow manner,*
> *From silver and sanguine shell,*
> *Where the scenes are little and terrible,*
> *Keyholes of heaven and hell.*

The portraits of the heroes are painted as brilliantly as the missal. More vivid even than Alfred are his chieftains, Eldred the Saxon, Mark the Roman, and Colan the Celt—a triple symbol of the forces that had gone to the making of England:

> *A mighty man was Eldred,*
> *A bulk of casks to fill,*
> *His face a dreaming furnace,*
> *His body a walking hill.*

This of Mark:

> *His fruit trees stood like soldiers*
> *Drilled in a straight line,*
> *His strange, stiff olives did not fail,*
> *And all the kings of the earth drank ale,*
> *But he drank wine.*
> *Wide over wasted British plains*
> *Stood never an arch or dome,*
> *Only the trees to toss and reel,*
> *The tribes to bicker, the beasts to squeal;*
> *But the eyes in his head were strong like steel,*
> *And his soul remembered Rome.*

Best of all, perhaps, is the picture of Colan the Celt:

> *His harp was carved and cunning,*
> *His sword prompt and sharp,*
> *And he was gay when he held the sword,*
> *Sad when he held the harp.*

As the chieftains had lived, so they fought, each after the manner of his kind, and so they died.

> *But like a cloud of evening*
> *To westward easily,*
> *Tall Eldred broke the sea of spears*
> *As a tall ship breaks the sea.*

. . . .

> *But while he moved like a massacre*
> *He murmured as in sleep,*
> *And his words were all of low hedges*
> *And little fields and sheep.*

He fell, pierced by a magic spear, and here enters a bit of latter-day psychology with effect like a calcium light. The Saxons, awed by the sweep of the enchanted weapon, fall back:

> *For the men were born by the waving walls*
> *Of woods and clouds that pass,*
> *By dizzy plain and drifting sea,*
> *And they mixed God with glamoury,*
> *God with the gods of the burning tree*
> *And the wizard's tower and glass.*
> *But Mark was come of the glittering towns*
> *Where white hot details show,*
> *Where men can number and expound,*
> *And his faith grew in a hard ground*
> *Of doubt and reason and falsehood found,*
> *Where no faith else could grow.*
> *Belief that grew of all beliefs*
> *A moment back was blown;*
> *And belief that stood on unbelief*
> *Stood up iron and alone.*

But though magic is powerless against the ingrain skepticism of the Roman, he falls at last overwhelmed by numbers, as does Colan the Celt. Colan's re-entrance upon the battle scene, borne "bare and bloody and aloft" before the band he had led in life, forms a last vigorous vignette:

> *And a strange music went with him,*
> *Loud and yet strangely far:*
> *The wild pipes of the Western land,*
> *Too keen for the ear to understand,*
> *Sang high and deathly on each hand*
> *When the dead man went to war.*[22]

Taken in its entirety, this was a very important review. There was true poetry here, the *Times* reviewer felt, and many instances of it. Still, though Chesterton was praised for attempting a great work, he was faulted for an abundance of repetition over the course of a poem that the reviewer thought excessive in length: *The Ballad of the White Horse* is too long. There is good stuff even in its redundancies, but that is beside the point. If Mr. Chesterton had had the resolution to lop it discriminately, he might have produced one of the most robustly picturesque poems of the century."[23]

A counterpoise to this conclusion was later offered by W. H. Auden, who admired *The Ballad of the White Horse* and thought it, perhaps, Chesterton's "greatest 'serious' poem."[24] Nor did he think, as some critics did, that the poem was overlong. "I do not, however, I am happy to say, find the length excessive. When, for example, Elf the Minstrel, Earl Ogier, and Guthrum express in turns their conceptions of the Human Condition, what they sing could not be further condensed without loss."[25]

But by far the most detailed and important critique of *The Ballad of the White Horse* appeared in Garry Wills's study *Chesterton*, published by Doubleday in 2001. Wills, a Pulitzer Prize–winning writer and critic, has long been a student of Chesterton's writings. His book is the best introduction yet written for Chesterton as a writer, and his considered reflections on *The Ballad of the White Horse* are the best assessment of that work to date.

From the outset, Wills revealed the depth of his understanding of Chesterton, the ballad form of poetry, and why this poetic form was ideally suited to Chesterton's artistic temperament and gifts. "Because Chesterton was a true balladeer," Wills wrote,

> he could use certain traditional forms with a spontaneity and a sense of the form's genius which is denied most poets by their very acuteness and personal accent. This was true not only of the drinking song but of the Christmas carol. Because of this, it was possible that Chesterton could write one kind of poem which would not only be jest or tour de force. He could restrain his loose and rapid spontaneity, yet work to a larger plan, polishing and reshaping its parts. He could stitch together the ballad stanzas as the original singers had done at the dawn of epic, when the stories of Robin Hood and Roland were fashioned from the old, sporadic material to a new and larger pattern.[26]

That this was Chesterton's intent is made clear in the prefatory note he wrote for *The Ballad of the White Horse* when it was published in 1911. King Alfred, Chesterton wrote,

> has come down to us in the best way (that is by national legends) solely for the same reason as Arthur and Roland and the other

giants of that darkness, because he fought for the Christian civilization against the heathen nihilism. But since this work was really done by generation after generation, by the Romans before they withdrew, and by the Britons while they remained, I have summarised this first crusade in a triple symbol, and given to a fictitious Roman, Celt, and Saxon, a part in the glory of Ethandune. I fancy that in fact Alfred's Wessex was of very mixed bloods: but in any case, it is the chief value of legend to mix up the centuries while preserving the sentiment; to see all ages in a sort of splendid foreshortening. That is the use of tradition: it telescopes history.[27]

As a young man, J. R. R. Tolkien greatly admired Chesterton's *Ballad*.[28] He was more receptive then to Chesterton's epic as a work of art that could be judged on its own merits, irrespective of any considerations of historicity. However, as he grew older and his scholarship regarding ancient myths and their historical origins increased, he found the utter lack of historicity in Chesterton's *Ballad* increasingly irksome. This can be clearly seen in a letter Tolkien sent to his son Christopher on September 3, 1944. Telling Christopher that he had been discussing Chesterton's poem with his daughter Priscilla, Tolkien wrote:

P[riscilla] . . . has been wading through *The Ballad of the White Horse* for the last many nights; and my efforts to explain the obscurer parts to her convince me that it is not as good as I thought. The ending is absurd. The brilliant smash and glitter of the words and phrases (when they come off, and are not mere loud colours) cannot disguise the fact that G. K. C. knew nothing whatever about the "North," heathen or Christian.[29]

This was fair enough on one level. Tolkien seems to have believed a poem with such literary virtues as the *Ballad* possessed could have been truly great if it were historically accurate. And Tolkien, as the acclaimed translator of *Sir Gawain and the Green Knight*, seems to have felt that Chesterton's epic was a missed opportunity to craft a modern poem that accurately carried forward ancient traditions and historical fact. All that one was left with, he lamented, was "the brilliant smash and glitter of the words and phrases."

But it bears repeating here that historicity was never a part of Chesterton's intent—something he had clearly stated in the prefatory note to the *Ballad*. "It is the chief value of legend," he had then written, "to mix up the centuries while preserving the sentiment; to see all ages in a sort of splendid foreshortening. That is the use of tradition."[30]

Here Tolkien and Chesterton clearly parted company, much as they had other affinities in their work as literary men. What Wills discerned, and what is certainly true, is that when it comes to weighing the merits of either man's approach to ancient myth, it is not an either/or proposition. There is room for both the Tolkienesque approach and the Chestertonian. Both have different purposes in view, but both have literary merit. And Chesterton, as Wills rightly understood, was acting in a literary tradition of ancient lineage, however lacking in historicity. He was acting as "the original singers had done at the dawn of epic."[31]

Wills also commented at length on another point of comparison made many times in discussion of Chesterton's *Ballad*: its similarities to Samuel Taylor Coleridge's *Rime of the Ancient Mariner*. This comparison was initially made by Maurice Baring in his review of the *Ballad* in 1911.[32] Baring had then stated that it was absurd to say that Chesterton's *Ballad* should have been more like *The Rime of the Ancient Mariner*. It was a wholly different kind of work, despite superficial similarities—an epic uniquely Chestertonian in character—and one that deserved to be judged as such.

Wills agreed with Baring's view and built upon what he had said. *The Ballad of the White Horse*, Wills argued, was in one important respect "unquestionably superior" to Coleridge's poem. "Coleridge's theme," Wills wrote,

> is not more complex and exalted than Chesterton's, but it is less "popular." Chesterton works from popular sentiment, as the ballad must, his poem is full of patriotism and the spirit of a single landscape:

> > *He sang of war in the warm wet shires*
> > *Where rain nor fruitage fails,*
> > *Where England of the motley states*
> > *Deepens like a garden to the gates*
> > *In the purple walls of Wales.*

> Coleridge filled the English ballad with Oriental horrors, but *The White Horse*:

> > *Seems like the tales a whole tribe feigns,*
> > *Too English to be true.*[33]

There was yet another way in which Chesterton's *Ballad* surpassed Coleridge's *Rime*. Coleridge's appropriation of Oriental motifs was one of several ways in which his poem moved away from the more traditional form of the English ballad. It was an innovative approach and one with artistic merits all its own, but it was nonetheless a departure from what had come before. Wills took note of this and observed that Chesterton's *Ballad* was praiseworthy because of its adherence to tradition. Indeed, Chesterton had recovered something in danger of being lost in modern poetry. Wills wrote:

> Chesterton recaptures, moreover, that moment when the primitive ballads were woven together to become a national epic. His poem is the record of a war from the heroic age; epic boasts and similes, a national hero, the hushed eve of battle and the screaming day that follows, make *The White Horse* echo the tales of Roland and Henry V as well as of Robin Hood. Coleridge's ballad, on the other hand, is a weird voyage into the self, its introversion making the "authentic" heroic more impossible.[34]

Wills's examination of Chesterton's *Ballad* concludes with an overview of the rich and vital Christian mysticism that infuses it from start to finish. In total, his critique runs to eleven pages. What is clear throughout is the high regard he holds for Chesterton's contribution to modern poetry and the act of literary recovery that the *Ballad* represented. Some years before, writing in *The Christian Century*, he expressed the depth of that regard in one phrase. *The Ballad of the White Horse*, he wrote, is a "neglected masterpiece in narrative verse."[35]

One other important voice should come into any discussion of the merits of Chesterton's *Ballad*. Late in his life, the novelist Graham Greene voiced what might be the most generous praise of the *Ballad* from a serious writer to appear in print. During an interview in March 1978, he called Chesterton an "underestimated poet," and to underscore that he meant he stated: "Put *The Ballad of the White Horse* against [T. S. Eliot's] *The Waste Land*. If I had to lose one of them, I'm not sure that . . . well, anyhow, let's just say I re-read *The Ballad* more often!"[36]

CHAPTER 17

Mr. Shaw's Insistent Demand

When one breathes Irish air, one becomes a practical man.
In England I used to say what a pity it was you did not
write a play.[1]

—GEORGE BERNARD SHAW, 1909

Chesterton's first play, *Magic: A Fantastic Comedy in a Prelude and Three Acts*, caused a considerable stir when it was first staged in 1913. Despite a mixed reaction from critics, it was in many ways an auspicious debut.

The critical responses were of three kinds. Some saw little merit in the play. Others felt it was at times flawed and uneven, but they discerned fine moments and much potential in Chesterton. Still others welcomed the advent of a new, talented, and highly inventive playwright from whom they wished to see more.

But a useful context for these responses can be provided by an overview of why it was written, where and how it was staged, how long it ran, and the general reception that it received.

Let's start, however, with a word about the reasons why Chesterton wrote it in the first place: the genial gadfly that was George Bernard Shaw. For some time prior to the play's debut in 1913, Shaw had been at his friend to try his hand at a play. As biographer Maisie

Ward phrased it, "Chesterton between 1911 and the [Great] War wrote the play that Shaw had been so insistently demanding."[2]

As it happened, Shaw had been making this demand for a long time—five years, in fact. As Maisie Ward wrote:

Meanwhile the private friendship between G. B. S. and G. K. C. was growing apace. Very early on, Shaw had begun to urge G. K. to write a play. G. K. was, perhaps, beginning to feel that newspaper controversy did not give him space to say all he wanted about Shaw (or perhaps it was merely that [his publisher] Messrs. Lane had persuaded him to promise them a book on Shaw for a series they were producing!). Anyhow, in a letter of 1908, Shaw again urges the play. . . .

Ayot St. Lawrence, Welwyn, Herts.

1st March 1908.

MY DEAR G. K. C.

What about that play? It is no use trying to answer me in *The New Age*: the real answer to my article is the play. I have tried fair means: *The New Age* article was the inauguration of an assault below the belt. I shall deliberately destroy your credit as an essayist, as a journalist, as a critic, as a Liberal, as everything that offers your laziness a refuge, until starvation and shame drive you to serious dramatic parturition. I shall repeat my public challenge to you; vaunt my superiority; insult your corpulence; torture Belloc; if necessary, call on you and steal your wife's affections by intellectual and athletic displays, until you contribute something to the British drama. You are played out as an essayist: your ardor is soddened, your intellectual substance crumbled, by the attempt to keep up the work of your twenties in your thirties. Another five years of this; and you will be the apologist of every infamy that wears a Liberal or Catholic mask. You, too, will speak of the portraits of Vecelli and the Assumption of Allegri, and declare that Democracy refuses to lackey-label these honest citizens as Titian and Correggio. Even that colossal fragment of your ruined honesty that still stupendously dismisses Beethoven as "some rubbish about a piano" will give way to remarks about "a graceful second subject in the relative minor." Nothing can save you now except a rebirth as a dramatist. I have done my turn; and I now call on you to take yours and do a man's work.[3]

Nor was this the only letter forthcoming from G. B. S. Chesterton received a similar letter on October 30, 1909—one full of practical advice as to the crafting of a play—on matters such as the length of the play, remuneration, and a choice of subject. "Could you not contract with me," Shaw asked, "to supply me within three months with a . . . stageable drama dealing with the experiences of St. Augustine after re-visiting England?"[4]

This letter, however artfully crafted, failed to have the desired effect. No play about Saint Augustine ever appeared—though one wonders what it would have been like if Chesterton had put pen to paper.

Shaw, however, would not take no for an answer. Two and a half years later, on April 5, 1912, he opted for a change in tactics and wrote to Frances. Saying he wished to visit them at Overroads in the near future, he sought to enlist her help in a friendly conspiracy. "I want to read a play to Gilbert," he said,

to insult and taunt and stimulate [him] with it. It is a sort of thing he could write and ought to write: a religious harlequinade.

In fact, he could do it better if a sufficient number of pins were stuck in him. My proposal is that I read the play to him on Sunday (or at the next convenient date), and that you fall into transports of admiration of it; declare that you can never love a man who cannot write things like that; and definitely announce that if Gilbert has not finished a worthy successor to it before the end of the third week next ensuing, you will go out like the lady in *A Doll's House*, and live your own life—whatever that dark threat may mean.[5]

Few first-time playwrights ever received such a noteworthy or persistent call to arms. Shaw genuinely wanted to see what Chesterton could do, and wouldn't take no for an answer. This is the more singular because artists can often be deeply jealous of anyone perceived as a rival—one thinks famously of Robert Frost's jealousy of other poets. However, Shaw's exhortations were wholly devoid of a desire to set up a straw man and then systematically set about dismantling him. Quite the reverse. For as events would prove, no one was happier to cheer Chesterton on than Shaw. This in itself was singular and revealing of the depth of a friendship no less cordial than it was unlikely.

But there also appears to have been another motive in play—a larger goal that Shaw had in view in so ardently soliciting a play from Chesterton. As Joseph Pearce has noted, Shaw had also written to Joseph Conrad, Rudyard Kipling, and H. G. Wells with a similar request. "Shaw," Pearce wrote, "was heavily involved with Hartley Granville-Barker in the revolutionising of the London theatre and, as part of his crusade to broaden the literary base of British drama . . . [he] was obsessed with getting as many well-known writers as possible to write plays."[6]

❖

Magic opened on November 7, 1913, at London's Little Theatre. A constant stream of handsomely accoutered guests alighted from cabs and walked briskly along the sidewalk past flickering gas lamps before entering under a marquee that displayed the night's featured performance.

Also on the evening's program were *Germinae*, a one-act farce written by George Calderon, and a program of music performed by a string trio—including Brahms's *Hungarian Dances*.[7]

The American critic Lawrence Gilman offered one of the best brief summaries of Chesterton's play. It was, he wrote, "quite simply and clearly a parable . . . a parable of haunting beauty and power."[8] In this instance, Chesterton's parable drew upon the convention of a drawing-room play and used elements of "comedy, drama, romance, suspense and debate" to explore the existence of hell and heaven, and powers infernal and divine—amid a cast of characters as motley as they were memorable: an American who was "a blatantly skeptical young atheist," a Conjurer who was "a master of devils," an extravagantly eccentric Duke, his beautiful young niece who wanders about the grounds of the Duke's estate seeing fairies, a clergyman who is "an honest man and not an ass," and an elderly agnostic named Dr. Grimthorpe. It was a parable such as only a writer like Chesterton could have conceived, and it made for a play unlike any other.[9]

A play, as it turned out, that was very well received by the audience that witnessed its first performance. "It was a memorable evening," Ada Jones (Cecil Chesterton's fiancée) remembered. "Gilbert and Frances were almost mobbed in the foyer, and at every interval were eagerly surrounded. . . . There was an immense ovation when the curtain rang down."[10]

Following the performance, the Chestertons were invited by the management of the Little Theatre to dine with cast and company at the Savoy. Grateful as they were for this mark of kindness, they decided instead to decamp with Cecil and Ada to the Chesterton family home at number 11 Warwick Gardens. When they arrived, "a huge sheaf of wires" was waiting to be opened.[11] Frances was prevailed upon to read the wires aloud, which she did to everyone's good pleasure.[12]

Magic then enjoyed a brief but respectable run. To mark its one hundredth performance, Bernard Shaw wrote a one-act play, *The Music Cure*, used thereafter as a curtain raiser at all performances to follow. The unique nature of this collaboration was cemented when, on March 2, 1914, a special souvenir edition of the play was presented by its director, Kenelm Foss, "to commemorate the one hundred and fiftieth performance of *Magic* by G. K. Chesterton and the fiftieth performance of *The Music Cure* by Bernard Shaw."[13]

Magic was soon after staged in Germany and would make its debut in America four years later, in 1917.[14] It would be revived in 1929, 1935, 1942, and, most famously, by Ingmar Bergman—who staged a production of it in the Göteborg City Theatre in March 1947.[15] Bergman later revisited themes suggested by Chesterton's play in his 1958 film *The Magician*.

✠

So far as the considered opinion of important writers and critics were concerned, one fine tribute appeared in a letter written by the Irish writer George Moore—a tribute all the more generous since Chesterton had criticized Moore eight years earlier in his book *Heretics*. With the kind of censorious flippancy that can lead to lasting resentment, Chesterton had then written: "Mr. Moore's egoism is not merely a moral weakness, it is a very constant and influential aesthetic weakness as well. We should really be much more interested in Mr. Moore if he were not quite so interested in himself."[16]

Moore, to his great credit, seems to have borne no trace of such resentment. In a letter to his friend Foster Bovill, written on November 24, 1913, he said of Chesterton's play:

> I have followed the comedy of *Magic* from the first line to the last with interest and appreciation, and I am not exaggerating when I say that I think of all modern plays I like it the best. Mr. Chesterton wished to express an idea and his construction and his dialogue are the best that he could have chosen for the expression of that idea: therefore, I look upon the play as practically perfect. . . .
>
> I hope I can rely upon you to tell Mr. Chesterton how much I appreciated his Play as I should like him to know my artistic sympathies.[17]

Shaw's considered opinion, making allowances for the mercenary nature of his perspective, was nonetheless generous and worth noting. In May 1916, when reviewing Julius West's book *G. K. Chesterton: A Critical Study*, he stated:

> I agree very heartily with Mr. West as to Mr. Chesterton's success in his single essay as a playwright. I shirk the theatre so lazily that I have lost the right to call myself a playgoer; but circumstances led to my seeing *Magic* performed several times, and I enjoyed it more and more every time. Mr. Chesterton was born with not only brains enough to see something more in

the world than sexual intrigue, but with all the essential tricks of the stage at his fingers' ends; and it was delightful to find that the characters which seem so fantastic and even ragdolly (stage characters are usually waxdolly) in his romances became creditable and solid behind the footlights, just the opposite of what his critics expected. The test is a searching one: an exposure to it of many moving and popular scenes in novels would reveal the fact that they are physically impossible and morally absurd. Mr. Chesterton is in the English tradition of Shakespeare and Fielding and Scott and Dickens, in which you must grip your character so masterfully that you can play with it in the most extravagant fashion. Until you can present an archbishop wielding a red-hot poker and buttering slides for policemen, and yet becoming more and more essentially archiepiscopal at every roar of laughter, you are not really a master in that tradition. The Duke in *Magic* is much better than Micawber or Mrs. Wilfer, neither of whom can bear the footlights because, like piping bullfinches, they have only one tune, whilst the Duke sets everything in the universe to his ridiculous music. That is the Shakespearian touch. Is it grateful to ask for more?[18]

The first notice of *Magic* in the American press appeared in the *New York Times*. It read, in full:

CHESTERTON PLAY PLEASES
"Magic," His New Paradoxical Comedy,
Is Like Nothing Else
By Marconi Transatlantic Wireless Telegraph
To The New York Times

LONDON. Nov. 7.—G. K. Chesterton's first essay as a dramatist has come up to expectations, so far as originality is concerned. "Magic," as his fantastic comedy, produced at the Little Theatre to-night, is called, is different from anything ever before seen on the stage.

In response to calls for the author Mr. Chesterton appeared before the footlights and declared that if anything was right in the piece it was his opinions. Those he held to, and hoped that others would share them. As most of the opinions expressed in the piece are voiced by such differently minded persons as an eccentric Duke, a conventional doctor, and a liberal parson, it is not easy to ascertain which are G. K.'s own particular views.

"Magic" is a paradox rather than a play, but it is amusing.[19]

Magic was staged in America for the first time in 1917. Reviewed in tandem with John Galsworthy's "gentle satire" of a play, *The Little Man*, the drama critic for the *New York Times* wrote:

"Magic," falls pretty short of being a fine play. It is a little skimpy in substance and very uncertain in gait, but there is so much that is rich and stimulating in many of its highly characteristic scenes that it need scarcely fear comparison with the more expert but less imaginative and original writings for the stage. Then it has much in it to delight the enthusiasts about the great Mr. Chesterton, for this comedy, his first, last, and only play, both in style and philosophic thought, is so extraordinarily and unmistakably his own.

"God and the demons and that Immortal Mystery which you deny have been in this room tonight," says the protagonist of "Magic" in the final scene, and they play their part in this mystical comedy which comes to us now more than three years after its first performance at the Little [Theatre] in London.

For "Magic" is a miracle play, and the miracle is one performed by a conjurer, who, taunted by an aggressive and insolent unbeliever, works an unbelievable mystery by calling to his aid a demon out of the spirit world. The boy is driven nearly to madness by the shattering experience, and it is to save the boy's reason that the conjurer calls at last upon Heaven to help him devise some natural explanation for the miracle he had wrought. And in the end he is really understood, not by the fighting young atheist, nor by the minister of little faith, nor by the scientist of no faith and no qualms, but only by the little Irish girl who has committed the indiscretion of seeing fairies outside of Ireland—as shocking a habit as gambling outside of Monte Carlo. For her it is all a fairy tale and it has ended in the only way a real fairy tale can ever end—by coming true.

So "Magic" is a reaffirmation of belief in the supernatural, and as that is Mr. Chesterton's whole business in life, it is scarcely surprising that his first and only play should be called "Magic."[20]

Something about Chesterton's play continued to capture this reviewer's imagination, for five days later, he took the unusual step of penning a second review that was, for the most part, an admonition to Chesterton to keep at this playwright business because he possessed great potential. Noting that there were "some stimulating and beautiful things" in the play, he observed:

What is especially interesting in Mr. Chesterton's first play is the complete persistence of his style in thought and expression when he turns his hand to a play. It is not always so. The essential quality and traits of Arnold Bennett as a novelist do not appear in his work for the theatre. Booth Tarkington, to take another example, becomes a very different writer when he turns from fiction to the stage. In his stories he is almost disconcertingly real and penetrating. His plays, on the other hand, are incredibly shallow and theatrical. . . . But Chesterton, like [J. M.] Barrie, undergoes no loss or change when he crosses the threshold of the stage door.[21]

The reviewer went on to offer suggestions for what "a more discerning director" could do with Chesterton's play. He chided Chesterton for his use of poorly conceived dialogue: "Chesterton's youth from the States 'reckons' in his second speech, 'guesses' in this third, and, before he has been on the stage five minutes, breaks out with 'tarnation,' and so confirms your haunting fear that another Englishman had taken to writing American dialect."[22]

In his concluding paragraph, the *Times* reviewer mingled praise with an attempt to rightly categorize what Chesterton had written. There was room in the theatrical world for such plays, though Chesterton needed to work at honing his craft:

These are some aspects of "Magic," a story beautifully conceived and dramatically, though inexpertly, told. It would seem to appeal only to a limited public. It is a highbrow play. That is a horrid phrase, but we have yet to coin a fitting substitute. Some catchword must be devised to describe what the naughty Louis Sherwin calls the Drier Drama, something to describe appreciatively the more rarified plays which await a producer with money in the bank and in his blood a priceless strain of Quixotism.[23]

Beyond this, it should be remembered that *Magic* was, after all, a first play. And therein lay much of its appeal. Since he was not by primary vocation a playwright, Chesterton was free, original, and inventive in the way he structured and composed his play—things several reviewers placed on the positive side of the ledger. And if the play was a kind of *Man Who Was Thursday* meets Broadway, or a sequel to *The Diabolist* set for the stage (descriptions not intended to be derogatory), it was no less devoid of genuine merits for all that. It was an exploration of themes the writer felt he not yet done with, and wished to take in new directions—even as he ventured into a new literary medium for the first time.

It bears repeating as well that following the first production of *Magic* in London in 1913, the theatrical world of New York City saw enough in the play to mount a Broadway production in 1917. Plays devoid of merit do not cross the pond.

Most significantly, *Magic* captured the imagination of Ingmar Bergman, inspiring a revival of the play under his direction, and serving as an important influence for Bergman's film *The Magician*. These are not negligible things. George Bernard Shaw had been the catalyst for Chesterton to write his play, and an artist of Bergman's stature kept revisiting the themes suggested by *Magic*. It was a play possessing an impressive pedigree and a no-less-impressive admirer and auteur.

The upshot of it all is well expressed in what the *Times* reviewer had discerned. He saw in Chesterton a playwright of great possibilities, possibilities that could perhaps be realized in a production of *Magic* staged under the guidance of the right director, or possibilities that Chesterton himself could realize with creative guidance from a director as he penned his next play. All in all, that is a considerable achievement for a first-time playwright. And, as subsequent revivals of the play would attest, other directors—most notably Bergman—saw the possibilities in *Magic* as well.

CHAPTER 18

The Toast of London

Though the knight-errant who seeks for giants and cuts their heads off is out of date, nothing can be more modern than Sir Chesterton of Overroads, who seeks for convictions and turns them inside out.[1]

—GEORGE BERNARD SHAW (1916)

It is one of Mr. Chesterton's jolly maxims that a man should be able to laugh at himself, poke fun at himself, enjoy his own absurdity. It is an excellent test of mental health. Man is a tragi-comedian. He should see himself the quaint "forked radish" that he is, fantastic as well as wonderful. He should see his mind ready to do battle and die, if need be, for an idea, but equally ready to get into a passion because his egg is boiled too hard. He should, in a word, see himself not as a hero, but as a man of strange virtues and stranger follies, a figure to move him to alternate admiration and laughter.[2]

—ALFRED GEORGE GARDINER (1914)

I n April 1914 A. G. Gardiner, editor of the *Daily News* and an accomplished essayist, published a new edition of his book of character portraits, a collection called *Prophets, Priests, and Kings*.[3] As its title indicated, people from all three groups were the subject of profiles—including King Edward VII, Kaiser Wilhelm, David Lloyd George, Winston Churchill, John Singer Sargent, George Bernard Shaw, Rudyard Kipling, Thomas Hardy, General William Booth of the Salvation Army, and Florence Nightingale. All were leading figures in the worlds of politics, the visual arts, literature, and philanthropy.

Chesterton was numbered among them, and the resulting prose portrait revealed the man who was G. K. C. at the height of his powers and celebrity. If ever someone wanted to see him as he was at this time, one could do no better than to read this well-wrought and closely observed essay. Gardiner knew Chesterton well, as Chesterton had once been a columnist for the *Daily News*. His prose portrait (all the better for not being uncritical) comes as close as any such contemporary essay has done to allowing the reader to meet Chesterton in the flesh. It captures Chesterton as he was in the time before the world was forever changed by the cataclysm of World War I. "Walking down Fleet Street some day," Gardiner began,

> you may meet a form whose vastness blots out the heavens. Great waves of hair surge from under the soft, wide-brimmed hat. A cloak that might be a legacy from Porthos floats about his colossal frame. He pauses in the midst of the pavement to read the book in his hand, and a cascade of laughter descending from the head notes to the middle voice gushes out on the listening air. He looks up, adjusts his pince-nez, observes that he is not in a cab, remembers that he ought to be in a cab, turns and hails a cab. The vehicle sinks down under the unusual burden and rolls heavily away. It carries Gilbert Keith Chesterton.
>
> Mr. Chesterton is the most conspicuous figure in the landscape of literary London. He is like a visitor out of some

fairy tale, a legend in the flesh, a survival of the childhood of the world. Most of us are the creatures of our time, thinking its thoughts, wearing its clothes, rejoicing in its chains. If we try to escape from the temporal tyranny, it is through the gate of revolt that we go. Some take to asceticism or to some fantastic foppery of the moment. Some invent Utopias, lunch on nuts and proteid at Eustace Miles', and flaunt red ties defiantly in the face of men and angels. The world is bond, but they are free. But in all this they are still the children of our time, fleeting and self-conscious. Mr. Chesterton's extravagances have none of this quality. He is not a rebel. He is a wayfarer from the ages, stopping Prophets, Priests, and Kings at the inn of life, warming himself at the fire and making the rafters ring with his jolly laughter.[4]

Gardiner had conceived a great respect for Chesterton the romantic, Chesterton the champion of fairy stories—and the Chesterton who walked the streets of London, swordstick in hand. Pessimism was in many quarters the dominant spirit of that age, and Chesterton stoutly resisted it. For, as Gardiner observed, his friend Chesterton possessed

the freshness and directness of the child's vision. In a very real sense indeed he has never left the golden age—never come out into the light of common day, where the tone is grey and things have lost their imagery. He lives in a world of romance, peopled with giants and gay with the light laughter of fairies. The visible universe is full of magic and mystery. The trees are giants waving their arms in the air. The great globe is a vast caravanserai carrying us all on a magnificent adventure through space. He moves in an atmosphere of enchantment, and may stumble upon a romance at the next street corner. Beauty in distress may call to him from some hollow secrecy; some tyrannous giant may straddle like Apollyon across the path as he turns into Carmelite Street. It is well that he has his swordstick with him, for one never knows what may turn up in this incredible world.[5]

Gardiner was unashamedly a cobelligerent with Chesterton. He, too, lamented modernity's tendency to cease to wonder at the world and to worship solely at the arid altar of science, a mind-set that centered on materialism—cold, implacable, and impersonal—a mind-set that could not, and could never, explain why humans possessed living souls.[6] If Chesterton was the kind of man who would insist that "the world, after all our science and sciences, is still a miracle; wonderful, inscrutable, *magical* and more, to whomsoever will *think* of it"—then he would gladly find common cause with him. Gardiner called this "the elemental faculty of wonder," of which the writer Thomas Carlyle had spoken. It was this, Gardiner insisted,

> that distinguishes Mr. Chesterton from his contemporaries, and gives him kinship at once with the seers and the children. He is anathema to the erudite and the exact; but he sees life in the large, with the eyes of the first man on the day of creation. As he says, in inscribing a book of Caldecott's pictures to a little friend of mine—

> *This is the sort of book we like*
> *(For you and I are very small),*
> *With pictures stuck in anyhow,*
> *And hardly any words at all.*

* * * * * * * *

You will not understand a word
Of all the words, including mine;
Never you trouble; you can see,
And all directness is divine
Stand up and keep your childishness:
Read all the pedants screeds and strictures;
But don't believe in anything
That can't be told in coloured pictures.

Life to him is a book of coloured pictures that he sees without external comment or exegesis. He sees it, as it were, at first hand, and shouts out his vision at the top of his voice. Hence the audacity that is so trying to the formalist who is governed by custom and authority. Hence the rain of paradoxes that he showers down.[7]

Chesterton's joy of living also held a strong appeal for Gardiner. It was, he argued, one of G. K. C's most singular traits. This prompted a comparison with Shakespeare's beloved character Falstaff—someone vibrantly alive, with a life full of the richly comic—set against the backdrop of a brief discussion of Chesterton's early life. "There are some men," Gardiner wrote,

who hoard life as a miser hoards his gold. . . . Mr. Chesterton spends life like a prodigal. Economy has no place in his spacious vocabulary. "Economy," he might say, with Anthony Hope's Mr. Carter, "is going without something you do want in case you should some day want something which you probably won't want." Mr. Chesterton lives the unconsidered, untrammelled life. He simply rambles along without a thought of where he is going. If he likes the look of a road he turns down it, careless of where it may lead to. "He is announced to lecture at Bradford to-night," said a speaker, explaining his absence from a dinner. "Probably he will turn up at Edinburgh." He will wear no harness, learn no lessons, observe no rules. He is himself, Chesterton not consciously or rebelliously, but unconsciously, like a natural element. St. Paul's School never had a more brilliant nor a less sedulous scholar. He did not win prizes, but he read more books, drew more pictures, wrote more poetry than any boy that ever played at going to school. His house was littered with books, filled with verses and grotesque drawings. All attempts to break him into routine failed. He tried the Slade School, and once even sat on a stool in an office. Think of it! G. K. C. in front of a ledger, adding up figures with romantic results—figures that turned into knights in armour, broke into song, and, added together, produced paradoxes unknown to arithmetic! He saw the absurdity of it all. "A man must follow his vocation," he said with Falstaff, and his vocation is to have none.

And so he rambles along, engaged in an endless disputation, punctuated with gusts of Rabelaisian laughter, and leaving behind a litter of fragments. You may track him by the blotting-pads he decorates with his riotous fancies, and may come up with him in the midst of a group of children, for whom he is drawing hilarious pictures, or to whom he is revealing the wonders of his toy theatre.[8]

Much as he admired the defiant joy that was so prominent a feature of Chesterton's character, Gardiner was no less admiring of the deep vein of seriousness that coexisted within his friend. Though no one loved his country more, Chesterton the patriot did not shy away from pointed criticism when he thought it warranted. As Gardiner wrote, Chesterton was a "lover of Little England, and the foe of the Imperialist"—and here Gardiner partially paraphrased one of Chesterton's better-known essays, "A Defence of Patriotism":

> "My country, right or wrong!" [Chesterton] cries. "Why, it is a thing no patriot could say. It is like saying, 'My mother, drunk or sober.'" No doubt, if a decent man's mother took to drink, he would share her troubles to the last; but to talk as if he would be in a state of gay indifference as to whether his mother took to drink or not is certainly not the language of men who know the great mystery. . . . We fall back upon gross and frivolous things for our patriotism. . . . Our school boys are left to live and die in the infantile type of patriotism which they learnt from a box of tin soldiers. . . . We have made our public schools the strongest wall against a whisper of the honour of England. . . . What have we done and where have we wandered, we that have produced sages who could have spoken with Socrates, and poets who could walk with Dante, that we should talk as if we had never done anything more intelligent than found colonies and kick [African natives]. We are the children of light, and it is we that sit in darkness.[9]

Gardiner moved next to a discussion of Chesterton's versatility and restless intellectual curiosity. And here Gardiner's essay recalls a description once given of the reformer and statesman William Wilberforce—of whom Sir James Mackintosh once said: "Now if I were called upon to describe Wilberforce in one word, I should say he was the most 'amusable' man I ever met with in my life. Instead of having to think what subjects will interest him, it is perfectly impossible to hit on one that does not. I never saw any one who touched life at so many points."[10] Gardiner's description of Chesterton was remarkably similar: "You may tap any subject you like: he will find it a theme on which to hang all the mystery of time and eternity."[11]

⌗

Gardiner closed his essay with a word picture of Chesterton as the knight-errant of Fleet Street. It was a sight many Londoners would have witnessed should they have seen Chesterton in full stride on that famous street at this time of his life. For Gardiner, his friend G. K. C. was in some ways a man born out of time—what with his Johnsonian manner, chivalrous notions, and love of medieval culture. All this was true enough. But Gardiner was grateful for a warm friendship with this unusual and unusually gifted writer. His essay concluded with a chivalrous tip of the cap to his friend.

> I sometimes think that one moonlight night, when he is tired of Fleet Street, he will scale the walls of the Tower and clothe himself in a suit of giant mail, with shield and sword to match. He will come forth with vizor up and mount the battle-steed that champs its bit outside. And the clatter of his hoofs will ring through the quiet of the city night as he thunders through St. Paul's Churchyard and down Ludgate Hill and out on to the Great North Road. And then once more will be heard the cry of "St. George for Merry England!" and there will be the clash of swords in the greenwood and brave deeds done on the King's highway.[12]

This was Chesterton as he was in April 1914—his star risen to a dizzying and dazzling height. He was just shy of his fortieth birthday. Few had ever enjoyed the literary celebrity and success that he had—and few had worked harder to get it. Five novels, one successfully staged play, two acclaimed literary biographies, studies of visual artists G. F. Watts and William Blake, book-length collections of essays, two works of apologetics—and the daily grind of writing articles for several newspapers. His had been a furious pace, and it could not last. Before the year came to a close, the tremendous strain of overwork, overeating, and the absence of proper exercise and rest would take its toll. It nearly took his life.

CHAPTER 19

A Near Closing of the Curtain

*Then his illness came upon him. . . . The doctor ordered a
water-bed, and almost the last words he heard before [G. K.]
sank into a coma were, "I wonder if this bally ship will ever
get to shore."[1]*

—MAISIE WARD, (1943)

For Americans who followed the life and writings of G. K.
Chesterton, the opening days of 1915 were days of grave concern. For on Sunday, January 3, a news flash printed on page 1 of
the *New York Times* reported that Chesterton was dying. The tersely
worded Special Cable to the *Times* left little room for hope:

G. K. CHESTERTON DYING
English Author Is Stricken with Paralysis at His Home

LONDON. Jan. 2.—Gilbert K. Chesterton is dying, according to information received today by The Times correspondent
from a relative of the famous essayist. For more than a month
Mr. Chesterton has been lying in a critical condition in his country home, Overroads, at Beaconsfield, Buckinghamshire.

The exact nature of his illness has not been disclosed, but it
is rumoured that he suffered a stroke of paralysis.[2]

Ten days later, anxious friends of Chesterton in America had the satisfaction of hearing in person from his brother, Cecil, that his condition had improved and that he was expected to survive his life-threatening illness.

CECIL CHESTERTON HERE;
To Lecture on War and Other Subjects—
Says His Brother Is Better

Cecil E. Chesterton, London editor and essayist and brother of G. K. Chesterton, arrived yesterday from Liverpool on the Cunard liner, *Orduna*, to deliver a series of lectures on the war and other subjects. His first appearance in New York will be at the Cort Theatre on Sunday night. . . . He said Gilbert K. Chesterton was much better when he left England and would pull through all right. He had a kidney complaint, and when the surgeons diagnosed his case they discovered that he had a weak heart, which caused anxiety for a few days.[3]

It had all started in late November 1914. On the twenty-fifth, Chesterton spoke to a large gathering of Oxford undergraduates "in defense of the English declaration of War." As he was speaking, he suddenly felt so dizzy that he had to leave the platform. Still feeling ill, he returned home. Perhaps to divert his mind, he began a letter to George Bernard Shaw. He wrote a few lines and laid down his pen. With great difficulty, he made his way to his bedroom. Just as he reached his bed, he collapsed, falling headlong with such force that his bed broke.[4]

Terribly frightened at finding her husband in such a state,

Frances called for the doctor. When he arrived, the initial diagnosis was a heart attack, with complications that impaired his mind and vital organs. It was a complete physical breakdown.

Then, on Christmas Eve, Chesterton lapsed into a coma, broken only by brief moments of consciousness. By mid-January 1915, the greatest danger had passed. On January 18, Frances wrote to Father O'Connor saying, "Gilbert has improved yesterday and again today. . . . He *asked* for me today, which is a great advance. He is dreadfully weak, but the brain-clouds are clearing, though the doctors won't allow him to make the slightest effort to think. Please God he will recover normally."[5]

On Easter Eve, Frances wrote again to Father O'Connor, this time with guarded optimism. "All goes well here," she said,

> though still very very slowly—G's mind is gradually clearing, but
> it is still difficult to him to distinguish between the real and the
> unreal. I am quite sure he will soon be able to think and act for
> himself, but I dare not hurry matters at all. I have told him I am
> writing to you often and he said, "That is right—I'll see him soon.
> I want to talk to him." He wanders at times, but the clear intervals
> are longer. He repeated the Creed last night, this time in English.[6]

By the summer of 1915, Chesterton was steadily gaining ground and strength. As Maisie Ward wrote, he "was taking up life again and with it the old friendships and the old debates, in the new atmosphere created by the war."[7]

On June 12, he wrote to George Bernard Shaw in lines that clearly conveyed he was feeling much more like himself. "My dear Bernard Shaw," Chesterton began,

I ought to have written to you a long time ago, to thank you for your kind letter which I received when I had recovered and still more for the many other kindnesses that seem to have come from you during the time before the recovery. I am not a vegetarian; and I am only in a very comparative sense a skeleton. Indeed I am afraid you must reconcile yourself to the dismal prospect of my being more or less like what I was before.[8]

Chesterton's letter also touched on their disagreement about the war. He thought it a grim necessity, while Shaw thought it profoundly wrong. Each tried to bring the other round to his point of view. But their disagreement did nothing to impair their friendship. Shaw's reply on June 22 makes this quite clear:

My dear Chesterton,

I am delighted to learn under your own hand that you have recovered all your health and powers with an unimpaired figure. You have also the gratification of knowing that you have carried out a theory of mine that every man of genius has a critical illness at 40, Nature's object being to make him go to bed for several months. Sometimes Nature overdoes it: Schiller and Mozart died. Goethe survived, though he very nearly followed Schiller into the shades. I did the thing myself quite handsomely by spending eighteen months on crutches, having two surgical operations, and breaking my arm. I distinctly noticed that instead of my recuperation beginning when my breakdown ended, it began before that. The ascending curve cut through the tail of the descending one; and I was consummating my collapse and rising for my next flight simultaneously.

It is perfectly useless for you to try to differ with me about the war. NOBODY can differ with me about the war: you might as well differ from the Almighty about the orbit of the sun. I have got the war right; and to that complexion, you too must come at last, your nature not being a fundamentally erroneous one....

Yours ever,

G.B.S.[9]

Another of Chesterton's great friends, H. G. Wells, was no less relieved that he had recovered, and would still be his friendly adversary on occasion. It was a better age when men who saw the world so differently could thus be so kind to one another. "Dear old G. K. C.," Wells wrote, "I'm so delighted to get a letter from you again. As soon as I can I will come to Beaconsfield and see you."[10]

Fortunate as he was in the gift of his friends, the close of World War I brought a great and lasting sorrow into Chesterton's life. In the summer of 1918 his brother, Cecil, who had enlisted as a soldier, took sick. Though his illness was known, he was not immediately sent to the hospital. Instead, he participated in a grueling twelve-mile march from Ypres in a pouring rain. He collapsed and was taken to a field hospital at Wimereux. His devoted wife, Ada, rushed to be with him as soon as she received word of his condition. She arrived in time but had only a few days with him before he died.

Chesterton was so overcome with grief that he could not bear to tell his parents. It was left to Frances to perform that sad task. In the years to come, Chesterton would try to honor his brother's memory by continuing to publish the *New Witness*, the paper Cecil had edited. It was a touching measure of devotion, though he could ill afford the added burden of work that it entailed.

He and Cecil had been closer than many brothers were. Eighteen more years were left to Chesterton, but he would always mourn the company of the brother he had so loved.

CHAPTER 20

What I Saw in America

For years [Chesterton] forbore visiting America, but [finally]
he decided to cross the Atlantic, in order, he announced, to
"lose my impressions of the United States."[1]

—NEW YORK TIMES (1936)

W hen Chesterton decided to visit America, Charles Lindbergh's celebrated solo flight across the Atlantic was six years in the future. And so it was that when the Chestertons commenced their journey west, they did so by ocean liner.

Their ship was the *Kaiserin Augusta Victoria*, and she left Liverpool on New Year's Day 1921. Almost immediately the ship encountered "fresh gales and rough seas." The weather did not improve as the crossing proceeded. On January 8, when the ship was but two days out of New York City, the conditions were still "decidedly squally."[2]

Inclement weather aside, the Chestertons seemed to have relished the prospect of this, their first trip to America. When Maisie Ward was researching her biography of Chesterton, she discovered that "Frances kept clippings of almost all their interviews" during their travels in the United States. G. K., for his part, seems to have looked on the first days following their arrival with a mixture of amusement and curiosity. For a start, a crowd of journalists met the couple as they disembarked—a welcome if somewhat startling experience. One writer long remembered his first sight of Chesterton, whom George Bernard Shaw had dubbed "the man-mountain"—an allusion to *Gulliver's Travels*.[3] Chesterton, the reporter said, was indeed a

> voluminous figure, quite imposing when he stands up, though not so abundantly Johnsonian as his pictures lead one to expect. He has cascades of grey hair above a pinkly beaming face, a rather straggly blond mustache, and eyes that seem frequently to be taking up infinity in a serious way.
>
> His falsetto laugh, prominent teeth and general aspect are rather Rooseveltian. . . .
>
> Mr. Chesterton, who is accompanied by Mrs. Chesterton, and who will deliver a lecture soon in Boston on the Ignorance of the Educated, said he did not expect to go further west than Chicago, since "having seen both Jerusalem and Chicago, I think I shall have touched on the extremes of civilization."[4]

Comparisons to Teddy Roosevelt, comments upon a supposed Johnsonian manner, eyes that immediately drew a spectator's attention as the one feature most sparkling with light and intensity—this reporter's description of Chesterton was proof positive that he was receiving the full celebrity treatment. Then, too, as Maisie Ward noted, Chesterton's brother journalists on the other side of the pond seem to have been rather chuffed that one of their number had become such a noted man of letters and lecturer.[5]

New York, Boston—as far west as Omaha and Oklahoma City—and as far south as Nashville—it was an ambitious itinerary for "the World Famous Literary Genius and his wife."[6]

And people came out to see him in great numbers. After spending part of January 1921 in Boston, Chesterton returned at the end of the month to give two additional lectures at the Times Square Theatre. "A large crowd," reported the *New York Herald*, "stormed the doors of the Times Square Theatre to hear the British essayist." The *New York World*, for its part, declared: "What [Mr. Chesterton] said was wholly to the liking of the really choice audience that gathered to hear him and he received sincere tributes of appreciation." Another paper concluded that Chesterton was "a crackling electric spark."[7]

There was no denying it, America liked the man mountain from overseas. America had its T. R. Now she was treated to a personal acquaintance with the man England had long since taken to calling G. K. C. And to round out the list, the *New York Times* was not least among the papers that had heralded his arrival:

We greet with a glad heart the landing of CHESTERTON, whose banner of whims o'er the world is unrolled. He has a plethora of friends here, who are too much inclined to regard him as the last enchantment of the Middle Age. He is only a medievalist in the sense that he venerates tradition and continuity, and that to him old things are young and dead things quick. Like Merlin, one of the few historical characters in this universal romance of the World as Fiction, he remembers the oak when it was an acorn and the Thunder Lizard when it was, so to speak, a chicken....

Mr. CHESTERTON is a ballad man and poet of originality and distinction. He has a vivid creative power as a romantic novelist. Those of us who swear by "The Man Who Was Thursday," "The Napoleon of Notting Hill," "The Ballad of the White Horse," and so on, are pained, but not surprised, to find him called an essayist. . . . A hearty stripling, a good young man, sir. We hope to hear him when he will be talking. Illustrious diplomatist of letters, he should have privileges. Not on lemonade were those mighty physical and mental thews built up and nourished.[8]

This was how America saw Chesterton. But, keenly observant journalist that he was, he was busy taking stock of all that he saw and heard. There was a book here, and he knew it.

What I Saw in America was published in 1922, and it contained many superlative passages. As one might have expected, it provided a near view of America as only Chesterton could have written it. There was, for a start, this reflection on America and her founding documents: "America is the only nation in the world that is founded on a creed. That creed is set forth with dogmatic and even theological lucidity in the Declaration of Independence; perhaps the only piece of practical politics that is also theoretical politics and also great literature."[9]

Chestertonian witticisms were not long in coming, as in this instance—a Johnsonism of which Samuel Johnson himself would have been proud. "It has long been recognised that America was an asylum," Chesterton quipped, "it is only since Prohibition that it has looked a little like a lunatic asylum."[10]

The American ideal called forth some of Chesterton's most deeply felt writing. After a spirited defense of Jefferson and Lincoln, he stated:

> [An Englishman] may realise equality is not some crude fairy
> tale about all men being equally tall or equally tricky; which

we not only cannot believe but cannot believe in any body believing. It is an absolute of morals by which all men have a value invariable and indestructible and a dignity as intangible as death. He may at least be a philosopher and see that equality is an idea; and not merely one of these soft-headed sceptics who, having risen by low tricks to high places, drink bad champagne in tawdry hotel lounges, and tell each other twenty times over, with unwearied iteration, that equality is an illusion.[11]

And then there were things that fired Chesterton's imagination—such as one unforgettable sight of Broadway. Lover of London that he was, he found that New York did take a bit of getting used to. It was a young city, and in many ways a brash young city, but there were things about this metropolis at the dawn of the jazz age that captured his fancy. Broadway by day was rather nondescript, but Broadway at night was something to behold, as Chesterton told his hosts one evening. As he spoke, they were treated to a glimpse of the unique way that he tended to see the world. Here was a genuine experience of Chesterton thinking outside the box. "When I looked at the lights of Broadway by night," he recalled,

I made to my American friends an innocent remark that seemed for some reason to amuse them. I had looked, not without joy, at that long kaleidoscope of coloured lights arranged in large letters and sprawling trade-marks, advertising everything, from pork to pianos, through the agency of the two most vivid and most mystical of the gifts of God; colour and fire. I said to them, in my simplicity, "What a glorious garden of wonders this would be, to any one who was lucky enough to be unable to read."[12]

211

Defiant Joy

Much of what Chesterton discussed in *What I Saw in America* concerned American democracy. Near the close of his book, he grew philosophical. He spoke of a testing time that would come to America, as it did to all nations. He spoke in words that echoed things America's founders had said about the necessity of a moral citizenry. He had conceived a great fondness for this young nation. He wished to see her do well and be well. And so he wrote:

> It would be the worst sort of insincerity, therefore, to conclude even so hazy an outline of so great and majestic a matter as the American democratic experiment, without testifying my belief that to this also the same ultimate test will come. So far as that democracy becomes or remains Catholic and Christian, that democracy will remain democratic. In so far as it does not, it will become wildly and wickedly undemocratic. Its rich will riot with a brutal indifference far beyond the feeble feudalism which retains some shadow of responsibility or at least of patronage. Its wage-slaves will either sink into heathen slavery, or seek relief in theories that are destructive not merely in method but in aim; since they are but the negations of the human appetites of property and personality.[13]

And so it went—Chicago, Philadelphia, Baltimore, Nashville, Oklahoma, Omaha, Albany, and on across the border to Canada. In all, Frances and G. K. traveled throughout America and Canada for a little over three months. They set sail for home aboard the liner *Aquitania* on April 12, 1921.

Aside from memories that would last a lifetime, the Chestertons had received one very practical benefit from their travels. Throughout the lecture tour, G. K. had been paid as much as a thousand dollars for each lecture that he gave. In total, the sum he had earned came to many thousands of dollars.

This made for a glad homecoming indeed. With such funds now available, the Chestertons were able to complete renovations to their new home, Top Meadow. They added a wing with a kitchen, a bathroom, and small bedrooms at the top of a winding stair. Chesterton could now have a proper studio and den that gave him comfort and solitude in which to write.[14]

Frances, for her part, reveled in domesticity—in surroundings that were at last what she and G. K. had long dreamt of. Their sister-in-law Ada remembered the "open brick fireplace with space for a small low chair on either side, where Frances would sit for hours, watching the logs crumble into fiery particles." And then there was the garden, "stretching luxuriantly" at the back of the house. Ada thought them a source of "undiluted happiness" for Frances, who delighted in their superintendence. The gardens were "lavishly kept" by "a local man who worked unremittingly." One summer day furnished the best of these memories. It was then that Ada remembered "flaming pokers, delphiniums, lupins, peonies, sunflowers—all the piled-up wealth of sun and colour—streamed across the lawn."[15]

CHAPTER 21

Saint Francis

The detail over which these monks went mad with joy was the universe itself; the only thing really worthy of enjoyment. The white daylight shone over all the world, the endless forests stood up in their order. The lightning awoke and the tree fell and the sea gathered into mountains and the ship went down, and all these disconnected and meaningless and terrible objects were all part of one dark and fearful conspiracy of goodness, one merciless scheme of mercy.[1]

—"Francis," from Varied Types (1903)

L ong ago in those days of boyhood my fancy first caught fire with the glory of Francis of Assisi."[2] So wrote Chesterton in the opening pages of one of his best-beloved books, *St. Francis of Assisi*, published in 1923.[3] This medieval saint, it seems, had always held a special place in his moral imagination, and the writing of this biographical study was fulfilling a debt of gratitude.

But it was an odd pairing of kindred souls, to be sure. Francis, the ascetic saint, and Chesterton the ebullient bon vivant—a man whose appearance and habits ran so dramatically counter to any notion of asceticism.

This, however, was to dwell on superficial appearances. For different as they were in appearance and habits, Chesterton had conceived a great and early reverence for Saint Francis, "the poet of life." And here these two sons of the Catholic Church could not have been more alike. In *Orthodoxy*, Chesterton had written, "the grass seemed signalling to me with all its fingers at once; the crowded stars seemed bent upon being understood."[4] This was language Saint Francis would have instantly understood, for he could easily have written, as Chesterton did, "the object of the artistic and spiritual life was to dig for this submerged sunrise of wonder; so that a man sitting in a chair might suddenly understand that he was actually alive, and be happy."[5] As it was, Saint Francis had written these lines in his beautiful *Canticle of the Sun*:

> *All praise be yours, my Lord, through Sister Moon and Stars;*
> *In the heavens you have made them, bright*
> *And precious and fair.*

But there were other, no less compelling reasons why Chesterton wished to write a book about Saint Francis. Chief among them was the "romance of religion" woven into every fiber of the faith Francis professed. "His figure," Chesterton wrote, "stands on a sort of bridge connecting my boyhood with my conversion to many other things; for the romance of his religion had penetrated even the rationalism of that vague Victorian time. In so far as I have had this experience, I may be able to lead others a little further along that road."[6]

And that, in brief, was his purpose in writing *St. Francis*: to lead others a little further along a road he had traveled. Perhaps the journey would be as fulfilling for them as it had been for him. He would try to make it so.

It was not the first time he had assayed to write about Saint Francis. Twenty years earlier, in 1903, the saint of Assisi had been the focus of an essay in his book *Varied Types* (published in England as *Twelve Types*). In this book, Chesterton had discussed the publication of Adderley's life of Saint Francis, a conventional study that spoke of Francis "primarily as the founder of the Franciscan Order."[7] As such Adderley's book commenced with "an admirable sketch of the history of Monasticism in Europe."[8] It was all undertaken with a view toward placing Francis in the context of his time, and that, Chesterton believed, was a good and helpful thing.

But it was the poetic genius of Francis that fascinated Chesterton most.[9] This seemed so decidedly at odds with the common perception of an ascetic—Chesterton called it "a fascinating inconsistency"—and he wanted to know more about why that inconsistency was a part of who Francis was. To his way of thinking, this saint had

> expressed in loftier and bolder language than any earthly thinker the conception that laughter is as divine as tears. He called his monks the mountebanks of God. He never forgot to take pleasure in a bird as it flashed past him, or a drop of water as it fell from his finger: he was, perhaps, the happiest of the sons of men. Yet this man undoubtedly founded his whole polity on the negation of what we think the most imperious necessities; in his three vows of poverty, chastity, and obedience, he denied to himself and those he loved most, property, love, and liberty. Why was it that the most large-hearted and poetic spirits in that age found their most congenial atmosphere in these awful renunciations?[10]

Chesterton then posed a series of questions about Saint Francis that he wished to see answered. "Why did he who loved where all men were blind, seek to blind himself where all men loved? Why was he a monk, and not a troubadour? These questions are far too large to be answered fully here, but in any life of Francis they ought at least to have been asked; we have a suspicion that if they were answered we should suddenly find that much of the enigma of this sullen time of ours was answered also."[11]

This passage is highly revealing. Chesterton was curious about the seeming enigma of a poet who willingly submitted to "awful renunciations." But more than this, he thought that the search for answers to this and the other questions he posed might yield an important message for his own time and questing souls, like him, who were trying to navigate an uncertain present.

⌗

The opportunity to fully explore all of these things was realized when Chesterton wrote his brief study of Saint Francis in 1923. However, the circumstances that allowed for the writing of this book were not ones that he initially welcomed.

Indeed, they were a source of sadness. For several years following his brother Cecil's death in 1918, he had edited the *New Witness*, the periodical Cecil had founded. Chesterton's stewardship of his brother's paper had been an act of filial devotion, but however devoted he was to his brother's memory, the paper ceased publication in 1922 due to lack of funds. Even as Chesterton lamented the paper's demise, he was now at a loose end professionally. Several months later he would launch *G. K.'s Weekly*, but until that time, he was free to pursue writing projects of his choosing.[12] Initially, these were trying circumstances. But he discovered through them that sometimes a gracious hand leads us in ways we know not.

And so his thoughts returned to Saint Francis. The atmosphere in which he wrote was well remembered by his friend and near neighbor Lawrence Solomon, whom he had known since boyhood. Chesterton, Solomon recalled, felt a sense of profound happiness following his conversion to the Catholic Church. He felt another feeling no less strongly. "Worry," Chesterton told his friend Maurice Baring, "[does] not worry so much as of old because of a fundamental peace."[13] A poem written about this time, "The Convert," expresses much of what he felt and opens a window on the atmosphere in which he wrote *St. Francis*:

> *After one moment when I bowed my head*
> *And the whole world turned over and came upright,*
> *And I came out where the old road shone white,*
> *I walked the ways and heard what all men said.*[14]

Biographer Maisie Ward wrote that *St. Francis* was one of two books that seemed to her the highest expression of Chesterton's mysticism (the other being *The Everlasting Man*). Seen in this light, several things stood out to her about why Chesterton was attracted to "the Little Poor Man of Assisi."

One aspect of the life of Saint Francis Chesterton deeply admired was his finding "the secret of life in being [a] servant."[15] In an earlier chapter, it was stated that following his youthful period of despair, Chesterton "was filled with both an enormous sense of thankfulness, and an enormous need for someone or something to thank."[16] A similar, no less profound sense of gratitude to God had also transformed the life of Saint Francis. So when

Chesterton wrote about this aspect of Franciscan spirituality in his book, he was writing a passage as deeply felt as it was powerfully descriptive. The true life of a servant, Chesterton wrote, flows from

the discovery of an infinite debt. It may seem a paradox to say that a man may be transported with joy to discover that he is in debt. But this is only because in commercial cases the creditor does not generally share the transports of joy; especially when the debt is by hypothesis infinite and therefore unrecoverable. But here again the parallel of a natural love-story of the nobler sort disposes of the difficulty in a flash. There the infinite creditor does share the joy of the infinite debtor; for indeed they are both debtors and both creditors. In other words debt and dependence do become pleasures in the presence of unspoilt love; the word is used too loosely and luxuriously in popular simplifications like the present; but here the word is really the key. It is the key of all the problems of Franciscan morality which puzzle the merely modern mind; but above all it is the key of asceticism. It is the highest and holiest of the paradoxes that the man who really knows he cannot pay his debt will be for ever paying it. He will be for ever giving back what he cannot give back, and cannot be expected to give back. He will be always throwing things away into a bottomless pit of unfathomable thanks. Men who think they are too modern to understand this are in fact too mean to understand it; we are most of us too mean to practise it. We are not generous enough to be ascetics; one might almost say not genial enough to be ascetics. A man must have magnanimity of surrender, of which he commonly only catches a glimpse in first love, like a glimpse of our lost Eden.[17]

A kindred renovation of the heart contributed no less meaningfully to the transformation of Saint Francis's life. Chesterton believed that this saint had recovered a way of seeing that is sadly too rare. This way of seeing "revolved round the idea of a new supernatural light on natural things."[18] Divine love, Chesterton maintained, "had called up [for Francis] every coloured creature one by one." Henceforth, "he saw everything as dramatic, distinct from its setting, not all of a piece like a picture but in action like a play. A bird went by him like an arrow; something with a story and a purpose . . . a purpose of life."[19]

Francis now understood that he and, indeed, all of humanity were caught up in a story (or drama) that had been unfolding since the world began. That story had an author—or, to put it another way, God was the Creator of the story, and he "illustrates and illuminates all things."[20] Since this was so, "all these things that God had given [were] something . . . precious and unique."[21]

Such an understanding ran very close to something Chesterton himself had already experienced and written about. In *Orthodoxy*, he wrote: "We have all read in . . . romances, the story of the man who has forgotten his name. This man walks about the streets and can see and appreciate everything; only he cannot remember who he is. Well, every man is that man in the story. Every man has forgotten who he is."[22]

Chesterton, like Saint Francis, had been given the grace to remember who he was—a beloved child of the Creator—someone precious and unique—an integral part (as indeed we all are) of the great cosmic story that God has been writing across all time. Thus each of our lives is imbued with profound meaning and significance. We are not solitary travelers left to our own devices—at the mercy of mere impersonal chance. God has written us into his story.

This was a transcendent truth that both Chesterton and Saint Francis wholeheartedly embraced. As Chesterton said in *Orthodoxy*, he had come to see that life "was an adventure because it was an opportunity . . . [I had come to see that] it was good to be in a fairy tale." For him, this realization yielded "enormous emotions which cannot be described," but of one thing he felt certain. "The test of all happiness," he wrote, "is gratitude; and I felt grateful." Then followed two sentences that captured the heart of the matter. "We thank people," he said, "for birthday presents of cigars and slippers. Can I thank no one for the birthday present of birth?"[23]

Chesterton had written of life as a story. The experience of Saint Francis had been much the same. For Chesterton, this resonated very powerfully. He had discovered someone who felt about the world as he did—someone who could help him better understand the world and its Maker. Chesterton felt profoundly grateful to have made this holy man's acquaintance. And so he concluded: "[St. Francis] was a poet and can only be understood as a poet. But he had one poetic privilege denied to most poets. In that respect indeed he might be called the one happy poet among all the unhappy poets of the world. He was a poet whose whole life was a poem."[24]

✠

Chesterton's study of Saint Francis proved a powerful complement to his embrace of Catholicism. As Maisie Ward wrote: "Faith, thanksgiving, love, surely these far above bodily asceticism can so clear a man's eyesight that he may fittingly be called a mystic since he sees God everywhere."[25] This new way of seeing shaped another of the finest passages in Chesterton's book:

When we say that a poet praises the whole creation, we commonly mean only that he praises the whole cosmos. But this sort of poet does really praise creation, in the sense of the act of creation. He praises the passage or transition from nonentity to entity; there falls here also the shadow of that archetypal image of the bridge, which has given to the priest his archaic and mysterious name. The mystic who passes through the moment when there is nothing but God does in some sense behold the beginningless beginnings in which there was really nothing else. He not only appreciates everything but the nothing of which everything was made. In a fashion he endures and answers even the earthquake irony of the Book of Job; in some sense he is there when the foundations of the world are laid, with the morning stars singing together and the sons of God shouting for joy.[26]

"Why," Chesterton had asked twenty years earlier, "did he who loved where all men were blind, seek to blind himself where all men loved? Why was [Francis] a monk, and not a troubadour?" The passage above reveals the answer Chesterton believed he had found to those questions. And for him, it was the answer, and the remedy, for the sullen time in which he lived.[27] Traveling down the road a little with Saint Francis had fostered within him a "belief in the superiority of childlike innocence over all forms of cynicism."[28] He had found a poetry of life. He commended that belief, and that poetry, to others through his book.

As noted above, Maisie Ward wrote as perceptively as anyone ever has about Chesterton's lifelong interest in Saint Francis. In her long study, *Gilbert Keith Chesterton* (published in 1943), she described how Chesterton was drawn to "the abundance of the mind's life." For him, that abundance consisted of many elements present in the life of Saint Francis: "logic and imagination, mysticism and ecstasy and poetry and joy."[29]

In Saint Francis, Chesterton had encountered a model to whom he could look for renewal and inspiration—a saint he could commend to others who were seekers as he once had been. There was, he fervently believed, a timelessness about the life of this great soul. A medieval man Francis may have been, but the spiritual ideals he held to were a store of reasons for hope in the modern world. "The mind must work in time," Maisie Ward had written,

> yet it can reach out into Eternity: it is conditioned by space but it can glimpse infinity. The modern world had imprisoned the mind. Far more than the body it needed great open spaces. And Chesterton, breaking violently out of prison, looked around and saw how the Church had given health to the mind by giving it space to move in and great ideas to move among. Chesterton, the poet, saw too that man is a poet and must therefore, "get his head into the heavens." He needs mysticism and among Her great ideas, the Church gives him mysteries.[30]

CHAPTER 22

Over to You, Mr. Wells

Lewis "would bid me study again Chesterton's Everlasting
Man; *would anxiously ask if the chaplains had really got it
into their heads that the ancients had got every whit as good
brains as we had."[1]*

—CHARLES GILMORE, ON C. S. LEWIS (1996)

The Everlasting Man, *published on 30 September [1925],
grew out of the controversy that had raged between [Hilaire]
Belloc and H. G. Wells ever since the latter had published his*
Outline of History.[2]

—JOSEPH PEARCE (1996)

Those who begin to delve more deeply into Chesterton's life
and writings soon learn that his book *The Everlasting Man*
proved a profoundly important catalyst in C. S. Lewis's return to
belief in Christianity.

More shall be said about that in due course. But at the outset
of a chapter dealing with this classic book, it is no less important
to consider what the catalyst was for Chesterton to put pen to
paper in the first place. And in this case, the answer is not hard

to find. *The Everlasting Man* is a literary reply to H. G. Wells's *Outline of History.*

Wells's book was originally published in twenty-four "fortnightly parts" (bound in color pictorial paper wraps) from 1919–1920.[3] It was then published to great acclaim as a two-volume hardcover in 1920.[4] A fourth revised edition was published in London by the distinguished house of Cassell and Company in 1925.

And so, when Chesterton's *The Everlasting Man* was published, Wells's book was still very much in the public eye. Indeed it could hardly have been otherwise, since Chesterton's friend Hilaire Belloc had from the first installments waged a very public and often bitter pamphlet controversy against Wells's book.[5]

With ruinous results, as it turned out. Wells and Belloc had formerly been on cordial terms. Once Belloc commenced his bellicose campaign, their relationship soured to the point that they became enemies.[6]

In writing *The Everlasting Man* Chesterton, a valued friend of both men, took a decidedly different tack. His book would initiate a dialogue, not a diatribe.[7] He would forcefully set out an intellectual case for Christianity but be guided by charity: his was a desire to conciliate and persuade. As he wrote in the prefatory note to the book:

> As I have more than once differed from Mr. H. G. Wells in his view of history, it is the more right that I should here congratulate him on the courage and constructive imagination which carried through his vast and varied and intensely interesting work; but still more on having asserted the reasonable right of the amateur to do what he can with the facts which the specialists provide.[8]

Given such a fair-minded and generous statement, it is not surprising that Wells always retained a warm friendship for the man he called "dear old G. K. C."[9] After Chesterton's death in 1936, Wells bore testimony to this, saying: "From first to last he and I were very close friends."[10]

❈

Aside from the absence of bombast, Chesterton's tone in *The Everlasting Man* was immediately conversational. The first lines of his introduction were rendered with a disarming blend of humor and paradox:

> There are two ways of getting home; and one of them is to stay there. The other is to walk around the whole world till we come back to the same place; and I have tried to trace such a journey in a story I once wrote. It is, however, a relief to turn from that topic to another story that I never wrote. Like every book I never wrote, it is by far the best book I have ever written. It is only too probable that I shall never write it, so I will use it symbolically here; for it was a symbol of the same truth.[11]

One of Chesterton's best gifts was his ability to describe something highly familiar as though one were seeing it for the first time or, to put it another way—with new eyes. In the case of Christianity, he could concede that it was something most people knew well, or thought they knew well. He could admit that this posed a difficulty in finding anything to appreciate about something so familiar and so often dismissed. Then he would pounce upon such preconceptions with a sudden originality:

In the specially Christian case we have to react against the heavy bias of fatigue. It is almost impossible to make the facts vivid, because the facts are familiar; and for fallen men it is often true that familiarity is fatigue. I am convinced that if we could tell the supernatural story of Christ word for word as of a Chinese hero, call him the Son of Heaven instead of the Son of God, and trace his rayed nimbus in the gold thread of Chinese embroideries or the gold lacquer of Chinese pottery, instead of in the gold leaf of our own old Catholic paintings, there would be a unanimous testimony to the spiritual purity of the story. We should hear nothing then of the injustice of substitution or the illogicality of atonement, of the superstitious exaggeration of the burden of sin or the impossible insolence of an invasion of the laws of nature. We should admire the chivalry of the Chinese conception of a god who fell from the sky to fight the dragons and save the wicked from being devoured by their own fault and folly. We should admire the subtlety of the Chinese view of life, which perceives that all human imperfection is in very truth a crying imperfection. We should admire the Chinese esoteric and superior wisdom, which said there are higher cosmic laws than the laws we know.[12]

Such a passage didn't by any means cut the Gordian knot of objections to Christianity in a thrice, but it did open a kind of door—it extended an invitation that said "Come in, and be welcome. If you're willing to sit by the fire and talk with me for a while, I'll ask nothing but that you bring an honest heart with you. Grant me a fair hearing, and you may find there is much for us to say and consider." Such an ability is a rare gift in a controversialist, and Chesterton possessed it.

One great virtue of *The Everlasting Man* is that Chesterton crafted it to flow in keeping with the nature of a dialogue. His book, therefore, would parallel Wells's *Outline of History*. And so, since Wells had commenced his work with a discussion of prehistoric man, Chesterton would as well.

This set the stage for one of the most famous passages in part 1 of *The Everlasting Man*, a passage that explored the difference between mankind and animals. "It is the simple truth," Chesterton wrote,

> that man does differ from the brutes in kind and not in degree; and the proof of it is here; that it sounds like a truism to say that the most primitive man drew a picture of a monkey and that it sounds like a joke to say that the most intelligent monkey drew a picture of a man. Something of division and disproportion has appeared; and it is unique. Art is the signature of man.
>
> That is the sort of simple truth with which a story of the beginnings ought really to begin. The evolutionist stands staring in the painted cavern at the things that are too large to be seen and too simple to be understood. He tries to deduce all sorts of other indirect and doubtful things from the details of the pictures, because he cannot see the primary significance of the whole; thin and theoretical deductions about the absence of religion or the presence of superstition; about tribal government and hunting and human sacrifice and heaven knows what.[13]

Moving forward from his discussion of the uniqueness of man, Chesterton turned next to a discussion of the uniqueness of Christ. And here, as Garry Wills has written, there was a distinction to be made between Wells's *Outline of History* and *The Everlasting Man*.

"Wells," Wills stated, "made of history a single rise and advance, uniformly gradated; a process self-explanatory and enclosed by reason of its internal symmetry. Chesterton moves from an attack on this philosophy of single direction and 'grey gradations' to the center of crisis in history, Christ."[14]

Chesterton had commenced *The Everlasting Man* with a discussion of the cave paintings at Lascaux. "The sketch of the human story," he wrote,

> began in a cave; the cave which popular science associates with the cave-man and in which practical discovery has really found archaic drawings of animals. The second half of human history, which was like a new creation of the world, also begins in a cave. There is even a shadow of such a fancy in the fact that animals were again present; for it was a cave used as a stable. . . . It was here that a homeless couple had crept underground with the cattle when the doors of the caravanserai [or roadside inn] had been shut in their faces; and it was here beneath the very feet of the passers-by, in a cellar under the very floor of the world, that Jesus Christ was born.[15]

Here was the kind of striking symmetry that readers of an apologia written for a popular audience could readily understand. In the cave paintings of Lascaux, man had shown why he was man and not an animal. In the cave of Bethlehem, God became man—and the moment when this happened became the still point of human history. Here a telling symbolism was in play. "God," Chesterton wrote in *The Everlasting Man*, "was also a Cave-Man, and had also traced strange shapes of creatures, curiously coloured, upon the wall of the world; but the pictures that he had made had come to life."

There was yet more fertile ground in exploring the implications of this line of thought. "A mass of legend and literature," Chesterton wrote,

has repeated and rung the changes on that single paradox; that the hands that had made the sun and stars were too small to reach the huge heads of the cattle. Upon this paradox, we might almost say upon this jest, all the literature of our faith is founded. It is at least like a jest in this, that it is something which the scientific critic cannot see. He laboriously explains the difficulty which we have always defiantly and almost derisively exaggerated; and mildly condemns as improbable something that we have almost madly exalted as incredible; as something that would be much too good to be true, except that it is true. When that contrast between the cosmic creation and the little local infancy has been repeated, reiterated, underlined, emphasised, exulted in, sung, shouted, roared, not to say howled, in a hundred thousand hymns, carols, rhymes, rituals, pictures, poems, and popular sermons, it may be suggested that we hardly need a higher critic to draw our attention to something a little odd about it; especially one of the sort that seems to take a long time to see a joke, even his own joke.[16]

Chesterton called this "the riddle of Bethlehem," saying that in this riddle, that is to say, Christ's being born in a cave, "it was heaven that was under the earth." He continued:

There is in that alone the touch of a revolution, as of the world turned upside down. It would be vain to attempt to say anything adequate, or anything new, about the change which this conception of a deity born like an outcast or even an outlaw had upon the whole conception of law and its duties to the poor and outcast. It is profoundly true to say that after that moment there could be no slaves. . . . Individuals became important, in a sense in which no instruments can be important. A man could not be a means to an end, at any rate to any other man's end. All this popular and fraternal element in the story has been rightly attached by tradition to the episode of the Shepherds; the hinds who found themselves talking face to face with the princes of heaven. But there is another aspect of the popular element as represented by the shepherds which has not perhaps been so fully developed; and which is more directly relevant here.

Men of the people, like the shepherds, men of the popular tradition, had everywhere been the makers of the mythologies. . . . They had best understood that the soul of a landscape is a story and the soul of a story is a personality. . . . Upon all such peasantries everywhere there was descending a dusk and twilight of disappointment, in the hour when these few men discovered what they sought. Everywhere else Arcadia was fading from the forest. Pan was dead and the shepherds were scattered like sheep. And though no man knew it, the hour was near which was to end and to fulfil all things; and though no man heard it, there was one far-off cry in an unknown tongue upon the heaving wilderness of the mountains. The shepherds had found their Shepherd.

And the thing they found was of a kind with the things they sought. The populace had been wrong in many things; but they had not been wrong in believing that holy things could have a habitation and that divinity need not disdain the limits of time and space.[17]

Here was an elegant, vivid, and reasoned exposition of the Christian faith. Memorable passages could be cited at length, but it is enough for our purposes here to say that many people found Chesterton's apologia profound and compelling.

One such reader was the Yale University critic and scholar William Lyon Phelps.[18] He wrote to Chesterton, saying that *The Everlasting Man* was "a magnificent work of genius and never more needed than now. . . . I took out my pencil to mark the most important passages, but I quickly put the pencil in my pocket for I found I had to mark every sentence."[19]

But by far the most celebrated reader of *The Everlasting Man* was C. S. Lewis. Following his reading of Chesterton's book, Lewis came to understand that here was someone who felt he had been given the answer to the greatest riddle of all: the riddle of the cosmos. The answer was Christianity—"the philosophy," Chesterton wrote, "in which I have come to believe. I will not call it my philosophy, for I did not make it. God and humanity made it; and it made me."[20] And in no place did he more eloquently describe what his faith meant to him than when he wrote: "The wise man will follow a star, low and large and fierce in the heavens, but the nearer he comes to it the smaller and smaller it will grow, till he finds it in the humble lantern over some little inn or stable. Not till we know the high things shall we know how lowly they are."[21]

Lewis had famously written that prior to his conversion he found "Chesterton had more sense than all the other moderns put together; bating, of course, his Christianity."[22] But Chesterton's writings would prove a powerful catalyst in the process of Lewis's embrace of Christianity. "In reading Chesterton," Lewis wrote, "as in reading [George] MacDonald, I did not know what I was letting myself in for. A young man who wishes to remain a sound Atheist

cannot be too careful of his reading. There are traps everywhere—
'Bibles laid open, *millions of surprises*,' as [George] Herbert says, 'fine
nets and stratagems.' God is, if I may say it, very unscrupulous."[23]
Lewis would later remember:

> I read Chesterton's *Everlasting Man* and for the first time saw the
> whole Christian outline of history set out in a form that seemed
> to me to make sense. Somehow I contrived not to be too badly
> shaken. You will remember that I already thought Chesterton the
> most sensible man alive "apart from his Christianity." Now, I veri-
> tably believe, I thought—I didn't of course *say*; words would have
> revealed the nonsense—that Christianity itself was very sensible.[24]

In the years following Lewis's conversion, he continually
praised *The Everlasting Man* or referred his correspondents to it.[25]
To Charles Williams he wrote in 1936: "I have just read your *Place
of the Lion* and it is to me one of the major literary events of my
life—comparable to my first discovery of George Macdonald, G. K.
Chesterton, or Wm. Morris."[26] Ten years later he told another correspondent, "I was brought back [to Christianity] . . . by the strong
influence of 2 writers, the Presbyterian George Macdonald & the
R.C. G. K. Chesterton."[27] In 1947, he advised a young woman
named Rhonda Bodle: "As for books, the v. best popular defence
of the full Christian position I know is G. K. Chesterton's *The
Everlasting Man*."[28]

One correspondent wrote saying that Chesterton could be rhetorical in a pejorative sense. Lewis conceded the point but then came
to Chesterton's defense. "Yes, Chesterton can be, in the bad sense,
rhetorical, but v. seldom is. As a man once said to me 'G. K. C. has
the same quality of becoming *more* eloquent the more exactly he

means what he says.'"[29] Late in his life, in May 1961, Lewis offered this commendation to a correspondent named Margaret Gray: "For a good ('popular') defence of our position against modern waffle, to fall back on, I know nothing better than G. K. Chesterton's *The Everlasting Man*."[30] And enigmatically, when one bears the book that would become *Mere Christianity* in mind, Lewis told Walden Howard in December 1947: "But Chesterton (whom I love) has done it: I could only water his wine. And the young people won't read Chesterton. I don't think they like paradox. They're all as grave as government paper now . . . yours very sincerely, C. S. Lewis."[31]

Lewis's continual recommendation of *The Everlasting Man* recalls the way people in later years would often commend his own book, *Mere Christianity*, to friends seeking a reasoned explanation of the Christian faith. His letter to Sheldon Vanauken in December 1950 is perhaps the best example of this. Here, Lewis described *The Everlasting Man* as "the best popular apologetic I know."[32]

Moreover, Lewis's affirmation of Chesterton's influence upon him is one supreme reason, among many, as to why Chesterton the apologist matters today. As an apologist, he helped to give the world C. S. Lewis, perhaps the most influential Christian apologist of all time. Lewis later underscored Chesterton's influence upon him as an apologist when he wrote: "The case for Christianity in general is well given by Chesterton; and I tried to do something [along the same lines] in my *Broadcast Talks*."[33] Lewis's *Broadcast Talks* later became the basis for his classic treatise *Mere Christianity*. And so the streams that Chesterton set in motion when giving the reasons for his hope are very much with us still—in his own writings and also in the works of Lewis.

And here it would perhaps be well to let H. G. Wells have the last word. His *Outline of History* had been the catalyst for *The Everlasting Man*. In the years following its publication, there had been no diminishing of their friendship. Eight years later, Wells was no less fond of his friend than he had been, as a letter written just before Christmas 1933 reveals. It speaks as well to how winsome Chesterton's apologia had been.

47 Chiltern Court, N.W.I.

Dec. 10, 1933

Dear old G. K. C.

An *Illustrated London News* Xmas cutting comes like the season's greetings. If after all my Atheology turns out wrong and your Theology right I feel I shall always be able to pass into Heaven (if I want to) as a friend of G. K. C.'s. Bless you.

My warmest good wishes to you and Mrs. G. K. C.

H. G.[34]

CHAPTER 23

Chaucer

There is at the back of all our lives an abyss of light, more
blinding and unfathomable than any abyss of darkness; and
it is the abyss of actuality, of existence, of the fact that things
truly are, and that we are ourselves incredibly and sometimes
almost incredulously real.[1]

—G. K. CHESTERTON

These were some of the most beautiful and life-affirming words that Chesterton ever wrote. They were a kind of centerpiece to one of the great works of his later career, *Chaucer* (published in 1932).

It is a book that continues to be much appreciated by some of the best writers and literary critics living today. Garry Wills quoted from it in several moving passages in his memoir *Why I Am a Catholic*. Harold Bloom wrote that his "favorite Chaucer critic still remains G. K. Chesterton."[2] Peter Ackroyd, in his acclaimed biography of Chaucer, wrote appreciatively of Chesterton's reflections on the author of *The Canterbury Tales* and *Troilus and Criseyde*. "Much has been said," Ackroyd wrote,

> concerning Chaucer as the "father of English poetry," so much
> in fact that it has become something of a literary and cultural

platitude; but Chaucer has become representative of so much else that, for writers like G. K. Chesterton, he turns into the figure of England or the face of Albion. He is the genial and smiling emblem of Englishness.[3]

Chesterton had been writing about Chaucer and medieval times for many years when he penned his study of Chaucer. One of his earliest essays to take up the subject was published in 1909, as part of the collection of essays called *Tremendous Trifles*. The essay was called "The Little Birds Who Won't Sing," and it captured much of Chesterton's lifelong appreciation for the Middle Ages. Remembering his return from a recent trip in Europe, he wrote:

> But if there was one thing the early mediaevals liked it was representing people doing something—hunting or hawking, or rowing boats, or treading grapes, or making shoes, or cooking something in a pot. . . . The Middle Ages is full of that spirit in all its monuments and manuscripts. Chaucer retains it in his jolly insistence on everybody's type of trade and toil. It was the earliest and youngest resurrection of Europe, the time when social order was strengthening, but had not yet become oppressive; the time when religious faiths were strong, but had not yet been exasperated. For this reason the whole effect of Greek and Gothic carving is different. The figures in the Elgin marbles, though often rearing their steeds for an instant in the air, seem frozen for ever at that perfect instant. But a mass of medieval carving seems actually a sort of bustle or hubbub in stone. Sometimes one cannot help feeling that the groups actually move and mix, and the whole front of a great cathedral has the hum of a huge hive.[4]

All his life Chesterton was drawn to the art and faith, the society, comedy, and sense of vibrant life that he saw in the Middle Ages. And his guide to all that mattered to him about this period of history was Geoffrey Chaucer. No one has expressed this idea better than the distinguished literary critic Harold Bloom, who wrote that Chesterton "was himself a Chaucerian pilgrim."[5]

So, when Chesterton began to write his study of Chaucer, he knew that he would be able to revisit at length a world that came alive for him in Chaucer's writings. They were kindred spirits well met, and because they were—rather, because Chesterton was such a kindred spirit—his intuitive reading of Chaucer's life and works serves him very well as a critic. For as Harold Bloom also wrote: "[Chesterton's] wonderful book *Chaucer* (1932) is popular and simple, as he intended, and seems to me to embody the spirit of Chaucer. I like it that there are more than fifty references to Shakespeare in the book, because only Shakespeare (in English) deserves to set the measure for Chaucer."[6]

⌗

Chesterton wasted little time in beginning to compare Chaucer and Shakespeare. As he did so, he demonstrated a unique ability to teach amidst the presentation of entertaining prose. He commenced his task of fostering a greater appreciation of Chaucer through writing that was at once lucid and provocative. And so he observed in the first chapter of *Chaucer* that while some critics

> have (if it were possible) overrated the greatness of Shakespeare, most of them have unaccountably underrated the greatness of Chaucer. Yet most of the things that are hinted in depreciation of

Chaucer could be said as easily in depreciation of Shakespeare. If Chaucer borrowed from Boccaccio and other writers, Shakespeare borrowed from anybody or anything, and often from the same French or Italian sources as his forerunner. The answer indeed is obvious and tremendous; that if Shakespeare borrowed, he jolly well paid back. But so did Chaucer, as in that very central instance I have named; when he turned the decorative picture-frame of the Decameron into the moving portrait-gallery of the ride to Canterbury.[7]

For a book that was intended to be popular and simple, *Chaucer* performed a remarkable feat: earning and retaining a high standing among modern critics and in widely respected sources of scholarly literature. Medievalist scholar Corinne Saunders described one of the reasons for this in her introduction to the volume on Chaucer for *The Blackwell Guide to Criticism* series. "For G. K. Chesterton," she wrote, "Chaucer was a 'great humorist,' 'a humorist in the grand style; a humorist whose broad outlook embraced the world as a whole, and saw even great humanity against a background of greater things.' Interestingly, Chesterton emphasizes the large 'design' of Chaucer's writing and the entirety of his cosmos, anticipating a later critical notion of the Gothic design of the *Canterbury Tales*."[8]

In specific terms, Chesterton artfully introduced the idea that the architecture of a Gothic cathedral could provide a highly useful context through which an exploration of *The Canterbury Tales* could be undertaken. This architectural analogy, according to *The Columbia Critical Guide to Geoffrey Chaucer*, is "now much used by Chaucer critics."[9] The passage where Chesterton introduced this analogy, which appears in chapter 5 of his book, subsequently became famous. It is an extended passage redolent with insight and discernment, showing Chesterton's best skills as a critic. As such, it amply warrants a citation in full. And so we read:

The Canterbury Tales do remain rather like a huge, hollow, unfinished Gothic cathedral with some of the niches empty and some filled with statues, and some part of the large plan traced only in lines upon the ground.

Just as in such a case, the arches would stand up more strongly than the statues, or the walls be made first and more firmly than the ornament, so in Chaucer's work the framework is finer than the stories which correspond to the statues. The prolonged comedy which we call the Prologue, though it includes many interludes and something like an epilogue, is made of much stronger material than the tales which it carries; the narrative is quite superior to the narratives. The Wife of Bath's Tale is not so good as the Wife of Bath; the Reeve's Tale is not so vivid as the Reeve; we are not so much interested in the Summoner's story as in the Summoner, and care less about Griselda than about the Clerk of Oxenford. The Miller does not prove even his own rather brutal energy, by telling a broad and rather brutal story, half so well as the poet conveys it in those curt and strong lines about his breaking a door by butting it with his red-bristled head. And the whole conception and cult of Chivalry is no better set forth, in all the seventy pages that unfold the Knight's Tale, than in the first few lines that describe the Knight. It is impossible to say for certain, of course, whether Chaucer realized how much more real and original were the passages which concern the Pilgrims than those which concern their imaginary heroes or martyrs. It is possible that, like many another original genius, he did not know which parts of his own work were really original, still less which were really great.... It may be that Chaucer did really regard the prologue as a mere frame, in the sense of a picture-frame. In that case, we can only say he invented a new kind of picture-gallery, in which the picture-frames are much better than the pictures. Still, a word must be said for the understanding of the pictures, even when he has stolen them out of other people's picture-frames. In other words, we must understand something about stories as stories, before we even open this medieval story-book.[10]

One seldom has the chance to so meaningfully advance the critical understanding of a seminal literary figure like Chaucer. And this is the more singular when one recalls that Chesterton did not have extensive academic training as a literary scholar. Forty years earlier, he had taken courses in Latin and English literature at University College, London—but he left the school without taking a degree.

He did, however, encounter a learned and greatly gifted professor during his time at University College: a man whose lectures were lively, often unconventional, and inspiring—all qualities that Chesterton's writing later possessed. The instructor was W. P. Ker, then Quain professor at University College, and later professor of poetry at Oxford. Looking back on this time of his life, Chesterton wrote: "I am able to boast myself among the many pupils who are grateful to the extraordinarily lively and stimulating learning of Professor W. P. Ker.... And I once had the honour of constituting the whole of Professor Ker's audience. But he gave as thorough and thoughtful a lecture as I have ever heard given, in a slightly more colloquial style; asked me some questions about my reading; and, on my mentioning something from the poetry of [Alexander] Pope, said with great satisfaction: 'Ah, I see you have been well brought up.'"[11]

All of this is to say that Chesterton's flair for the unconventional in his literary criticism may have received an early and important influence from Professor Ker—though it is just as likely that Ker's lively, unconventional, and inspiring instructional technique may have reinforced similar tendencies already present in Chesterton's approach to literature. But when all this is said, and it is noteworthy, it is still remarkable that Chesterton hit upon the highly original idea of undertaking an exploration of Chaucer's *Canterbury Tales* by means of an architectural analogy centered on the design of a Gothic cathedral. His was a mind that often ran in untraveled paths, or blazed trails then unexplored in literary criticism. It was a unique and highly intuitive gift. And as Chesterton would later demonstrate in his study of Saint Thomas Aquinas, although he had not received a full and thorough academic training as a literary scholar, he could craft literary or more philosophically oriented studies that practiced and well-regarded scholars found highly useful and compelling. Such was certainly the case when it came to his study of Chaucer.

⌗

Given the appreciation among modern critics that Chesterton's study of Chaucer enjoys, it is also interesting to note that Chesterton himself had little appreciation for the reflections of his contemporary critics about Chaucer. Writing with brio and panache, he took them to task. "Now Chaucer," he said,

> is a particularly easy mark for the morbid intellectual or the mere innovator. He is very easily pelted by the pedants, who demand that every eternal poet should be an ephemeral philosopher. . . .

He is as awakening as a cool wind on a hot day, because he breathes forth something that has fallen into great neglect in our time, something that very seldom stirs the stuffy atmosphere of self-satisfaction or self-worship. And that is gratitude, or the theory of thanks. He was a great poet of gratitude; he was grateful to God; but he was also grateful to Gower. He was grateful to the everlasting Romance of the Rose; he was still more grateful to Ovid and grateful to Virgil and grateful to Petrarch and Boccaccio. He is always eager to show us over his little library and to tell us where all his tales come from. He is prouder of having read the books than of written the poems.[12]

Another literary trait in Chaucer with which Chesterton closely identified is what Harold Bloom has called his "mastery of psychological realism." This, Bloom wrote, "was grounded upon his ironic sense that the chivalric ideal was a lost illusion, to be affirmed only in the mode of nostalgia. Everything that existed represented a falling away from a more generous vision, though Chaucer, profoundly comic in his genius, declined to become a master of regret. Chesterton's own fictions and poems move me because he had learned from Chaucer to long for this abandoned field of romance."[13]

Taking up this theme at the close of chapter 1 of *Chaucer*, Chesterton produced one of the finest passages in his study. "It is true," he wrote,

that the true poet is ultimately dedicated to Beauty, in a world where it is cleansed of beastliness, and it is not either a new scheme or theory on the one hand, nor a narrow taste or technique on the other. It is concerned with ideas; but with ideas that are never new in the sense of neat, as they are never old in the sense of exhausted. They lie a little too deep to find perfect expression in any age; and great poets can give great hints of them in any. I would say no more of Chaucer than that the hints that he gave were great.[14]

Chaucer was a master of the comic, and Chesterton's appreciation for this aspect of his artistry was no less profound than his appreciation for the medieval poet's other gifts. In a passage where he considered whether or not Chaucer was a satirist, he introduced a comparison to Charles Dickens that helped to make his point. "Chaucer," he wrote,

> often sounds satirical; yet Chaucer was not strictly a satirist. Perhaps the shortest way of putting it is that he already inhabits a world of comicality and not a world of controversy. He makes fun of people, in the exact sense of getting fun out of them for himself. . . . He is already on the road to the Dickensian lunatic-asylum of laughter; because he is valuing his fools and knaves and almost wishing (as it were) to preserve them in spirits—in high spirits.[15]

Wherein lay Chaucer's claim to immortality? Chesterton believed he knew. At the close of his chapter on "The Greatness of Chaucer," he offered an extended reflection that readily explains why readers return to and reread passages of his book. "Chaucer," he wrote,

> was a child of light and not merely of twilight, the mere red twilight of one passing dawn of revolution, or the grey twilight of one dying day of social decline. He was the immediate heir of something like what Catholics call the Primitive Revelation;

that glimpse that was given of the world when God saw that it was good; and so long as the artist gives us glimpses of that, it matters nothing that they are fragmentary or even trivial; whether it be in the mere fact that a medieval Court poet could appreciate a daisy, or that he could write, in a sort of flash of blinding moonshine, of the lover who "slept no more than does the nightingale." These things belong to the same world of wonder as the primary wonder at the very existence of the world; higher than any common pros and cons, or likes and dislikes, however legitimate. Creation was the greatest of all Revolutions. It was for that, as the ancient poet said, that the morning stars sang together; and the most modern poets, like the medieval poets, may descend very far from that height of realization and stray and stumble and seem distraught; but we shall know them for the Sons of God, when they are still shouting for joy. This is something much more mystical and absolute than any modern thing that is called optimism; for it is only rarely that we realize, like a vision of the heavens filled with a chorus of giants, the primeval duty of Praise.[16]

CHAPTER 24

The Pillar of the Apennines

*[Chesterton] had, said Mr. Eccles, an intuitive mind. He
had, too, read more than was realized.[1]*

—MAISIE WARD (1943)

*Mr. Chesterton's little volume makes one of the pleasantest
introductions to St. Thomas that could be desired.*

—TIMES LITERARY SUPPLEMENT (1933)

I t would be easy to say that Chesterton was drawn to Saint Thomas
Aquinas because they were much alike. Both men, it is true, were
men of prodigious bulk—Aquinas was likened in his lifetime to an ox,
while Chesterton was the recipient of many oxlike or boxlike quips.
Both were men of great intellect; though Aquinas's was by far the
greater, Chesterton, as Lawrence of Arabia remembered, was called a
"colossal genius" by George Bernard Shaw.[2] Aquinas has been called
"a genius whose claim to that accolade is barely debatable." Anthony
Kenny, the eminent analytical philosopher, has written that "Aquinas
is . . . one of the dozen greatest philosophers of the western world. . . .
His metaphysics, his philosophical theology, his philosophy of mind,
and his moral philosophy entitle him to rank with Plato and Aristotle,
with Descartes and Leibniz, with Locke and Hume and Kant."[3]

All similarities aside, there were stark differences between Chesterton and Aquinas. Where Aquinas was taciturn, Chesterton was outgoing and gregarious. Where one (Aquinas) preferred to be alone with his thoughts and to pursue unfettered scholarship, the other (Chesterton) loved to write and think in the midst of a restaurant or tavern. Aquinas was a deeply disciplined man—in terms of both his intellectual pursuits and his personal habits. He was a focused man, if ever there was one. Chesterton was famously unkempt in appearance, and though a dedicated writer, was often spendthrift in his use of time, his intellectual energy, and in taking on a staggering workload throughout his professional life. Aquinas poured a lifetime of study and reflection into his *Summa Theologica*. Chesterton poured himself into many books simultaneously.

The two men were in this sense an odd couple, but they had one great thing in common. As Chesterton said of St. Thomas in chapter 1 of his book: "Thomas was a very great man who reconciled religion with reason . . . who insisted that the senses were the windows of the soul and that the reason had a divine right to feed upon facts, and that it was the business of the Faith to digest the strong meat of the toughest and most practical of pagan philosophies."

It was Chesterton's abiding admiration for this sterling achievement, and the deeply human tale that attended it, which moved Chesterton to write *St. Thomas Aquinas*, published in September 1933.

⌖

That Chesterton's study of Saint Thomas has become a classic of its kind is widely acknowledged.[4] That it would prove so when he first announced his intention to write a book to his American publisher, Sheed & Ward, was anything but certain. As Maisie Ward remembered:

> When we were told that Gilbert was writing a book on St. Thomas and that we might have the American rights, my husband felt a faint quiver of apprehension. Was Chesterton for once undertaking a task beyond his knowledge? Such masses of research had recently been done on St. Thomas by experts of such high standing and he could not possibly have read it all. Nor should we have been entirely reassured had we heard what Dorothy Collins told us later concerning the writing of it.
>
> He began by rapidly dictating to Dorothy about half the book. So far he had consulted no authorities but at this stage he said to her:
>
> "I want you to go to London and get me some books."
>
> "What books?" asked Dorothy.
>
> "I don't know," said G. K.
>
> She wrote therefore to Father O'Connor and from him got a list of classic and more recent books on St. Thomas. G. K. "flipped them rapidly through," which is, says Dorothy, the only way she ever saw him read, and then dictated to her the rest of his own book without referring to them again.[5]

This was not an auspicious beginning, but it was from such seemingly haphazard origins that a very fine book was written. The reason that it was such a fine piece of interpretive writing was that Chesterton had a profoundly intuitive mind. As Bernard Bergonzi wrote in *The Oxford Dictionary of National Biography*, "Chesterton had no philosophical training, [but] his book shows his intuitive grasp of Aquinas."[6]

Chesterton had a great gift. He could also isolate the pith and importance of a book with great rapidity, relate what he had learned to an overarching theme, or detect the interconnectedness of ideas he had encountered. And while his reading, research, and preparation for the writing of his book on Saint Thomas were rather limited, he was otherwise very well read.

This was largely the reason that he could almost immediately begin dictating to his secretary Dorothy Collins. His thinking about Aquinas had been underway for a long time. As his reading in earlier years had continued, he had been all the while thinking about what he had read and forming conclusions or theories about Saint Thomas. When the time came to write his book, not long after the very stimulative and helpful task of completing his study of Geoffrey Chaucer, he could at last give his mind fully to something that he had previously only been able to think about in snatches here and there. But he *had* thought much about Saint Thomas; that much was clear. And what he had been thinking rightly centered on the heart of Aquinas's thought and its significance in history and the development of ideas.

This was confirmed almost immediately when the distinguished Thomist scholar Étienne Gilson offered his considered opinion of Chesterton's book. When *St. Thomas* appeared, Maisie Ward remembered, "[Gilson] said to a friend of mine 'Chesterton makes one despair. I have been studying St. Thomas all my life and I could never have written such a book.'"[7]

Following Chesterton's death in 1936, Gilson was again asked for an estimate of *Saint Thomas*. His respect for what Chesterton had written had only grown with the years. "I consider it," Gilson said,

> as being without possible comparison the best book ever written on St. Thomas. Nothing short of genius can account for such an

achievement. Everybody will no doubt admit that it is a "clever" book, but the few readers who have spent twenty or thirty years in studying St. Thomas Aquinas, and who, perhaps, have themselves published two or three volumes on the subject, cannot fail to perceive that the so-called "wit" of Chesterton has put their scholarship to shame. He has guessed all that which they had tried to demonstrate, and he has said all that which they were more or less clumsily attempting to express in academic formulas. Chesterton was one of the deepest thinkers who ever existed; he was deep because he was right; and he could not help being right; but he could not either help being modest and charitable, so he left it to those who could understand him to know that he was right, and deep; to the others, he apologized for being right, and he made up for being deep by being witty. That is all they can see of him.[8]

Chesterton's own aspirations for *St. Thomas* were much more modest in character. "This book," he wrote in an introductory note, "makes no pretence to be anything but a popular sketch of a great historical character who ought to be more popular."[9] Second, he had written his book "very largely [for] those who are not of the communion of St. Thomas"—that is to say he was writing for non-Catholics.[10] Finally, it was his intent merely to give samples of Saint Thomas's philosophy—that in so doing he might give only what was needed (and no more) to foster a just appreciation of Aquinas's genius and his contribution to the history of thought and religion. "I have," he wrote,

> only . . . given samples of [St. Thomas's] philosophy. . . . It is practically impossible to deal adequately with the theology. A lady I know picked up a book of selections from St. Thomas with

a commentary; and began hopefully to read a section with the innocent heading, "The Simplicity of God." She then laid down the book with a sigh and said, "Well, if that's His simplicity, I wonder what His complexity is like." With all respect to that excellent Thomistic commentary, I have no desire to have this book laid down, at the very first glance, with a similar sigh. I have taken the view that the biography is an introduction to the philosophy, and that the philosophy is an introduction to the theology; and that I can only carry the reader just beyond the first stage of the story.[11]

What Chesterton had to say about Saint Thomas was eminently worth saying. Almost immediately he set about clearing away the clutter of fuzzy thinking about who Aquinas was and who he was not. Aquinas had been, Chesterton said,

> one of the great liberators of the human intellect. . . . The truth of historical proportion . . . begins to reappear as quarrels begin to die down. Simply as one of the facts that bulk big in history, it is true to say that Thomas was a very great man who reconciled religion with reason, who expanded it towards experimental science, who insisted that the senses were the windows of the soul and that the reason had a divine right to feed upon facts, and that it was the business of the Faith to digest the strong meat of the toughest and most practical of pagan philosophies.[12]

At other times Chesterton was decidedly provocative—relishing the role of an iconoclast vis-à-vis traditionally held views of Aquinas within the academy. "The Thomist movement in metaphysics," he wrote, like the Franciscan movement in morals and manners, was an enlargement and a liberation, it was emphatically a growth of Christian theology from within; it was emphatically not a shrinking of Christian theology under heathen or even human influences. The Franciscan was free to be a friar, instead of being bound to be a monk. But he was more of a Christian, more of a Catholic, even more of an ascetic. So the Thomist was free to be an Aristotelian, instead of being bound to be an Augustinian. But he was even more of a theologian; more of an orthodox theologian; more of a dogmatist, in having recovered through Aristotle the most defiant of all dogmas, the wedding of God with Man and therefore with Matter. Nobody can understand the greatness of the thirteenth century, who does not realise that it was a great growth of new things produced by a living thing. In that sense it was really bolder and freer than what we call the Renaissance, which was a resurrection of old things discovered in a dead thing. In that sense medievalism was not a Renascence [variant spellings used by Chesterton], but rather a Nascence. It did not model its temples upon the tombs, or call up dead gods from Hades. It made an architecture as new as modern engineering; indeed it still remains the most modern architecture. Only it was followed at the Renaissance by a more antiquated architecture. In that sense the Renaissance might be called the Relapse. Whatever may be said of the Gothic and the Gospel according to St. Thomas, they were not a Relapse. It was a new thrust like the titanic thrust of Gothic engineering; and its strength was in a God who makes all things new.[13]

This turning of traditional Thomist constructs on their head was important and necessary. But beyond this, one of the best elements of *St. Thomas* was the way in which Chesterton evoked a sense of Aquinas's world—his struggle to find himself and a sense of calling—and how his decision to become a Dominican monk outraged his family. Chesterton the visual artist could still render landscapes in words with great skill. His was an artist's gift of immersing a reader at once in a world of his making.

"Some miles from the monastery of Monte Cassino," Chesterton wrote,

> stood a great crag or cliff, standing up like a pillar of the Apennines. It was crowned with a castle that bore the name of The Dry Rock, and was the eyrie in which the eaglets of the Aquino branch of the Imperial family were nursed to fly. Here lived Count Landulf of Aquino, who was the father of Thomas Aquinas and some seven other sons. In military affairs he doubtless rode with his family, in the feudal manner; and apparently had something to do with the destruction of the monastery. But it was typical of the tangle of the time, that Count Landulf seems afterwards to have thought that it would be a tactful and delicate act to put in his son Thomas as Abbot of the monastery. This would be of the nature of a graceful apology to the Church, and also, it would appear, the solution of a family difficulty.
>
> For it had been long apparent to Count Landulf that nothing could be done with his seventh son Thomas, except to make him an Abbot or something of that kind. Born in 1226, he had from childhood a mysterious objection to becoming a predatory eagle, or even to taking an ordinary interest in falconry or tilting or any other gentlemanly pursuits. He was a large and heavy and quiet boy, and phenomenally silent, scarcely opening his mouth

except to say suddenly to his schoolmaster in an explosive manner, "What is God?" . . .

In so far as we may follow rather dim and disputed events, it would seem that the young Thomas Aquinas walked into his father's castle one day and calmly announced that he had become one of the Begging Friars, of the new order founded by Dominic the Spaniard; much as the eldest son of the squire might go home and airily inform the family that he had married a gypsy; or the heir of a Tory Duke state that he was walking tomorrow with the Hunger Marchers organised by alleged Communists. . . . He said he wished to be a Friar, and his family flew at him like wild beasts; his brothers pursued him along the public roads, half-rent his friar's frock from his back and finally locked him up in a tower like a lunatic.[14]

With such passages in view, one can see why a contemporary reviewer for the *Times Literary Supplement* (TLS) wrote that "Chesterton not only awakens the mind in this little volume [but he also] keeps it awake."[15]

St. Thomas is also a book rendered with great insight. As the TLS reviewer observed: "There is a world of wisdom in one of [Chesterton's] observations."[16] Then followed a passage that showed why this was so. "As the nineteenth century," Chesterton had written,

clutched at the Franciscan romance, precisely because it had neglected romance, so the twentieth century is already clutching at the Thomist rational theology, because it has neglected reason. In a world that was too stolid, Christianity returned in the form of a vagabond; in a world that has grown a great deal too wild, Christianity has returned in the form of a teacher of logic.[17]

Twenty-three years after *St. Thomas* was first published, the American firm of Doubleday brought out a new edition of the book. Featured in its opening pages was an appreciation written by Anton C. Pegis, the renowned Thomist scholar.[18] It was as fine a summation of Chesterton's achievement as ever appeared. "There are not," Pegis wrote,

> many brief portraits of St. Thomas, the humble Dominican monk, who dedicated his mind to God and the cause of Christian truth. There are the little introductory works on St. Thomas of the late Monsignor Grabmann, of Maritain, Waltz and Chenu. Yet none of these admirable books is the artistic triumph that G. K. Chesterton achieved in writing his *St. Thomas Aquinas.* . . . Those who read [it] will see a true and living St. Thomas emerge from its pages. They will catch the spirit of the man.[19]

CHAPTER 25

Men Must Endure
Their Going Hence

Tonight I'll watch the stars and smile
I know I'm
Watching eternity
Sometime not far from me
In my heart I will be laughing.

—CHARLIE PEACOCK (1984)

I n her biography of Chesterton, Maisie Ward recalled a day in
1935 when Dorothy Collins, his secretary, told her that he had
begun writing an autobiography some years earlier but had set it
aside. Collins, who realized the literary importance of this unfinished manuscript, was nonetheless conflicted about it. She had a
sense of foreboding "about urging him to get on with it—as though
the survey of his life and the end of his life would somehow be tied
together."[1] In reply, Ward

> urged [Dorothy] to get over this feeling because of all the book
> would mean to the world. After this talk she got out the manu-
> script and laid it on Gilbert's desk. He read what he had written
> and immediately set about dictating the rest of the book.

Early in 1936 he told a group of friends that the book was finished. One of them said "Nunc dimittis" and Edward Macdonald, who was present, commented: "The words were chilling, though he seemed to be in fairly good health. But certainly he was tired."[2]

Sadly, Dorothy Collins's fears proved well founded.

Chesterton's *Autobiography*, published posthumously in the autumn of 1936, was the last flowering of his literary gifts. It was a bittersweet achievement but a very worthy addition to the Chesterton canon. And since it was completed before his passing, it seems fitting here to discuss its contents and something of the critical reception it had.

For a start, there was a bit of irony connected with the book's publication that Chesterton would have loved. He had once quipped "that the English should have instituted an annual Thanksgiving Day, to celebrate the fact that the Pilgrim Fathers had left."[3] The fifth impression I have before me of the first British edition of 1936 states that it was "made and printed in Great Britain at *The Mayflower Press, Plymouth.*"

As for the contents of *Autobiography*, Maisie Ward noted that "the book showed no sign of fatigue. High-spirited and intensely amusing, it seemed to [revive] the imagination and energy in which as a very young man we saw his resemblance to the youthful Dickens."[4]

The *New York Times*, for its part, published a 2,300-word review under the title "The Rewarding Autobiography of G. K. Chesterton." Written by Edward M. Kingsbury, its subtitle stated: "Humor and highest seriousness will endear this book to all good Chestertonians."

And so it should not have been surprising that what followed was a largely sympathetic review. The parallels to Dickens, noted by Maisie Ward, continued in the *Times* review when Kingsbury wrote:

> Mr. Chesterton was "firmly of the opinion that he was born on the 29th of May, 1874, on Campden Hill, Kensington." He was baptized "in the little church of St. George opposite the large Waterworks Tower that dominated the ridge." He denies that "the church was chosen because it needed the whole Watertower of West London to turn me into a Christian." He was born in the right place. The Waterworks Tower dominates not only the ridge but the glorious military campaign of *The Napoleon of Notting Hill*. He was born at the right time. Dickens died only four years before. It was a Dickensian world upon which young Gilbert looked. His grandfather kept up the old Christian custom of singing at the dinner table. The grandson was a happy triller of songs and catches. One day a strange gentleman called on the grandfather, bowed to him reverentially and uttered this noble phrase: "You are a Monument, Sir, you are a Landmark." Almost one feels that this must be a quotation from Dickens.[5]

Following this, Kingsbury observed that Chesterton had been singularly fortunate in the environment in which he was raised. *Autobiography* vividly recalled the Kensington of Chesterton's youth, a place steeped in history and literature. Amid such surroundings, Kingsbury wondered aloud:

> Why did boys have to go to school in that favored day and region? The whole Kensington district was a history and an education. It was "laid out like a chart or plan to illustrate Macaulay's Essays." Every day the boy walked past Holland House and the statue of

Lord Holland, "inscribed with the boast that he was the nephew of Fox and the friend of Gray." Addison Street was just opposite the first house of the Chestertons. Afterward they lived in the street named after Warwick, Addison's stepson. Cromwell, Russell, Argyll—what memories for a lad devouring Macaulay. Chesterton's father was moderate, tolerant, liberal. He loved French cathedrals and Gothic architecture as expounded by Mr. Ruskin. Chesterton was fortunate in his inheritance.[6]

One aspect of Chesterton's childhood, Kingsbury rightly discerned, prefigured the man and writer he would become. "His philosophy of childhood," Kingsbury wrote, "and its memory, its delight in 'make-believe,' perfectly apprehended as different from reality, is rich in insight and imagination."[7] The following passage from chapter 2 of *Autobiography* embodies this dynamic: a moment when the image of the White Horse first captured Chesterton's imagination and forever after lingered in memory:

> One of these glimpses of my own prehistoric history is a memory of a long upper room filled with light (the light that never was on sea or land) and of somebody carving or painting with white paint the deal head of a hobby-horse; the head almost archaic in its simplification. Ever since that day my depths have been stirred by a wooden post painted white; and even more so by any white horse in the street; and it was like meeting a friend in a fairytale to find myself under the sign of the White Horse at Ipswich on the first day of my honeymoon. But for that very reason, this image has remained and memory has constantly returned to it; and I have even done my best to deface and spoil the purity of the White Horse by writing an interminable ballad about it.[8]

But by far the most profound and most richly rendered passage of chapter 2 (indeed, one of the most richly rendered passages of the entire *Autobiography*) is Chesterton's description of his first memory and all that it held for him thereafter. Briefly referenced earlier, it amply repays an exploration in full. "The very first thing I can ever remember seeing with my own eyes," he wrote,

> was a young man walking across a bridge. He had a curly moustache and an attitude of confidence verging on swagger. He carried in his hand a disproportionately large key of a shining yellow metal and wore a large golden or gilded crown. The bridge he was crossing sprang on the one side from the edge of a highly perilous mountain chasm, the peaks of the range rising fantastically in the distance; and at the other end it joined the upper part of the tower of an almost excessively castellated castle. In the castle tower there was one window, out of which a young lady was looking. . . .
>
> This was the sight on which my eyes first opened in this world. And the scene has to me a sort of aboriginal authenticity impossible to describe; something at the back of all my thoughts; like the very back-scene of the theatre of things. I have no shadow of recollection of what the young man was doing on the bridge, or of what he proposed to do with the key; though a later and wearier knowledge of literature and legend hints to me that he was not improbably going to release the lady from captivity. . . . All the rest is gone; scenes, subject, story, characters; but that one scene glows in my memory like a glimpse of some incredible paradise; and, for all I know, I shall still remember it when all other memory is gone out of my mind. . . .

If psychologists are still saying what ordinary sane people have always said—that early impressions count considerably in life—I recognise a sort of symbol of all that I happen to like in imagery and ideas. . . . I can no longer behold the beauty of the princess; but I can see it in the bridge that the prince crossed to reach her. And I believe that in feeling these things from the first, I was feeling the fragmentary suggestions of a philosophy I have since found to be the truth. . . . If some laborious reader of little books on child-psychology cries out to me in glee and cunning, "You only like romantic things like toy-theatres because your father showed you a toy-theatre in your childhood," I shall reply with gentle and Christian patience, "Yes, fool, yes. Undoubtedly your explanation is, in that sense, the true one. But what you are saying, in your witty way, is simply that I associate these things with happiness because I was so happy. It does not even begin to consider the question of *why* I was so happy." . . . [I reject] the horrible and degrading heresy that our minds are merely manufactured by accidental conditions, and therefore have no ultimate relation to truth at all.[9]

Less successful for Kingsbury in his *New York Times* review were the portions of Chesterton's *Autobiography* that discussed his "activities as a pro-Boer and as a rebuker of the Marconi scandals." These passages, Kingsbury wrote, "seem a little mildewed. The Liberal Party is reasonably dead. Mention of the Fabian Society almost tempts one to make the well-known Virgilian line read: *Cunctando postposuit rem*—it preferred dawdling to doodling."[10]

For Kingsbury, far more important than Chesterton's discursions into his social and political views was his account of the circumstances that resulted in "that strange, powerful and rather inexplicable book, *The Man Who Was Thursday*." Kingsbury's discussion of this book distilled its essence and at the same time related a story that would have rejoiced Chesterton's heart had he known of it. The novel's title, Kingsbury began,

> invited disaster. The neglected subtitle "A Nightmare" explains. The story "is a nightmare of things not as they are but as they seem to the young half-pessimist of the Nineties." A distinguished psychoanalyst paid [Chesterton] a curious compliment: "I know a number of men who nearly went mad," he said quite gravely, "but were saved because they had really understood *The Man Who Was Thursday*."[11]

There had been a time in Chesterton's youth, as recounted earlier, when his sanity had been sorely tried by a hurtful flirtation with the occult, his separation from his friends among the JDC, and the oppressive weight he felt upon his mind stemming from the cultural pessimism that dominated the world of art and literature. Before this time of his life had ended, he had inhabited the nightmarish world depicted in *The Man Who Was Thursday*. That his novel might in any way have freed others from a cell of despair would have been welcome news indeed.

Then there were the stories—stories, Kingsbury noted, such as it is given to few men to remember. The famous wander through them, vying with moments of humor for the greatest effect. There was, to be sure, a slightly melancholy feeling in that Chesterton was describing a world that was no more, but therein lay much of its special character. Kingsbury seems to have been rather caught up in it all, wishing to linger indefinitely:

at one of those little places off Leicester Square where "in those days a man could get half a bottle of perfectly good red wine for sixpence." [The young Chesterton] makes his way in journalism. His whimsical recipe for success in it is to send to every paper the kind of article most suited to it. He lives in Clapham, becomes a friend of W. B. Yeats, "perhaps the best author I ever met except his old father, who, alas! will talk no more in this earthly tavern, though I hope he is still talking in Paradise." He is a half-hearted socialist for a time. He meets with Anglo-Catholic clergymen who belong to a little company of English eccentrics. One wore correct clerical garb "surmounted with a sort of hairy or furry cap making him look like an eccentric rat-catcher." Another had designed for himself a cassock and biretta of the sixteenth century. To little wanton boys who hooted it, unaware of its traditional exactitude, he would say, "Are you aware that this is the precise costume in which Latimer went to the stake?" One day Chesterton, wearing the big hat and cloak his wife had designed for him, walked between the hairy cap and the Latimerian biretta. Behind them walked Charles Masterman, derisively waving his umbrella and crying, "Could you see three backs like that anywhere in God's creation?"

These were nights and days of the gods and the playboys. The all-accomplished Maurice Baring celebrated the fiftieth anniversary of his birthday by dancing a Russian dance with incredible contortions and taking a bath in evening dress.[12]

Kingsbury's review treated the subject of Chesterton's embrace of Catholicism with great sympathy, calling it "the central fact of Chesterton's life." It was there, Kingsbury wrote, that "he found certainty, freedom, peace." This set the stage for a graceful transition to the close of *Autobiography*—which recalled once more the image of "the man with the golden key." Here Chesterton had written:

> There starts up again before me, standing sharp and clear in shape as of old, the figure of a man who crosses a bridge and carries a key, as I saw him when I first looked into fairyland through the window of my father's [toy-theatre]. But I know that he who is called Pontifex, the Builder of the Bridge, is called also Claviger, the Bearer of the Key; and that such keys were given him to bind and loose when he was a poor fisher in a far province, beside a small and almost secret sea.

It had all been a glimpse of a world that was gone, but Chesterton had given his readers one last gift—a chance to revisit that world any time of their choosing.

Chesterton, who had very early taken to radio as a medium ideally suited for his talents, made what would prove his last radio broadcast on March 15, 1936. By this time, he had become a fixture on the BBC. This last appearance was part of a series of talks entitled "The Spice of Life," and this particular talk was called "We Will End with a Bang." One sentence was the highlight of his remarks—a flash of the Chestertonian flair for paradox. "A great many people," he said, "are at this moment paying rather too much attention to the spice of life, and rather too little attention to life."[13]

By this time Chesterton's health, which had been worsening, experienced a precipitous decline. In May, he undertook a pilgrimage to Lisieux and Lourdes where, it was hoped, he might purchase more time.

All his life, Chesterton had written about pilgrims, Bunyan and Chaucer among the rest. Now he had become one. Before his departure, he and Frances visited their friends the Nicholl sisters, who lived in a home called Christmas Cottage. The Chestertons' visit was brief, but it lingered long in the sisters' memory:

> It was a particularly beautiful night, flower-scented, sunlit and enchanted, as only a May night in England can be. G. K. arrived looking for the first time in our memory dreadfully tired. We made the excuse of drinking him *bon voyage* to produce brandy, which brought some colour, but not much, back into his face.
>
> For some reason on this one occasion we stood together in the porch to see him off, and neither walked to the gate. The dusk was still gold in a lingering and splendid sunset. G. K. went through the wooden gate and turned, his hand still on the latch. He looked back at us; then he stretched out his hand in the strangest prolonged gesture—it was like a mixture of benediction and farewell.[14]

Sadly, though Lourdes had been the site of many miraculous cures, Chesterton left the holy shrine still unwell. Home once again at Top Meadow in Beaconsfield, he began to lose concentration and often fell asleep at his desk. The doctor was called for. His heart had begun to fail. Now confined to bed, he began to drift in and out of consciousness. Lucid moments were rare, but during one such moment he said: "The issue is now quite clear. It is between light and darkness and every one must choose his side."[15]

By early June Top Meadow had become the scene of a sad vigil. Chesterton lingered, but the end was near. Frances, utterly devastated by her husband's condition, had to leave all details connected with running the house with Dorothy Collins, who, despite her own sense of grief, performed heroically.

On June 12 one of Chesterton's oldest friends, E. C. Bentley, came to visit. He was unable to see G. K. but very kindly stayed with Dorothy for a time.

Meanwhile, the news of Chesterton's condition was only just becoming known. A journalist from the *Daily Mail* called to make inquiries. Dorothy confirmed that Chesterton was gravely ill, but she asked that the news be kept in confidence because absolute silence was of the utmost necessity. "We must not have telephones and doorbells," she said. In clear break with convention, the journalist promised not to publicize Chesterton's illness. It was a signal act of kindness, and one Dorothy never forgot.

Later that day, Monsignor Smith, the parish priest, arrived. Chesterton had strength enough to receive communion. Soon after, Father Vincent McNabb came, arriving from St. Dominic's Priory in London. He went to Chesterton's bedside and recited the *Salve Regina*, as was customary in the Dominican order to honor a priest in his final hours. Chesterton was at this time unconscious.

Frances, there all the while, showed great courage amidst her grief. For a few moments on June 13, Chesterton regained consciousness. Seeing her, he said: "Hello, my darling." Upon seeing that Dorothy Collins was sitting to one side in the room, his sense of fatherly regard flickered briefly. "Hello, my dear," he said.[16]

These were his last words—kind words of greeting. At ten o'clock the following morning, Sunday, June 14, he entered a world he had long desired to see.

One day before his death, Chesterton had an article published in the *Illustrated London News*. He had no way of knowing it would be the last word from him to appear in print before his passing. But it proved to be so—one last reply in a conversation he had kept up with his readers for the better part of forty years. He referred to the great novel of his youth, *The Man Who Was Thursday*, saying that it "was not intended to describe the real world as it was, or as I thought it was. . . . It was intended to describe the world of wild doubt and despair which the pessimists were generally describing at that date; with just a gleam of hope in some double meaning of the doubt, which even the pessimists felt in some fashion."[17]

At the last, Chesterton found one more way to come alongside fellow pilgrims and offer a hand of friendship. He had found a "sort of moonshine" in the night. Would they not walk further with him? A gleam of hope beckoned.

A Near View
of the Man as He Was

*[Chesterton's] energy and his versatility were amazing; his
exuberant intellect ran riot over letters, art, religion,
philosophy, and current affairs.*

—TIMES OF LONDON, 15 JUNE 1936

*Gilbert Keith Chesterton spent his whole life in teaching
others how to live. The very sound of his name is like a
trumpet-call. . . . He was the kind of man of whom Bunyan
was thinking when he drew the picture of Mr. Greatheart.
His sword was at the service of pilgrims.*[1]

—SIR ARTHUR BRYANT (1936)

On Sunday, June 28, 1936, John B. Kennedy, a *New York Times*
correspondent formerly based in England, published a three-
thousand-word tribute to the man who had been G. K. C. He
recalled a day in 1915 when he had received word that Chesterton
was converting to Catholicism. It was a story his managing editor
back in New York wanted him to investigate. Chesterton by this
time was such a fixture on the American literary scene that this was

a story deemed highly newsworthy, which attests to the stature and standing Chesterton had then attained.

Kennedy's article was one of the better prose portraits written about Chesterton in his lifetime. It commenced with a paragraph that brought summer in Britain home to the reader. Outside Chesterton's home,

> bees and birds of England hummed and twittered over flowery meadows and trimmed hedges on one of those August after-noons that give Summer the scene and fragrance of its truest meaning. A large man played with a shaggy collie, and when he bent over the dog it was not easy to distinguish the iron-gray shocks of either. The man was Gilbert Keith Chesterton. As he moved about you observed a neat house in the background— a low, rambling red house amid leaning trees and velvet lawns. It was at a little village in Buckinghamshire, a village named Beaconsfield....
>
> Mine was an alien mission that afternoon—that is, alien to the robust English tradition, so thoroughly personified in this robust Englishman: that personal curiosity is not a virtue. I had a hot tip that G. K. C. had gone over to the Catholic Church— this was excessively premature to that event, 1915 to be exact. My orders from a relentless managing editor in New York were to get the story.

⚜

> Chesterton welcomed me with a cheery smile. He was huge as he stood his full height, his great face with its ragged mus-tache suggesting a snub-nosed lion. He led me into a wide room

whose ceiling lowered as he strode. There were cabinets of precious Goss, bright rugs and sunlit pictures.

He waved me to a sturdy chair with a hand delicately pro-
portioned to his bulk. He seated himself in another sturdy chair,
which creaked complainingly. I told him my mission—to find
out whether or not he, whom Robert Hugh Benson, I think,
dubbed the bell of the Church which rang for it while remaining
outside, had finally embraced Catholicism.

He emitted a high, bubbling laugh.

"Would you mind," he said, leveling at me a burning cigar,
forbidden by his doctors, for he was then convalescing from
serious illness—"would you mind minding your own business?
And," he added, "join me in a cup of tea?"

Before the visit was concluded there came to that small
house containing so large a man a serious-miened delega-
tion. They resembled a group of pall-bearers on a picnic.
Each man looked in his frock-coat as if he were the rival of
the next as a model for mustache-cups. They had come, their
spokesman said between four-syllable coughs, to request Mr.
Chesterton to accept the honorary post of under-sheriff for
Bucks—Buckinghamshire County. Mr. Chesterton's roll-top
torso writhed nervously. He shrank, he said, from honorary
appointments of whatever kind. He bore not title to which
he did not deliver duty. And would they be so good as to tell
him the principal duty of an under-sheriff? The spokesman
coughed and defined:

"To suppress riots against His Majesty's peace."

"Quite impossible," chanted Mr. Chesterton, for his speaking voice was a rising rhythm, cadenced and lofty. "It wouldn't do
at all." He beamed explanatorily. "If there is ever any riot around

here," he added, "I couldn't conscientiously suppress it, for I should be the principal rioter."

❊

The man was paradox personified. He thought about all things backward to reach their beginnings, to penetrate their truth. As with his casual essays, so with his fiction—their mere titles were paradoxes, sharp and challenging. "Tremendous Trifles," "The Napoleon of Notting Hill," "The Man Who Was Thursday," "The Defendant"—which latter was a devil's advocate assault upon the superciliously civilized. He has been frequently compared to Samuel Johnson, but the only apparent likeness between them—saving a magnificent mastery of the language—were two ears and more chins. There was nothing stodgy or pompous or affected about Chesterton. His enormous personal paradox was that so huge a man, who relished good living with unflagging gusto, could be a vessel of pure poetic fire.

I recall Joyce Kilmer in the *New York Times* office after a particularly calorific lunch, burst into exhortation:

"Wordsworth, Shelley, Browning—and the moderns—forget them. The poet for you is Chesterton."

❊

So we read "The Flying Inn" and "The Ballad of St. Barbara" and "The Ballad of the White Horse" and more. It was easily detectable, while skirting "The Ball and the Cross" and others of his prodigious creation, especially for those of us who happened to profess the faith he was seeking, that he made plain

271

his personal spiritual odyssey in that singular and arresting poem, "The Three Wise Men." This is stamped by the mark of his intellect, his inspiration and his style quite as much as anything he wrote. There is the swinging gait of the lines measuring his stride from nowhere to somewhere, to find himself a child amid a plethora of paradox—for he suddenly came upon what he considered:

> *The house from which the heavens are fed,*
> *The old strange house, that is our home.*
> *Where tricks of words are never said,*
> *Where mercy is as plain as bread,*
> *And honor is as hard as stone.*
> *Hark, laughter like a lion wakes,*
> *To roar to the resounding plain,*
> *And the whole heaven shouts and shakes,*
> *For God himself is born again.*
> *And we are little children walking,*
> *Through the snow and rain.*[2]

Following Chesterton's death, his widow Frances received a letter of condolence that she treasured ever after. George Bernard Shaw had been her husband's opponent in several epic debates. Their worldviews were as different as their physical appearance: Shaw, the rail-thin "heathen mystic"; Chesterton, the rotund, Johnsonian champion of orthodoxy.

But Shaw had a "deep affection" for his departed friend, which was warmly returned. He mourned Chesterton's loss greatly.

Shaw was mindful as well of a practical concern that might soon confront his widow. Chesterton had never been careful about money, and Shaw was worried that Frances's grief might be compounded by the revelation of unexpected debt. He wasted no time in writing to her. "It seems the most ridiculous thing in the world," he wrote on June 15, "that I, 18 years older than Gilbert, should be heartlessly surviving him. However, this is only to say that if you have any temporary bothers that I can remove, a line on a postcard (or three figures) will be sufficient."

It was an act of quiet kindness—and soon followed by a word of great tenderness. "The trumpets are sounding for him," Shaw wrote in closing his letter—a lovely allusion to *The Pilgrim's Progress* and Christian's entry into the Celestial City.

Frances was profoundly moved by this—the final seal on Shaw's unlikely but very genuine friendship with her husband. Shaw did not share Chesterton's hope of heaven, but something of that hope had found a place in his memory. And this says much about how faith, wedded to a great heart, can be winsome and compelling— despite great differences in how people look at the world.[3]

⌗

"What matters here is [Chesterton's] lonely moral battle against his age."[4] So wrote T. S. Eliot in the *Tablet*, on June 20, 1936. His words were part of an obituary for Chesterton, a tribute that would have been unlikely, to say the least, had Chesterton died twenty-five years before.

Indeed for many years, Chesterton had been little more than a literary punching bag for Eliot. In 1918, he had written caustically: "Mr. Chesterton's brain swarms with ideas. . . . I see no evidence that it thinks."[5] As late as December 1927, Eliot declared that Chesterton's writing style was "exasperating to the last point of endurance"[6] and his "cheerfulness . . . depressing."[7]

Eliot's tribute of 1936 was only possible because of his conversion in the late 1920s. In the years following, he came to see Chesterton, as he did so many things, in a new light. In matters of literary style they might still differ widely, but when it came to matters of faith, he now understood that they were co-belligerents. Writing in the *Criterion* about the same period as the *Tablet* obituary, Eliot was candid about his change of heart: "With Mr. Chesterton I naturally have sympathies which I did not have twenty-five years ago, and an increasing respect and regard for a man who has been, in every respect but as a man of letters, fighting against the current."[8]

Chesterton himself had contributed to this rapprochement in 1929, when he had praised Eliot for an "admirably sane, subtle, and penetrating article" on "The Humanism of Irving Babbitt."[9] Chesterton was extending a hand of friendship. It was taken.

That Chesterton and Eliot were able to better understand each other prior to Chesterton's death is testament to the ways in which grace can bridge a formerly unbridgeable gulf. Would that such moments were more frequent and more public today.

Beyond this, it is often the case that many writers and their writings are never valued at their true worth until their passing. Even then, decades may pass before anything like a proper and just appreciation emerges. Eliot contributed in no small measure to the task of regarding Chesterton at his true worth in the lines of his *Tablet* obituary.

"I never met Gilbert Chesterton," Eliot wrote in the opening sentence of this tribute, "but his disappearance, from a world such as that we live in, is one of those which give even to us who did not know the man, a sense of personal loss and isolation."[10]

Such a statement was itself a revelation. Eliot had once held only derision and scorn for Chesterton. He now felt genuine grief at the passing of a man for whom he had come to have "an increasing respect and regard."[11]

After this graceful opening, Eliot offered a considered estimate of Chesterton's legacy that set the stage for all that was to follow. "The notices I have seen in the general Press seem to me to have exaggerated Chesterton's achievements in some obvious respects, and to have ignored his achievements in much more important ones."[12]

As a poet, Eliot judged that Chesterton's achievements were more modest in scale than many had written. "His poetry was first-rate journalistic balladry, and I do not suppose that [Chesterton] took it more seriously than it deserved."[13]

More fulsome praise was reserved for Chesterton's fictional works. Two works in particular prompted comparisons with the writings of Robert Louis Stevenson. Chesterton, Eliot wrote, "reached a high imaginative level with *The Napoleon of Notting Hill*, and higher with *The Man Who Was Thursday*, romances in which he turned the Stevensonian fantasy to more serious purpose."[14] At the same time, Eliot greatly admired Chesterton's powers as a literary critic, saying, "His book on Dickens seems to me the best essay on that author that has ever been written."[15]

Chesterton's accomplishments as an essayist were, to Eliot's mind, of lesser note. For while his gifts in this vein were considerable, he was at times spendthrift in writing so much. "Some of his essays can be read again and again," Eliot stated, "though of his essay writing as a whole, one can only say that it is remarkable to have maintained such a high average with so large an output."[16]

One would think that Eliot would have pointed to one of Chesterton's literary achievements as the capstone of his legacy, but that was the not the case. Instead, he stated:

> It is not, I think, for any piece of writing in particular that Chesterton is of importance, but for the place he occupied, the position that he represented, during the better part of a generation.... To judge Chesterton on his "contributions to literature," then, would be to apply the wrong standards of measurement. It is in other matters that he was importantly and consistently on the side of the angels.[17]

What were these "other matters"? Eliot spoke first of Chesterton's writings on economics and society. He saw them as the natural extension of Chesterton's faith. "Even if," Eliot wrote, "[his] social and economic ideas appear to be totally without effect, even if they should be demonstrated to be wrong—which would perhaps only mean that men have not the good will to carry them out—they were the ideas for his time that were fundamentally Christian and Catholic."[18]

Ultimately, Eliot reserved his most generous praise for Chesterton the champion of orthodoxy. All of his writings, taken together, were a cultural apologetic. Therein lay his greatness:

> He did more, I think, than any man of his time—and was able to do more than anyone else, because of his peculiar background, development, and abilities as a public performer—to maintain the existence of the important minority in the modern world.[19]

As touching the totality of Chesterton's life, and the essence of his writings, it would seem that Eliot's assessment of Chesterton is best: "What matters here is his lonely moral battle against his age."[20] Cast in this light, Chesterton was much like Bunyan—a man who was far from perfect, a pilgrim who often walked "with halting steps and slow"—but ultimately, a man who sought "to light such a candle as by God's grace should never be put out."[21]

Acknowledgments

M y debts of gratitude regarding this book are many. First and foremost, I should like to thank Joel Miller, vice-president of acquisitions and editorial at Thomas Nelson, for his invitation to write a full-length Chesterton biography. I had originally envisioned this study as a more modestly sized monograph for Thomas Nelson's Christian Encounters series—a companion volume in its own way to *John Bunyan* and *D. L. Moody*, two other books I had previously written. Joel urged me to consider writing a more substantial work, and I thank him most sincerely for his vision and encouragement.

As ever, my agent, Bucky Rosenbaum, has been a steadfast friend and advocate. His enthusiasm for this project and his good counsel throughout its creation have been invaluable.

Bryan Norman, editor at Thomas Nelson, has helped this book in every way to become the best book that it could be. At each stage of this book's development, he has given good and wise counsel. I am greatly indebted as well to the care and skill of copy editor extraordinaire Cheryl Dunlop.

Lastly, I wish to thank each member of the Thomas Nelson team who played a part in the creation of this book. Across the board, I deeply appreciate their commitment to excellence.

Apart from a grateful acknowledgment of my colleagues at Thomas Nelson, I wish to pay tribute to the memory of Tom Howard (1950–2010), a greatly gifted pianist and composer whose recordings are a treasured part of my musical library. I listened to them many times as I was writing this book.

We met once, during my undergraduate years, when he performed at my alma mater, Gordon College. At that time one of his finest solo piano recordings, *The Harvest*, had just been released. As he was beginning to set up for his performance, I overcame my shyness and walked up to the stage. "Excuse me," I said, "Are you Tom Howard?"

He turned and smiled. "Yes, I am," he said.

"Would you mind if I took your picture?" I asked.

"Not at all," he replied, and he waved as I snapped the picture.

I wish I had that picture now (sadly lost in one of my many moves since college). But what I do have is the memory of a gifted musician taking a few moments to show kindness to a college student whom he'd never met. Each time I listen to one of his recordings, I remember that brief meeting—and the music which meant so much to me then. It still does. *Requiescat in pace.*

⊞

This book bears a dedication to my wife, Kelly. Throughout its creation, I often shared passages from Chesterton's works with her. In many ways, her appreciation for the "big things" in him has come to be as great as my own. Kelly is a gifted writer herself, and the dedication of this book to her is one way of saying how deeply grateful I am for the hours she has given me to write—and the moments when I have seen Chesterton through her eyes. She has helped me understand the great man better and to have a heightened appreciation for the poet who walked about in the cloak of a "rollicking journalist." Together we have laughed at his jokes, and—in company with our four-year-old son, Sam—gazed with renewed wonder upon stars that "seemed bent upon being understood."

A Chesterton Timeline[1]

1874 – 29 May. Gilbert Keith Chesterton is born at 32 Sheffield Terrace, Campden Hill, London.

1879 – Chesterton, age five, moves with his family to 11 Warwick Gardens, Kensington, London.

c. 1883 – Chesterton begins his formal schooling at Colet House.

1887 – January. Chesterton begins attending St. Paul's School.

1892 – Autumn. Having graduated from St. Paul's School, Chesterton begins attending the Slade School of Art. In 1893, he begins taking courses in Latin and English literature at University College, London.

1893 – Just prior to Long Vacation, the three months in the summer when college and university students do not have classes, Chesterton begins to experience a "dark night of the soul."

1894 – Summer. Chesterton's "dark night of the soul" comes to an end.

1895–1901 – Chesterton begins his professional life, first

working for the publisher Redway's, then after one year, for Fisher Unwin.

1900 – October. *Greybeards at Play* is published, as are *The Wild Knight* (November) and *The Defendant* (December).

1901 – 28 June. Gilbert Chesterton weds Frances Blogg.

1902 – October. *Twelve Types* is published.

1903 – May. *Robert Browning* is published.

1904 – March. *The Napoleon of Notting Hill* is published, as is *G. F. Watts*.

1905 – June. *Heretics* is published.

1906 – August. *Charles Dickens* is published.

1908 – February. *The Man Who Was Thursday* is published, as is *Orthodoxy* (September).

1909 – August. *George Bernard Shaw* is published, as is *Tremendous Trifles* (September).

1910 – February. *The Ball and the Cross* is published, as are *What's Wrong with the World* (June) and *William Blake* (November).

1911 – February. *Appreciations and Criticisms of Charles Dickens* is published, as are *The Innocence of Father Brown* (July) and *The Ballad of the White Horse* (August).

1912 – February. *Manalive* is published.

1913 – February. *The Victorian Age in Literature* is published, as is *Magic* (November).

1914 – January. *The Flying Inn* is published.

1915 – April. *Poems* is published.

1917 – October. *A Short History of England* is published.

1919 – November. *Irish Impressions* is published.

1920 – October. *The Uses of Diversity* is published.

1921 – 10 January to 12 April. Gilbert and Frances
Chesterton tour America.

1922 – March. *Eugenics and Other Evils* is published, as are
The Ballad of St. Barbara (October), *The Man Who Knew
Too Much* (November), and *What I Saw in America*.

1923 – October. *St. Francis of Assisi* is published.

1925 – September. *The Everlasting Man* is published, as is
William Cobbett (November).

1926 – June. *The Incredulity of Father Brown* is published.

1927 – May. *The Return of Don Quixote* is published, as are
Collected Poems (June), *The Secret of Father Brown*
(September), and *Robert Louis Stevenson* (November).

1928 – October. *Generally Speaking* is published.

1932 – April. *Chaucer* is published. The second edition of
Collected Poems is also published.

1933 – September. *St. Thomas Aquinas* is published.

1935 – March. *The Scandal of Father Brown* is published.

1936 – 14 June. Chesterton dies at his home, Top
Meadow, in Beaconsfield, Buckinghamshire.

Notes

Epigraph

1. Edward M. Kingsbury, "The Rewarding Autobiography of G. K. Chesterton," *New York Times*, 8 November 1936, BR3.
2. Ibid.
3. John Gross, "Books of the Times," review of *G. K. Chesterton* by Michael Ffinch (San Francisco: Harper & Row, 1986), *New York Times*, 10 February 1987.
4. Ibid.
5. "Three Literary Giants of Today: Critical Studies of Kipling, G. K. Chesterton and G. B. Shaw Present an Interesting Picture of Contemporary Literature," *New York Times Book Review*, 7 May 1916, BR189.
6. John Updike, as quoted in *Conversations with John Updike*, ed. James Plath (Univ. Press of Mississippi, 1994), 187. Updike's comments appeared originally on 4 January 1987 in Section VI, l, 4 of the *Los Angeles Times*, as part of the interview: "John Updike Still Finds Things to Say About Life, Sex, and Religion," conducted by Katherine Stephen.

Author's Note

1. Garry Wills, "A Chesterton for the Religious Right," *The Christian Century*, 16–23 May 1990, 532.
2. Paul Schlicke, as quoted in *The Oxford Reader's Companion to Dickens* (Oxford: Oxford Univ. Press, 1999), 130.
3. William Oddie, *Chesterton and the Romance of Orthodoxy: The Making of G.K.C. 1874–1908* (New York: Oxford Univ. Press, 2009), 12–13.
4. Richard Ingrams, as quoted in Joseph Pearce, *Wisdom and Innocence: A Life of G. K. Chesterton* (San Francisco: Ignatius Press, 1996), ix. This sentiment is also expressed by William Oddie in *Chesterton and the Romance of Orthodoxy*, 377. Here, Oddie wrote of "Chesterton's continuing relevance to our own age." See also page 379, where Oddie states: "Chesterton's times were much more like our own than we imagine."

Prologue

1. Mark Twain to William Dean Howells (28 December 1877). See Henry Nash Smith and William M. Gibson, eds., *Mark Twain-Howells Letters: The Correspondence of Samuel L. Clemens & William D. Howells, 1869–1910* (Cambridge: Harvard Univ. Press, 1960), 215.

I also wish to acknowledge here that after I decided to use Twain's quote with reference to Chesterton, my research led me to "God's Fool," Stefan Kanfer's excellent review of Alzina Stone Dale's biography of Chesterton, *The Outline of Sanity*, in *Time*, 14 February 1983.

2. http://en.wikipedia.org/wiki/G._K._Chesterton.

3. See J. D. Douglas, "G. K. Chesterton, the Eccentric Prince of Paradox," *Christianity Today*, 24 May 1974. The text of this article is posted at: http://www.christianitytoday.com/ct/2001/augustweb-only/8-27-52.0.html.

4. See *Heretics*, 4th ed. (London: John Lane, 1907), 97, where Chesterton wrote: "A man who has faith must be prepared not only to be a martyr, but to be a fool." Aside from Chesterton's writings, see Garry Wills, *Chesterton* (New York: Image/Doubleday Books, 2001). Here Wills refers often to Chesterton as a jester. See Kanfer, "God's Fool." Here Kanfer wrote: "Chesterton came to regard life as a moral melodrama. In it he appropriated the role of God's Fool." See also Douglas, "G. K. Chesterton, the Eccentric Prince of Paradox." Here Douglas wrote: "A reputation for mild eccentricity is a tremendous asset, and Chesterton made the most of it. His sartorial quirks were pressed into the same service. If he made fun of others he laughed most of all at himself."

5. G. K. Chesterton, *Autobiography*, fifth impression (London: Hutchinson & Co., 1936), 141. Here it is worth clearing up a common misconception. Reportedly, about 1910, the *Times* of London asked for letters in reply to the question "What's Wrong with the World?" Chesterton is rumored to have written in response: "Dear Sirs, I am. Yours sincerely, G. K. Chesterton." However, no documentary proof of this has ever been found, nor has a search of back issues of the *Times*, which I have undertaken, yielded any such letter, or anything remotely like it. In fact, it is almost certain that Chesterton never wrote such a letter to the *Times*.

However, in June 1910, Chesterton did publish a book bearing the title *What's Wrong with the World?* In a dedicatory letter to Charles Masterman, which is reproduced in this book, Chesterton wrote:

My dear Charles,
I originally called this book "What is Wrong," and it would have satisfied your sardonic temper to note the number of social misunderstandings that arose from the use of the title. Many a mild lady visitor opened her eyes when I remarked casually, "I have been doing 'What is Wrong' all this morning."

This then, appears to be the origin of the famous rumor that Chesterton wrote a letter to the *Times*. The dedicatory letter in which he said he had "been doing 'What is Wrong' all this morning" seems to provide the solution to this common misconception. Here, Chesterton facetiously confessed to "doing wrong"—which is very similar to his "rumored reply" to the question from the *Times*.

6. Chesterton greatly admired Twain and was a charter member of the International Mark Twain Society, founded by Twain's kinsman Cyril Clemens in 1930. In that same year, Chesterton's tribute to Twain was published in *Tributes to Mark Twain* (Paris: Mark Twain Society, 1930). Some years before, Chesterton had referenced Twain in an illustration appearing on page 66 of *Orthodoxy* (New York: John Lane Company, 1908). He also praised Twain in his book *Varied Types* (New York: Dodd, Mead and Company, 1903), 182 and 185. Chesterton's thoughts on Twain are also referenced in Ron Powers,

Mark Twain: A Life (New York: Simon and Schuster/The Free Press, 2005), 89. Lastly some observers, noting similarities, have called Chesterton "the Catholic Mark Twain."

7. "During my year of European travels," wrote Twain's cousin Cyril Clemens, "I had heard much of Shakespeare, Browning, and Dante societies. Strolling on deck while returning to New York, I came to the conclusion that America's best known author deserved a society named in his honor. Upon my return to St. Louis I founded the International Mark Twain Society among whose charter members were Hilaire Belloc, G. K. Chesterton, Alfred Noyes, Maurice Baring, Shane Leslie, Rt. Rev. Ronald A. Knox, Agnes Repplier, Rene Bazin, Giovanni Papini. In 1936 the Mark Twain Quarterly was established with myself as editor. When a distinguished member dies, a whole quarterly is often devoted to his memory. This was done in the case of Chesterton with many of his friends participating." This recollection by Cyril Clemens, originally published in Walter Romig, *The Book of Catholic Authors* vol. 3 (1945), is posted online at: http://www.catholicauthors.com/clemens.html.

8. G. K. Chesterton on Mark Twain, as quoted in Archibald Henderson, *Mark Twain* (New York: Frederick A. Stokes Company, 1912), 110.

9. "Always, however, his animus was directed against policies and ideas, not against people." J. D. Douglas, "G. K. Chesterton, the Eccentric Prince of Paradox," *Christianity Today*, 24 May 1974. See also Michael Ffinch, *G. K. Chesterton: A Biography* (San Francisco: Harper & Row, 1986), 3. Here, Ffinch wrote: "Chesterton was avidly listened to and, it appears, was one of the few men who never made an enemy. The reason was that everything he said was said with such good humour. Even those whose opinions he attacked felt confident that it was only their opinions that were under attack."

10. See Karl Keating, *Controversies: High-Level Catholic Apologetics* (San Francisco: Ignatius Press, 2001), 46. Here Keating wrote: "[As an apologist] Chesterton came to be known for gentleness and jocularity."

11. See M. D. Aeschliman, "Chesterton's Marvelous Year," *National Review*, 14 July 2008. Here Aeschliman wrote: "The wise and witty *Orthodoxy* proved to be not only a classic nonsectarian defense of the Christian religion, and a forerunner to his admirer C. S. Lewis's *Mere Christianity*."

12. Chesterton's massive literary output is discussed in "Books: Orthodoxologist," *Time*, 11 October 1943, which states that Chesterton authored nearly 100 books. However, a more accurate tally of 78 books was provided by Alzina Stone Dale in 1982. See Kanfer, "God's Fool."

13. G. K. Chesterton, *Orthodoxy* (New York: John Lane, 1908), 136.

Chapter 1: "My Earliest Path"

1. G. K. Chesterton, *Autobiography*, fifth impression (London: Hutchinson & Co., 1936), 19.

2. The story of Churchill and Chesterton's meeting is recounted in Joseph Pearce, *Wisdom and Innocence: A Life of G. K. Chesterton* (San Francisco: Ignatius Press, 1996), 74.

3. Chesterton, *Autobiography*, 10.

4. Ibid., 11.

5. See William Oddie, *Chesterton and the Romance of Orthodoxy: The Making of G. K. C. 1874–1908* (New York: Oxford Univ. Press, 2009), 16. Here Oddie quotes the following description given by Chesterton of his father: "He was known to the world,

and even the next-door neighbours, as a very reliable and capable though rather
unambitious business man."

6. The best discussion of Edward Chesterton's heart condition is given in Oddie, *The Romance of Orthodoxy*, 15.

7. As quoted in Michael Ffinch, *G. K. Chesterton: A Biography* (San Francisco: Harper & Row Publishers, 1986), 8.

8. Chesterton, *Autobiography*, 35.

9. For Chesterton's account of an incident demonstrating his father's personal integrity in business dealings, see Chesterton, *Autobiography*, 24.

10. Ibid., 10.

11. Ibid., 35.

12. Ibid., 24.

13. Ibid., 11.

14. Ibid., 15.

15. The description of Chesterton as a "dreamy" child appears in Bernard Bergonzi's essay for *The Oxford Dictionary of National Biography* (2004).

16. Chesterton, *Autobiography*, 31. Chesterton's use of the word *proscenium* here refers specifically to the foreground of a toy theater.

17. Ibid., 32.

18. Ibid.

19. Ibid., 34.

20. C. S. Lewis, *Surprised by Joy* (New York: Harcourt Brace Jovanovich, 1955), 7.

21. Chesterton, *Autobiography*, 35.

22. Ibid., 36.

23. As quoted in Ffinch, *G. K. Chesterton*, 9.

24. Ffinch, *G. K. Chesterton*, 9.

25. Maisie Ward, *Gilbert Keith Chesterton* (London: Sheed & Ward, 1943), 18.

26. Ibid., 17–18.

27. Ibid., 9.

28. Chesterton, *Autobiography*, 18.

29. Ibid.

30. Ada Chesterton, *The Chestertons* (London: Chapman and Hall, 1941), 19–20.

31. From Bernard Bergonzi's essay for *The Oxford Dictionary of National Biography* (2004).

32. The information given in the first three sentences of this paragraph, including the quote in the first sentence, is taken from Bernard Bergonzi's essay for *The Oxford Dictionary of National Biography* (2004).

33. The information given here about Marie-Louise Chesterton's cavalier attitude towards order and cleanliness, including the quote about her dress habits, is from Oddie, *Chesterton and Romance*, 17. See also Ward, *Gilbert Keith Chesterton*, 18.

34. Ffinch, *G. K. Chesterton*, 10.

35. Alzina Stone Dale, *The Outline of Sanity: A Life of G. K. Chesterton* (Grand Rapids, Michigan: William B. Eerdmans, 1982), 7.

36. Ffinch, *G. K. Chesterton*, 10.

37. Ibid.

38. Ibid.

39. Ibid.

40. Ibid.

41. Chesterton, *Autobiography*, 35–36.

42. From Bernard Bergonzi's essay for *The Oxford Dictionary of National Biography* (2004).

Chapter 2: "From Childhood to Boyhood"

1. G. K. Chesterton, *Autobiography*, fifth impression (London: Hutchinson & Co., 1936), 57.

2. William Oddie, *Chesterton and the Romance of Orthodoxy: The Making of G. K. C. 1874–1908* (New York: Oxford Univ. Press, 2009), 43.

3. Edmund Clerihew Bentley, *Those Days* (London: Constable, 1940), 54. See also Oddie, *Chesterton and Romance*, 43–44.

4. H. A. Sams, *Pauline and Old Pauline* (Cambridge, 1933), 7.

5. Chesterton, *Autobiography*, 57.

6. Ibid., 58.

7. Ibid., 56.

8. From the signed obituary article by E. C. Bentley entitled "G. K. C.," *Spectator*, 19 June 1936, 1125.

9. Ibid., 1126.

10. Bentley, *Those Days*, 46.

11. Oddie, *Chesterton and Romance*, 46.

12. Maisie Ward, *Return to Chesterton* (London: Sheed & Ward, 1952), 13–14.

13. Ibid.

14. G. K. Chesterton, *The Victorian Age in Literature* (London: Williams and Norgate, 1913), 152.

15. Oddie, *Chesterton and Romance*, 48.

16. The information in this paragraph, as well as the quote therein, is taken from Oddie, *Chesterton and Romance*, 50–52.

17. Oddie, *Chesterton and Romance*, 55. Here Oddie confirms Cecil Chesterton's statement that the formation of the JDC was "the most important event of [Gilbert's] school career, so far as its influence on his own future [was] concerned."

18. The best and most comprehensive list of the members of the JDC appears in *The Collected Works of G. K. Chesterton*, vol. 10, bk. 2, *Collected Poetry* (San Francisco: Ignatius Press, 2008), 119. See also Michael Coren, *Gilbert: The Man Who Was G. K. Chesterton* (New York: Paragon House, 1990), 33.

19. The discussion of Lucian Oldershaw's matriculation to Oxford appears in Alzina Stone Dale, *The Outline of Sanity: A Life of G. K. Chesterton* (Grand Rapids, MI: William B. Eerdmans, 1982), 39.

20. Maisie Ward, *Gilbert Keith Chesterton* (New York: Sheed & Ward, 1943), 21 and 31.

21. Ibid., 31.

22. The achievements in later life of Vernède and Fordham are given in Coren, *Gilbert*, 33.

23. Salter's full name, which seldom appears in Chesterton biographies, is given by Chesterton himself in *The Collected Works of G. K. Chesterton*, vol. 10, bk. 1, *Collected Poetry*, Part One (San Francisco: Ignatius Press, 1994), 287.

24. See Coren, *Gilbert*, 33.

25. The names and subsequent careers of Digby d'Avigdor, Hubert Arthur Sams, Francis George Lawder Bertram, and Bernard Noël Langdon-Davies are discussed in *The Collected Works of G. K. Chesterton*, vol. 10, bk. 2, *Collected Poetry*, 119.

26. Oddie, *Chesterton and Romance*, 55.

27. Ibid., 55–57.

28. Ward, *Gilbert Keith Chesterton*, 29.
29. Oddie, *Chesterton and Romance*, 56.
30. Ibid., 60. Here Oddie refers the reader to *The Debater*, ii. 4.
31. Sams, *Pauline and Old Pauline*, 46.

Chapter 3: A Perfect Storm

1. G. K. Chesterton, as quoted in Maisie Ward, *Gilbert Keith Chesterton* (New York: Sheed & Ward, 1943), 158.
2. Frederick Buechner, *Speak What We Feel* (New York: HarperCollins, 2001), 92–93.
3. William Oddie, *Chesterton and the Romance of Orthodoxy: The Making of G. K. C. 1874–1908* (New York: Oxford Univ. Press, 2009), 101.
4. Buechner, *Speak What We Feel*, 93.
5. Oddie, *Chesterton and Romance*, 103.
6. These quotes are taken from Dr. George P. Landow's posting on the scholarly web site, the Victorian Web. Dr. Landow is professor of English and art history at Brown University. His discussion of decadence in the 1890s appears online at: http://www.victorianweb.org/victorian/decadence/decadence.html.
7. G. K. Chesterton, *The Man Who Was Thursday* (New York: Dodd, Mead and Company, 1908), iii.
8. Ibid.
9. G. K. Chesterton, The *Autobiography of G.K. Chesterson* (London: Hutchinson and Co., 1936), 92–93.
10. Ward, *Gilbert Keith Chesterton*, 44.
11. Ibid., 45.
12. Buechner, *Speak What We Feel*, 95.
13. Chesterton, *Autobiography*, 92.
14. Ibid., 93–94.
15. Ibid., 94.
16. Ibid., 94–95.
17. Buechner, *Speak What We Feel*, 119.
18. Oddie, *Chesterton and Romance*, 156.
19. As quoted in Ward, *Gilbert Keith Chesterton*, 62.
20. Ibid., 61.
21. Oddie, *Chesterton and Romance*, 110. Here Oddie offers the suggestion that Chesterton was recording his thoughts in a manner reminiscent of Pascal's *Pensées*.
22. As quoted in Ward, *Gilbert Keith Chesterton*, 62.
23. Ibid.
24. Oddie, *Chesterton and Romance*, 122. Here, Oddie states that Chesterton had come through his dark night of the soul by the summer of 1894.

Chapter 4: And Now for a Career

1. Paul Dwight Moody (1879–1947) was the youngest son of famed evangelist Dwight L. Moody. The quotation from Paul Dwight Moody given here is taken from an article describing a sermon he preached on Sunday, 18 August 1929, at the Madison Avenue Presbyterian Church in New York City. "Dr. Moody Urges a Spirit of Inquiry," *New York Times*, 19 August 1929, 26.

2. G. K. Chesterton, as quoted in Maisie Ward, *Gilbert Keith Chesterton* (New York: Sheed & Ward, 1943), 69.

3. A characterization given of Chesterton's Ruskin review in William Oddie, *Chesterton and the Romance of Orthodoxy: The Making of G. K. C. 1874–1908* (New York: Oxford Univ. Press, 2009), 157.

4. "The Ruskin Reader," *Academy* 47 (22 June 1895), no. 1207: 523.

5. "Robert Bridges," *Academy*, 48 (19 Oct. 1895), no. 1224, 315.

6. Chesterton stayed at Redway's from September 1895 to October 1896. All of the information in this paragraph is taken from Oddie, *Chesterton and Romance*, 160, 162.

7. Joseph Pearce, *Wisdom and Innocence: A Life of G. K. Chesterton* (San Francisco: Ignatius Press, 1996), 37.

8. As quoted in Ward, *Gilbert Keith Chesterton*, 104–5.

9. Both quotes in this paragraph are taken from Michael Ffinch, *G. K. Chesterton: A Biography* (San Francisco: Harper and Row, 1986), 50.

10. Pearce, *Wisdom and Innocence*, 39.

11. As quoted in Maisie Ward, *Return to Chesterton* (London: Sheed & Ward, 1952), 67.

12. G. K. Chesterton, "Velasquez and Poussin," *Bookman* (Dec. 1899), 87.

13. Ibid.

14. Michael Coren, *Gilbert: The Man Who Was G. K. Chesterton* (New York: Paragon House, 1990), 108.

15. Oddie, *Chesterton and Romance*, 198.

16. W. H. Auden, "The Gift of Wonder," in John Sullivan, ed., *G. K. Chesterton: A Centenary Appraisal* (London, 1974), 78. In the full text of Auden's essay, he mentions Lear, as well as Lewis Carroll.

17. G. K. Chesterton, "The Oneness of the Philosopher with Nature," in *Greybeards at Play: Literature and Art for Old Gentlemen* (London: R. Brimley Johnson, 1900), 2, 6, 10.

18. G. K. Chesterton, "A Christmas Carol," in *The Wild Knight*, fourth edition with additional poems (London: J. M. Dent & Sons, Ltd., 1914), 46–47.

19. The publishing house of R. Brimley Johnson had issued Chesterton's first book *Greybeards at Play*. *The Wild Knight* was published in London by the publishing firm Grant Richards. Later editions, such as the fourth edition of 1914, were published by J. M. Dent & Sons, of London.

20. As quoted in Ward, *Return to Chesterton*, 143.

21. Oddie, *Chesterton and Romance*, 202–3.

Chapter 5: An Artist in Words

1. As quoted in Maisie Ward, *Gilbert Keith Chesterton* (New York: Sheed & Ward, 1943), 154.

2. G. K. Chesterton, *The Defendant* (New York: Dodd, Mead & Co., 1902; British edition London: R. Brimley Johnson, 1902).

3. Ibid., 1–2.

4. Ibid.

5. "Fantastic Reasoning: G. K. Chesterton's Smart but Rather Nonsensical Essays," *New York Times* in the *Saturday Review of Books*, 27 September 1902, BR16.

6. Ibid.

7. G. K. Chesterton, *Heretics* (New York: John Lane Company, 1905), 217.

8. "Fantastic Reasoning."

9. Ibid.
10. Ibid.
11. Sir Arthur Quiller-Couch, as quoted in D. J. Conlon, ed., *G. K. Chesterton: The Critical Judgements* (Antwerp Belgium: Studies in English Literature, 1976) 38–39.
12. Chesterton, *The Defendant*, 23.
13. Quiller-Couch, as quoted in Conlon, ed., *G. K. Chesterton*, 39.

Chapter 6: Eternal Ideas

1. Maisie Ward, *Gilbert Keith Chesterton* (New York: Sheed & Ward, 1943), 158.
2. "Alvin Langdon Coburn was born in Boston in 1882, and his interest in photography began eight years later. In addition to being a founding member of the Photo-Secession in 1902, he became a member of the Linked Ring in 1903. He was also associated with Wyndham Lewis and the Vorticist group in 1917–18. Having emigrated to England in 1912, he became a naturalized British citizen in 1932. He died in Colwyn Bay, Wales in 1966. He is known for the pictorial effects he achieved in his portraits and views, thus helping to confirm the medium's place as an art form." This information is taken from the web page for the Alvin Langdon Coburn Collection at the Harry Ransom Humanities Research Center. See http://research.hrc.utexas.edu:8080/hrcxtf/view?docId=ead/00260.xml.
3. Ward, *Gilbert Keith Chesterton*, 158.
4. William Oddie, *Chesterton and the Romance of Orthodoxy: The Making of G.K.C., 1874–1908* (New York: Oxford Univ. Press, 2009), 310.
5. Joseph Pearce, *Wisdom and Innocence: A Life of G. K. Chesterton* (San Francisco: Ignatius Press, 1996), 81.
6. G. K. Chesterton, *The Autobiography of G.K. Chesterton* (London: Hutchinson & Co., Ltd., 1936), 99.
7. Ibid. See also Pearce, *Wisdom and Innocence*, 81.
8. "Review 4," *New York Times* in *Saturday Review of Books and Art*, 27 June 1903, BR1. Clement King Shorter (1857–1926), referred to in this block quote, was a noted English journalist, editor, and avid collector of material related to the Brontës. Shorter's collection and research eventually developed into several books on this literary family. In 1891 he was made editor of the *Illustrated London News*, where he also edited *Album* and *Pick-me-up*. In addition to editing, Shorter founded three papers: *Sketch* (1893), *Sphere* (1900), and *Tatler* (1903). For more, see the biographical note on C. K. Shorter at the following University of Delaware web site: http://www.lib.udel.edu/ud/spec/findaids/shorterc.htm.
9. G. K. Chesterton, *Robert Browning* (New York: The Macmillan Company, 1903), 178.
10. Ibid., 16.
11. "Mr. Chesterton's Browning," review in *Vanity Fair*, 28 May 1903. The full text of this review is given in D. J. Conlon, ed., *G. K. Chesterton: The Critical Judgments 1900–1937* (Antwerp, Belgium: Antwerp Studies in English Literature, 1976), 60–61.
12. Bernard Bergonzi, "Chesterton, Gilbert Keith (1874–1936)," *Oxford Dictionary of National Biography*. Online ed., accessed 18 August 2009. Dr. Bergonzi, an expert on T. S. Eliot, is emeritus professor of English at the University of Warwick. Several of his books are published by Oxford University Press. For the source of the sentence from Chesterton Bergonzi cites in this block quote, see G. K. Chesterton, *Robert Browning* (London: Macmillan, 1903), 118.

13. Chesterton, *Robert Browning*, 165.
14. "Mr. Chesterton's *Robert Browning*," review in *Sunday Sun*, 31 May 1903. The complete text is presented in Conlon, ed., *Chesterton: The Critical Judgments*, 61–64.
15. Ibid.
16. Chesterton, *Robert Browning*, 37–39.
17. "Mr. Chesterton's *Robert Browning*."
18. Ibid.
19. Ibid.
20. Ibid.
21. Ibid.
22. Chesterton, *Robert Browning*, 201–2.
23. "Mr. Chesterton's *Robert Browning*."
24. Ibid.
25. Ibid.
26. Chesterton, *Autobiography*, 99.
27. Ibid.
28. Iain Finlayson, *Robert Browning: A Private Life* (London: HarperCollins, 2004), 9.

Chapter 7: *Varied Types*

1. *Twelve Types*, as its title implies, contains only twelve essays. *Varied Types* has nineteen.
2. John White Chadwick, "Paradoxical Chesterton: A New Volume of Piquant Essays by a Young Writer Whose Influence Will Be Felt," review in *New York Times* in *Saturday Review of Books and Art*, 2 January 1904, BR1.
3. "Mr. Chesterton's Essays," *New York Times*, in the *Saturday Review of Books*, 7 March 1903, BR15.
4. Ibid.
5. G. K. Chesterton, *Varied Types* (New York: Dodd, Mead and Company, 1903), 44.
6. The phrase "graceless age" was first made popular by the singer/songwriter Don Henley in the song "The Heart of the Matter, 1988."
7. Chesterton, *Varied Types*, 47–48. Chesterton is referring here to the poet and journalist William Ernest Henley (1849–1903).
8. Ibid., 48.
9. Ibid., 49–50.
10. Ibid., 50.
11. Ibid., 54. See also *The Works of Alexander Pope, Volume II. Containing His Imitations, Moral Essays, Satires, &c.* (New York: William Durell, 1808), 183–84. The lines cited from this poem ("Epistle to Dr. Arbuthnot, Being the Prologue to Satires") are lines 198–200, and 209–12.
12. Chesterton, *Varied Types*, 54–55.
13. H. Bellyse Baildon, *Robert Louis Stevenson: A Life Study in Criticism* (London: Chatto & Windus, 1901).
14. Chesterton, *Varied Types*, 97.
15. Ibid., 98.
16. Ibid., 98–99.
17. Ibid., 104–5.
18. *Casa Guidi Windows* is Elizabeth Barrett Browning's "two-part poem about the

Italian struggle to end Austrian domination, on September 12, 1847, her first wedding anniversary and the end of her first year in Italy with Robert Browning. Part One is a commentary on the hopeful early events in the Risorgimento, her adopted country's struggle for political autonomy and unification. Part Two, written two or three years later, records Barrett Browning's recognition that the Risorgimento will in fact be painful and protracted, and that the results are uncertain. The poem was an eye-witness view of history." This information is taken from Mary Pollock in *The Literary Encyclopedia*. Pollock's article is posted online at: http://www.litencyc.com/php/sworks.php?rec=true&UID=14956.

19. Chesterton, *Varied Types*, 261.
20. Ibid., 261–62.
21. Ibid., 262–63.
22. Ibid., 263–64.
23. Ibid., 267.

Chapter 8: The Tower That Strikes the Stars

1. G. K. Chesterton, *The Napoleon of Notting Hill* (New York: John Lane, 1904), 136.
2. Quoted in Cyril Clemens, *Chesterton as Seen by His Contemporaries* (Webster Groves, MO: Mark Twain Society, 1939), 16–17.
3. G. K. Chesterton, as quoted in Maisie Ward, *Gilbert Keith Chesterton* (New York: Sheed & Ward, 1943), 166.
4. The complete text of Bettany's review appears in D. J. Conlon, ed., *G. K. Chesterton: The Critical Judgments 1900–1937* (Antwerp, Belgium: Antwerp Studies in English Literature, 1976), 87.
5. From Eliot's signed obituary for Chesterton in the *Tablet*, 20 June 1936, 785.
6. In its review of 25 March 1904, the *Times* of London stated that "*The Napoleon of Notting Hill* enshrines a parable." This should be taken together with F. G. Bettany's assertion in the *Sunday Times*, 27 March 1904, that Chesterton had "struck a new vein of romance." Both observations were equally true. See D. J. Conlon, ed., *G. K. Chesterton: The Critical Judgments 1900–1937* (Antwerp, Belgium: Antwerp Studies in English Literature, 1976), 85–87, wherein the text of both reviews is given.
7. Chesterton, *Napoleon of Notting Hill*, 22.
8. Ibid., 72.
9. A description of London and its boroughs given on the back cover of the Oxford World's Classics edition of *The Napoleon of Notting Hill* (Oxford: Oxford Univ. Press, 1994).
10. Chesterton, *Napoleon of Notting Hill*, 104–6.
11. Points made in text appearing in the Oxford World's Classics edition of *The Napoleon of Notting Hill*.
12. "Doings of English Authors and Publishers—The Latest Announcements," Special Cable to *New York Times*, 12 March 1904. Featured in Part Two of the *Saturday Review of Books*, page BR 169.
13. See "Mr. Chesterton," review of *The Napoleon of Notting Hill*, the *New York Times Review of Books*, 28 May 1904, BR360.
14. Ibid.
15. Chesterton, *Napoleon of Notting Hill*, 21.

Chapter 9: Heretics and First Things

1. Philip Yancey, introduction to G. K. Chesterton, *Orthodoxy* (New York: Doubleday, 2001), xx.
2. G. K. Chesterton, *Heretics*, 4th ed. (London: John Lane, 1907), 16.
3. A point made cogently by Garry Wills, *Chesterton* (New York: Image/Doubleday Books, 2001), 108–9.
4. Chesterton, *Heretics*, 17.
5. See Ron Powers, *Mark Twain: A Life* (New York: Simon and Schuster/The Free Press, 2005), 89. See also page 396, where Powers states that Chesterton was one of the few to take note of the seriousness and sorrow present in Twain's writing.
6. Michael Ffinch wrote of the reception that Chesterton's novel *The Man Who Was Thursday* received: "The critics were mostly agreed that Chesterton had produced an extraordinary fantasy, behind which, as Frank Harris noted, lurked 'a great, serious mission (for Mr. Chesterton, like all clowns, is intensely serious).'" *G. K. Chesterton: A Biiography* (San Francisco: Harper & Row, 1986), 161.
7. Chesterton, *Heretics*, 18–19.
8. Ibid., 12.
9. Ibid., 12–13. Concerning Chesterton's taking the intellectual "measure" of Shaw, Garry Wills wrote with great perception in *Chesterton*, 143 and the pages immediately preceding.
10. Chesterton, *Heretics*, 14–15.
11. Ibid., 15.

Chapter 10: No Definite Image of Good

1. T. S. Eliot, *Selected Prose of T. S. Eliot* (New York: Harcourt, 1975), 291.
2. H. I. Brock, "G. K. Chesterton: An Interview with the Great Paradoxist . . . ," *New York Times*, in the *Sunday Review of Books*, 18 August 1912, BR449.
3. G. K. Chesterton, *Heretics*, 4th ed. (London: John Lane, 1907), 22. See Garry Will's comments in *Chesterton* (New York: Image/Doubleday, 2001), 143 and the pages immediately preceding. Wills is particularly excellent in his assessment of Shaw's devotion to "progress" and why Chesterton chose his foe well in Shaw because Shaw was such a hero to the Fabians—and those who continue to revere the Fabians today.
4. Chesterton, *Heretics*, 22–24.
5. Ibid., 28.
6. Ibid.
7. Ibid., 28–29.
8. Ibid., 32.
9. Ibid.
10. Ibid., 32–33.
11. Ibid., 33.
12. Moore published a celebrated three-volume memoir entitled *Hail and Farewell* (New York, Appleton & Co., 1914).
13. Chesterton, *Heretics*, 128.
14. Ibid., 129.
15. Ibid., 130.
16. Ibid., 131.

17. Ibid., 133.
18. Ibid., 132.
19. Ibid., 131.
20. Ibid., 171.
21. Ibid., 172.
22. Ibid., 171.
23. Chapter 13 of Lewis's autobiography, *Surprised by Joy* (London: Geoffrey Bles, 1955).
24. Owen Barfield, *History in English Words* (London: Faber & Faber, 1953; revised edition Grand Rapids, MI: Eerdmans, 1967), 164.
25. See the article posted at http://en.wikipedia.org/wiki/Chronological_snobbery#cite_note-0.
26. G. K. Chesterton, *Orthodoxy* (New York: John Lane, 1909), 135–36.
27. Chesterton, *Heretics*, 196–97.
28. Ibid., 208–9.
29. Ibid., 36–37.

Chapter 11: Mr. Dickens's Champion

1. George Bernard Shaw to G. K. Chesterton, 6 September 1906, as quoted in Maisie Ward, *Gilbert Keith Chesterton* (New York: Sheed & Ward, 1943), 178.
2. William Oddie, *Chesterton and the Romance of Orthodoxy: The Making of G.K.C. 1874–1908* (New York: Oxford Univ. Press, 2009), 311.
3. Paul Schlicke, as quoted in *The Oxford Reader's Companion to Dickens* (Oxford: Oxford Univ. Press, 1999), 130.
4. Michael Slater, as quoted in *Oxford Reader's Companion to Dickens*, 86–87.
5. Paul Schlicke, as quoted in *Oxford Reader's Companion to Dickens*, 130.
6. Michael Slater, as quoted in *Oxford Reader's Companion to Dickens*, 86–87.
7. T. S. Eliot to G. K. Chesterton, private correspondence, 8 May 1929, The Wade Center, Wheaton College, Wheaton, Illinois.
8. T. S. Eliot, *Selected Essays*, 3rd enlarged ed. (London: Faber, 1951). See also T. S. Eliot, *Selected Essays*, 1927 essay "Wilkie Collins and Dickens" (New York: Harcourt, Brace and Company, 1932), 374.
9. For an excellent discussion of Lewis's gift for wide-ranging literary criticism written with brio, arresting originality, and erudition, see Alan Jacobs, *The Narnian* (San Francisco: HarperSanFrancisco, 2005), xvi–xvii.
10. G. K. Chesterton, *Charles Dickens: A Critical Study* (New York: Dodd, Mead & Co., 1906), 85–87.
11. Jacobs, *The Narnian*, xvi–xvii.
12. Chesterton, *Charles Dickens*, 85–87.
13. J.R.R. Tolkien, "On Fairy-Stories," 57–58, an essay in *Tales from the Perilous Realm* (London: HarperCollins, 2008), 372–74.
14. See Peter Kreeft, *The Philosophy of Tolkien* (San Francisco: Ignatius Press, 2005), 83.
15. G. K. Chesterton, *Orthodoxy* (New York: John Lane, 1909), 105–6.
16. Tolkien, "On Fairy-Stories," 57.
17. Ibid., 58–59.
18. Ibid., 57–58.
19. "'Impressionistic' Criticism Rampant: Mr. Gilbert K. Chesterton's Smart Book About Charles Dickens and His Works Carries the Undefined Art of the

Irresponsible Critic to Its Limit," review of G. K. Chesterton, *Charles Dickens: A Critical Study* (New York: Dodd, Mead & Co., 1906), *New York Times Review of Books*, 29 September 1906, BR598.

20. Ibid.

21. Ibid.

22. Ibid.

23. Michael Slater, as quoted in *Oxford Reader's Companion to Dickens*, 86–87.

24. Ibid.

25. Hamilton Carr, "Chesterton on Dickens," a 614-word review (sent as a letter) of G. K. Chesterton, *Charles Dickens: A Critical Study* (New York: Dodd, Mead & Co., 1906), *Review of Books* in the *New York Times*, 29 December 1906, BR912. Though published December 29, Carr's letter was dated December 26, 1906.

26. See Jacqueline Banerjee, "G. K. Chesterton," posted online at http://www .victorianweb.org/authors/chesterton/bio.html.

Chapter 12: Why *Orthodoxy* Matters

1. Francis Bacon, "Of Atheism," in *The Essays of Francis Bacon* (New York: Charles Scribner's Sons, 1908), 71.

2. A description of and quotations from John Updike in *The John Updike Encyclopedia*, ed. Jack De Bellis (Westport, CT: Greenwood Press, 2000), 49. For more, see Updike's book *Self-Consciousness*.

3. G. K. Chesterton, *Introduction to the Book of Job*, as quoted in Maisie Ward, *Gilbert Keith Chesterton* (New York: Sheed & Ward, 1943), 208.

4. Ward, *Gilbert Keith Chesterton*, 208.

5. *Orthodoxy* was published in September 1908. Chesterton was born on 29 May, 1874.

6. G. K. Chesterton, *Orthodoxy* (New York: John Lane, 1909), 13.

7. Ibid., vii–viii.

8. R. A. Scott-James, "Mr. Chesterton's Masterpiece," review in the *Daily News* of London, 25 September 1908. Rolfe Arnold Scott-James (1878–1959) was the influential author, critic, and editor of the *London Mercury*. The text of Scott-James's review appears in D. J. Conlon, ed., *G. K. Chesterton: The Critical Judgments 1900–1937* (Antwerp: Antwerp Studies in English Literature, 1976), 159–61.

9. Philip Yancey, "The 'Ample' Man Who Saved My Faith," *Christianity Today*, 3 September 2001, vol. 45, no. 11. This article, accessed 24 March 2010, is posted online at: http://www.christianitytoday.com/ct/2001/september3/6.66 .html?start=1.

10. Ibid.

11. Ibid.

12. Chesterton, *Orthodoxy*, 146–47.

13. This portion of the review in *Outlook* appears in the endpapers to the 1915 British edition of *Orthodoxy* (London: John Lane, 1915).

14. Richard R. Lingeman, "Defender of the Faith," review of Dudley Barker, *G. K. Chesterton, New York Times*, 1 September 1973.

15. Yancey, "'Ample' Man."

16. G. K. Chesterton, *St. Francis of Assisi* (London: Hodder and Stoughton, 1933), 88.

17. Yancey, "'Ample' Man."

18. Ibid.

19. Philip Yancey's introduction appears in G. K. Chesterton, *Orthodoxy* (New York: Image/Doubleday Books, 2001), xii–xxi.

20. Jack Miles, "The Loyal Opposition," review of Garry Wills, *Why I Am A Catholic*, *The New York Times*, 14 July 2002.

21. Garry Wills, *Why I Am a Catholic* (New York: Mariner Books, 2003), 27.

22. G. K. Chesterton, chapter 1, "The Greatness of Chaucer," *Chaucer* (London: Faber & Faber Ltd., 1932).

23. Wills, *Why I Am a Catholic*, 35.

24. Ibid.

25. Ibid., 27–28.

26. From *St. Francis of Assisi*, contained in *The Collected Works of G. K. Chesterton*, vol. 2 (San Francisco: Ignatius Press, 1986), 73.

27. Wills, *Why I Am a Catholic*, 311.

28. Ibid. The Chesterton poem, "The Holy of Holies," is in the public domain, having been anthologized originally in *The Oxford Book of Mystical Verse*, ed. Nicholson & Lee (Oxford: Clarendon Press, 1917). This poem is posted online at http://www.bartleby.com/236/313.html.

29. Lewis's love of *The Ballad of the White Horse* is richly recounted in the Preface to George Sayer, *Jack: C. S. Lewis and His Times* (San Francisco: Harper & Row, 1988), xvi.

30. Wills, *Why I Am a Catholic*, 312.

31. Ibid., 41–42.

32. Garry Wills, *Chesterton* (New York: Image/Doubleday Books, 2001), 8.

Chapter 13: A Melodramatic Sort of Moonshine

1. Welles said this during his introduction to *The Mercury Theatre on the Air's* presentation of *The Man Who Was Thursday*, originally broadcast throughout America by the network of affiliates comprising the Columbia Broadcasting System (CBS) and a "coast to coast network" of the CBC in Canada on Monday, 5 September 1938. Welles (who had penned the radio play adaptation of Chesterton's novel) offered his spoken tribute during the time period lasting from 1 minute 28 seconds into the program to 1 minute 53 seconds into the program. This celebrated radio theater adaptation of Chesterton's novel was described in critic Richard Corliss's *Time* magazine article "That Old Feeling: Mercury, God of Radio," posted online at: http://www.time.com/time/arts/article/0,8599,172672-4,00.html.

2. The information provided about the CBS radio network is taken from http://www.cbs.com/specials/cbs_75/timeline/1930.shtml.

3. This information about the history of the CBC is provided through a web page of *The Canadian Encyclopedia*, which states: "In 1937 . . . 50-kw transmitters were built in Montréal and Toronto, increasing coverage to about 76% of the population." See the web page posted at: http://www.thecanadianencyclopedia.com/index.cfm?PgNm =TCE&Params=a1ARTA0001266.

4. Introduction to G. K. Chesterton, *The Man Who Was Thursday* (New York: Modern Library Classics, 2001).

5. Ibid.

6. Ibid.

7. In 2007, the British journalist and critic Gilbert Adair joined earlier writers and critics like C. S. Lewis in contending that Chesterton was at times much like Kafka.

Adair wrote: "It is, at any rate, his flesh-creeping proximity to Poe and Kafka and indeed Borges that makes him not just still readable but still curiously modern." Adair's remarks here, which originally appeared on Saturday, 20 October 2007 in the British newspaper *The Guardian*, are posted online at: http://www.guardian.co.uk/ books/2007/oct/20/featuresreviews.guardianreview31.

8. This sentence contains thoughts from several important sources. For the comparison of Chesterton to Poe I am indebted to Jorge Luis Borges. For the comparison of Chesterton to Kafka I am indebted to C. S. Lewis. And for the description of *The Man Who Was Thursday* as a metaphysical thriller I am indebted to Kingsley Amis.

   "Chesterton," Borges wrote, "restrained himself from being Edgar Allan Poe or Franz Kafka, but something in the makeup of his personality leaned toward the nightmarish, something secret, and blind, and central." See Garry Wills, *Chesterton* (New York: Image/Doubleday Books, 2001), 273. Lewis's comparison of Chesterton to Kafka appears in *On Stories* (New York: Mariner Books, 2002), 116–17. Here, Lewis offered a comparison to the surrealist writings of Kafka: "While both give a powerful picture of the loneliness and bewilderment which each one of us encounters in his (apparently single-handed) struggle with the universe, Chesterton, attributing to the universe a more complicated disguise, and admitting the exhilaration as well as the terror of the struggle, has got in rather more; is more balanced: in that sense, more classical, more permanent."

   Kingsley Amis called *The Man Who Was Thursday* "not quite a political bad dream, nor a metaphysical thriller, nor a cosmic joke in the form of a spy novel, but it has something of all three." See Amis, introduction to G. K. Chesterton, *The Man Who Was Thursday* (London: Penguin Books, 1986). Amis also called *The Man Who Was Thursday* a "metaphysical adventure" in "Speaking of Books: 'The Man Who Was Thursday,'" the *New York Times Book Review*, BR2.

9. G. K. Chesterton, *Charles Dickens* (London: Methuen & Co., 1917), 23.

10. The summary of Chesterton's art college years in this paragraph, and the quotes cited within it, are taken from Frederick Buechner, *Speak What We Feel* (San Francisco: HarperCollins, 2001), 92–96, 119.

11. G. K. Chesterton, *Orthodoxy* (New York: John Lane, 1909), 18.

12. G. K. Chesterton, *Tremendous Trifles* (New York: Dodd, Mead and Co, 1909), 7.

13. Buechner, *Speak What We Feel*, 119.

14. A point cogently argued by David Stewart in his review of Buechner, *Speak What We Feel*, in *Books and Culture* 29 July 2002. This article is posted online at: http://www .christianitytoday.com/bc/columns/bookculturecorner/020729.html?start=2.

15. See Lewis, *On Stories*, 116–17.

16. Hildegarde Hawthorne, "G. K. Chesterton's Fantastic Novel," review in the *New York Times*, 2 May 1908, BR 253. The poet and author Hildegarde Hawthorne (1871–1952) was the granddaughter of Nathaniel Hawthorne and the daughter of Julian Hawthorne, also a writer. She wrote many books for children.

17. Interestingly, John Updike traces the "pedigree" of magic realism to "Borges, back through the fantasy of Chesterton and Stevenson . . . clear to Hawthorne and Poe." This description of and quotation from John Updike in *The John Updike Encyclopedia*, ed. Jack De Bellis (Westport, CT: Greenwood Press, 2000), 258.

18. Hawthorne, "G. K. Chesterton's Fantastic Novel."

19. G. K. Chesterton, *The Man Who Was Thursday* (New York: Dodd, Mead and Company, 1908), 109.

20. Hawthorne, "G. K. Chesterton's Fantastic Novel."

21. Amis, "Speaking of Books."
22. Ibid.
23. C. S. Lewis to Charles Williams, 11 March 1936, in C. S. Lewis, *The Collected Letters of C. S. Lewis, volume 2* (San Francisco: HarperSanFrancisco, 2004), 183.
24. Amis, "Speaking of Books."
25. Ibid.
26. Ibid.
27. Ibid.
28. Ibid.
29. Chesterton, *Man Who Was Thursday*, 65–66.
30. Amis, "Speaking of Books."
31. Ibid.
32. From an article published by Chesterton in the *Illustrated London News*, 13 June 1936.

Chapter 14: Chesterton, Mencken, and Shaw

1. Henry Wadsworth Longfellow, as quoted in *The Prose Works of Henry Wadsworth Longfellow* (London: Chatto and Windus, Publishers, 1878), 778.
2. Both quotes in this sentence are taken from H. L. Mencken, "A Faded Charmer," review of G. K. Chesterton, *Alarms and Discursions*, in *The Smart Set: A Magazine of Cleverness*, May 1911. See William H. Nolte, ed., *H. L. Mencken's Smart Set Criticism* (Washington, D.C.: Regnery, 1987), 162–63.
3. Ibid.
4. Ibid.
5. From the close of David Stewart, review of Terry Teachout, *The Skeptic: A Life of H. L. Mencken*, in *Christian Century*, 5 April 2003.
6. H. L. Mencken, "Chesterton's Picture of Shaw," review in *The Smart Set*, January 1910. The full text of this review appears in Nolte, ed., *Mencken's Smart Set*, 57–59.
7. Chesterton calls his book a "rough study," in *George Bernard Shaw* (New York: John Lane, 1910), 7.
8. Mencken, "Chesterton's Picture of Shaw."
9. Ibid.
10. Mencken, "A Faded Charmer."
11. Ibid.
12. See Stewart, review of Teachout, *The Skeptic*. Here, Stewart wrote, "[Mencken] lacked the capacity for self-criticism—a lack that energized him to write fearlessly and spitefully about the absurdities of others while completely overlooking the limits of his own insight."
13. G. K. Chesterton, "Mr. Mencken and the New Physics," *Illustrated London News*, 14 June 1930. See volume 35 of *The Collected Works of G. K. Chesterton: The Illustrated London News 1929–1931*, ed. Lawrence J. Clipper (San Francisco: Ignatius Press, 1991), 323–26.
14. Ibid.
15. Ibid.
16. "Mencken on Democracy," *Illustrated London News*, 13 November 1926, 198. The full text of this article is given in *The Collected Works of G. K. Chesterton*, vol. 34, *The Illustrated London News, 1926–1928* (San Francisco: Ignatius Press, 1991).
17. Stewart, review of Teachout, *The Skeptic*.

18. Cosmo Hamilton, on his debating opponent, G. K. Chesterton, as quoted in Alan Jacobs, *The Narnian* (San Francisco: HarperSanFrancisco, 2005), 121. Jacobs states: "One of Lewis's favorite writers in these days was G. K. Chesterton, that indefinable man."

19. G. B. Shaw, "George Bernard Shaw Replies to Chesterton and Analyzes Himself," *New York Times Magazine*, 12 September 1909, SM10 issue. For the entire text of this review in a scholarly text, see D. J. Conlon, ed., *G. K. Chesterton: The Critical Judgments (1900–1937)* (Antwerp, Belgium: Antwerp Studies in Literature, 1976), 201–6. Shaw's review first appeared in the British publication *The Nation*, 25 August 1909.

20. Ibid.

21. Ibid.

22. Ibid.

23. G. K. Chesterton, *George Bernard Shaw*, "Introduction to the First Edition" (New York: John Lane, 1909), 5.

24. Ibid., 23.

25. Ibid., 101–2. *Vanitas vanitatum* means "vanity of vanities."

26. Ibid., 102–3.

27. Ibid., 95–96.

28. In *Man and Superman*, Shaw lamented the consequences that would result "unless we have a Democracy of Supermen." Immediately afterward, he stated that "the production of such a Democracy is the only change that is now hopeful enough to nerve us to the effort that Revolution demands." These quotations appear in *The Revolutionist's Handbook*, under the heading "The Political Need for the Superman." See George Bernard Shaw, *Man and Superman* (London: Penguin Classics, 2000), 228.

    Writing of "Shaw's discovery of Nietzsche," Chesterton stated that Nietzsche "has had an influence upon Shaw and his school which it would require a separate book adequately to study." From Chesterton, *George Bernard Shaw*, 196.

    See also Dan Stone, *Breeding Superman: Nietzsche, Race and Eugenics in Edwardian and Interwar Britain* (Liverpool: Liverpool Univ. Press, 2002), 127. Here, Stone wrote: "on 3 March 1910 Bernard Shaw, one of the more wayward supporters of eugenics with his notion of a 'democracy of supermen,' delivered a lecture to the Eugenics Education Society."

    Lastly, *The Stanford Encyclopedia of Philosophy*, in its scholarly article on Nietzsche, states: "Specific 20th century figures who were influenced, either quite substantially, or in a significant part, by Nietzsche include painters, dancers, musicians, playwrights, poets, novelists, psychologists, sociologists, literary theorists, historians, and philosophers: Alfred Adler, Georges Bataille, Martin Buber, Albert Camus, E. M. Cioran, Jacques Derrida, Gilles Deleuze, Isadora Duncan, Michel Foucault, Sigmund Freud, Stefan George, André Gide, Hermann Hesse, Carl Jung, Martin Heidegger, Gustav Mahler, André Malraux, Thomas Mann, H. L. Mencken, Rainer Maria Rilke, Jean-Paul Sartre, Max Scheler, Giovanni Segantini, George Bernard Shaw . . ." This article, accessed 7 May 2010, is posted online at: http://plato.stanford.edu/entries/nietzsche/.

29. G. K. Chesterton, *George Bernard Shaw*, Chapter 6, "The Philosopher," 199. Chesterton wrote this in 1909, eight years before Lenin led the Communists to power in Russia, thirteen years before Mussolini became Italy's Fascist leader, and fully twenty-four years before Hitler led the Nazi Party to power in Germany.

    That Hitler was profoundly influenced by Nietzsche is beyond dispute. Nietzsche's sister Elisabeth wrote a letter to a member of the Nietzsche Archive board in which she said: "If my brother had ever met Hitler his greatest wish would have been fulfilled. . . . What I like most about Hitler is his simplicity and naturalness. . . . I admire him utterly." See Ben Macintyre, *Forgotten Fatherland: The Search for Elisabeth Nietzsche* (New York: Farrar Straus Giroux, 1992), 183.

The *Stanford Encyclopedia of Philosophy's* scholarly article on Nietzsche states: "During the 1930's, aspects of Nietzsche's thought were espoused by the Nazis and Italian Fascists, partly due to the encouragement of Elisabeth Förster-Nietzsche through her associations with Adolf Hitler and Benito Mussolini. It was possible for the Nazi interpreters to assemble, quite selectively, various passages from Nietzsche's writings whose juxtaposition appeared to justify war, aggression and domination for the sake of nationalistic and racial self-glorification." This article, accessed on 7 May 2010, is posted online at: http://plato.stanford.edu/entries/nietzsche/.

30. Chesterton, *George Bernard Shaw*, 23.
31. Ibid., 174.
32. Ibid., 250.

Chapter 15: The Advent of Father Brown

1. "Mr. Chesterton's Priest-Detective," *New York Times Review of Books*, 17 December 1911, BR836.
2. V. S. Pritchett, as quoted on the front cover of *Father Brown: The Essential Tales* (New York: The Modern Library, 2005). Sir Victor Sawdon Pritchett (1900–1997) was a noted British writer and critic. Famous for his short stories, he also taught at Princeton, the University of California, Columbia University, and Smith College. He also published acclaimed biographies of Honoré de Balzac, Ivan Turgenev, and Anton Chekhov. In recognition of his services to literature, he was knighted in 1975.
3. See Martin Gardener, ed., *The Annotated Innocence of Father Brown* (Oxford Univ. Press, 1987), 279, wherein it is stated that the story "Valentin Follows a Curious Trail" was published on 7/23/1910. This story later appeared as "The Blue Cross" in the first collection of Father Brown mystery stories, *The Innocence of Father Brown* (London: Cassell, 1911/New York: John Lane Company, 1911). Chesterton scholar Hugh Robson has traced the initial publication of the first twelve Father Brown stories to *Saturday Evening Post* in 1910–11, where they appeared under different titles than those given them in *The Innocence of Father Brown*.
4. Chesterton, *The Innocence of Father Brown*, 1–2.
5. Ibid., 4–5.
6. V. S. Pritchett, as quoted on the front cover of *Father Brown: The Essential Tales*.
7. John O'Connor, as quoted in Michael Coren, *Gilbert: The Man Who Was G. K. Chesterton* (New York: Paragon House, 1990), 148.
8. Maisie Ward, *Gilbert Keith Chesterton* (New York: Sheed & Ward, 1943), 252.
9. Ibid.
10. John O'Connor, as quoted in Michael Coren, *Gilbert*, 147.
11. Ward, *Gilbert Keith Chesterton*, 252–53.
12. A tally confirmed by author Sinclair McKay in the 19 December 2009 issue of *The Spectator*. This article is posted online at: http://www.spectator.co.uk/essays/5635928/bring-back-father-brown.thtml.
13. From P. D. James's introduction to *Father Brown: The Essential Tales* (New York:

Modern Library Classics, 2005), xiii.

14. "Mr. Chesterton's Priest-Detective."

15. Ibid.

16. Ibid.

17. Walter Goodman, "Books of the Times," review of G. K. Chesterton, *The Father Brown Omnibus* (New York: Dodd, Mead & Co., 1983), *New York Times*, 7 June 1983.

18. Ibid.

19. Ibid.

20. A statement Father Brown makes in "The Oracle of the Dog," a story contained in *The Incredulity of Father Brown* (New York: Dodd, Mead & Co., 1926).

21. Walter Goodman, "Books of the Times."

22. Ibid.

23. Ibid.

24. Ibid.

25. Ibid.

26. James, introduction to *Father Brown*, xiv–xv.

27. Ibid., xv.

28. G. K. Chesterton, "The Song of the Flying Fish," in *The Collected Works of G. K. Chesterton*, volume 13, Father Brown Stories, Part 2 (San Francisco: Ignatius Press, 2005), 267–68.

29. James, introduction to *Father Brown*, xv. Here, James wrote: "In one respect G. K. Chesterton was ahead of his time. He was one of the first writers of detective fiction to realize that this popular genre could be a vehicle for exploring and exposing the condition of society and of saying something true about human nature."

30. James, introduction to *Father Brown*, xv–xvi.

Chapter 16: The Great Ballad

1. Lines from the close of Book One of G. K. Chesterton's epic poem *The Ballad of the White Horse* (London: Methuen, 1911).

2. This story is recounted in Joseph Pearce, *Wisdom and Innocence: A Life of G. K. Chesterton* (San Francisco: Ignatius Press, 1996), 166–67.

3. Pearce, *Wisdom and Innocence*, 167. See also Maisie Ward, *Gilbert Keith Chesterton* (New York: Sheed & Ward, 1943), 286.

4. Lines from the second half of Book Seven of *Ballad of the White Horse*.

5. C. S. Lewis to George Sayer, as quoted in Pearce, *Wisdom and Innocence*, 165. Lewis's exchange with Sayer appeared originally in George Sayer, *Jack: C. S. Lewis and His Times* (London: Macmillan, 1988), xvi.

6. C. S. Lewis, *On Stories and Other Essays on Literature*, ed. Walter Hooper (New York: Harcourt Books, 1982), 116.

7. Ibid.

8. See Garry Wills, *Chesterton* (New York: Image/Doubleday Books, 2001), 171.

9. Ibid.

10. See Ward, *Gilbert Keith Chesterton*, 282; and also Wills, *Chesterton*, 171.

11. G. K. Chesterton, "Fragment from a Ballad Epic of Alfred," *Albany Review*, Volume I, April–September 1907 (London: Published by John Lane, The Bodley Head, 1907), 81–85.

12. Ward, *Gilbert Keith Chesterton*, 283.
13. G. K. Chesterton, as quoted in Ward, *Gilbert Keith Chesterton*, 283.
14. Chesterton, *Ballad of the White Horse*, v.
15. This information and the plot below are taken from a summary given by Ward in *Gilbert Keith Chesterton*, 244, 284.
16. Chesterton, *Ballad of the White Horse*, xvi.
17. Words from King Alfred's *Addition to Boethius*, which appear on the title page of G. K. Chesterton, *Ballad of the White Horse*.
18. Ward, *Gilbert Keith Chesterton*, 283.
19. Christopher Hollis, "G. K. Chesterton, 1874–1936," in Ian Scott-Kilvert, ed., *British Writers*, volume 6 (New York: Charles Scribner's Sons, 1983), 338. Hollis (1902–77) was educated at Eton and Balliol College, Oxford. For ten years (1925–35) he taught history at Stonyhurst College, and from 1935 to 1939 was a visiting professor at the University of Notre Dame in Indiana. He was the author of two books on Chesterton: *G. K. Chesterton* (London: Longmans, Green & Co., 1950), and *The Mind of Chesterton* (London: Hollis & Carter, London, 1970; and in America, Univ. of Miami Press, 1970).
20. Quoted in "Through the Poetic Hall of Fame," review of Theodore Maynard's book *Our Best Poets* (New York: Henry Holt & Co., 1922) in *The New York Times Book Review*, 31 December 1922, 42.
21. "New York and King Alfred," review of G. K. Chesterton, *Ballad of the White Horse*, *Review of Books* for *New York Times*, 4 February 1912.
22. Ibid.
23. Ibid.
24. Bernadette Sheridan, introduction to G. K. Chesterton, *The Ballad of the White Horse* (San Francisco: Ignatius Press, 2001), xxix.
25. Auden's assessment appears in ibid.
26. Wills, *Chesterton*, 170.
27. Chesterton, *Ballad of the White Horse*, viii.
28. Joseph Pearce, ed., "Tolkien and the Catholic Literary Revival," in *Tolkien—A Celebration: Collected Writings on a Literary Legacy* (San Francisco: Ignatius Press, 2001), 117. This book was originally published in Great Britain in 1999 by HarperCollins.
29. An airgraph from J. R. R. Tolkien to Christopher Tolkien, dated 3 September 1944, and published in Humphrey Carpenter, ed., *The Letters of J. R. R. Tolkien* (New York: Houghton Mifflin, 2000).
30. Chesterton, *Ballad of the White Horse*, viii.
31. Wills, *Chesterton*, 170.
32. See D. J. Conlon, ed., *G. K. Chesterton: The Critical Judgments 1900–1937* (Antwerp, Belgium: Antwerp Studies in Literature, 1976), 274. Baring's 7 September 1911 review of *The Ballad of the White Horse* for the *Eye-Witness* is given in full on pages 272–74.
33. Wills, *Chesterton*, 172.
34. Ibid., 172–73.
35. Garry Wills, "A Chesterton for the Religious Right," *Christian Century*, 16–23 May 1990, 532.
36. Graham Greene, as interviewed in the *Observer*, dated 12 March 1978. See also Pearce, *Wisdom and Innocence*, 166.

Chapter 17: Mr. Shaw's Insistent Demand

1. George Bernard Shaw to G. K. Chesterton, 30 October 1909, as quoted in Maisie Ward, *Gilbert Keith Chesterton* (New York: Sheed & Ward, 1943), 234.

2. Ward, *Gilbert Keith Chesterton*, 368.

3. Ibid., 226.

4. Ibid., 235.

5. Ibid., 239–40.

6. Joseph Pearce, *Wisdom and Innocence: A Life of G. K. Chesterton* (San Francisco: Ignatius Press, 1996), 198.

7. Ibid., 193.

8. Lawrence Gilman, "Drama and Music: Mr. Chesterton's 'Magic.' A New American Sonata. The Philharmonic's Seventy-Fifth Birthday," in the *North American Review*, vol. 205, No. 736 (March 1917): 455–61. This review article is posted online at: http://www.jstor.org/stable/25121497.

9. I am indebted to the following sources for the quotations used in the brief summary of *Magic* that I gave here: Dale Ahlquist, "Chesterton's play *Magic*," a lecture posted online by the American Chesterton Society; Julius West's critique of *Magic*, in *G. K. Chesterton: A Critical Study* (London: Martin Secker, 1915), 59–71; and lastly, Lawrence Gilman, "Drama and Music: Mr. Chesterton's 'Magic.' A New American Sonata. The Philharmonic's Seventy-Fifth Birthday," in *The North American Review* vol. 205, No. 736 (March 1917): 455–61. This review article is posted online at: http://www.jstor.org/stable/25121497.

10. Ada Chesterton, *The Chestertons* (London: Chapman and Hall, 1941), 134–35.

11. Ibid.

12. Pearce, *Wisdom and Innocence*, 194.

13. Ibid., 198.

14. Ward, *Gilbert Keith Chesterton*, 369.

15. For a complete overview of Bergman's production of Chesterton's play *Magic*, see Birgitta Steene, *Ingmar Bergman: A Reference Guide* (Amsterdam Univ. Press, 2005), 534–35. For the various revivals of *Magic*, see the following sources: "'Magic' is revived at the Gansevoort," review in the *New York Times*, 17 December 1929, 28. "'Magic' Seen in Dublin," review in the *New York Times* 14 March 1935, page 19 of the Amusements section. "Gossip of the Rialto," the *New York Times*, 21 June 1942, page X1 of the Drama, Screen, Music, Etc. section.

16. See "The Moods of Mr. George Moore," chapter 9 of *Heretics* (New York: John Lane Company, 1907), 131.

17. As quoted in Ward, *Gilbert Keith Chesterton*, 369.

18. From George Bernard Shaw's signed review of Julius West, *G. K. Chesterton: A Critical Study*, in the *New Statesman*, May 13, 1916.

19. "Chesterton Play Pleases," the *New York Times*, 8 November 1913, 5.

20. "A Miracle Play by Mr. Chesterton," review in the *New York Times*, 13 February 1917, 13.

21. "Second Thoughts on First Nights," review in the *New York Times*, 18 February 1917, X6 of the Arts and Leisure section. Of this production, the unnamed reviewer notes: "which Mrs. Hapgood presented last Monday at the Maxine Elliott."

22. Ibid.

23. Ibid.

Chapter 18: The Toast of London

1. "The Case Against Mr. Chesterton," review of Julius West, *G. K. Chesterton: A Critical Study*, 13 May 1916. The text of this review is reprinted in full in Brian Tyson, ed., *Bernard Shaw's Book Reviews Volume Two 1884 to 1950* (Pennsylvania State Univ. Press, 1996), 329.

2. A. G. Gardiner, *Prophets, Priests, and Kings* (London: J. M. Dent & Sons Ltd., 1914), 220–21.

3. Ibid. I am indebted to Joseph Pearce for drawing my attention to the significance of Gardiner's book. See Joseph Pearce, *Wisdom and Innocence: A Life of G. K. Chesterton* (San Francisco: Ignatius Press, 1996), 212–13.

4. Gardiner, *Prophets, Priests, and Kings*, 322–23.

5. Ibid., 323–24.

6. Here, I am indebted to a reflection penned by A. N. Wilson, who returned to the Christian faith after a lengthy period of atheist belief. "The real category mistake made by atheists," Wilson wrote, "is not about God, but about human beings. Turn to the Table Talk of Samuel Taylor Coleridge—'Read the first chapter of Genesis without prejudice and you will be convinced at once.... *The Lord God formed man of the dust of the ground, and breathed into his nostrils the breath of life.*' And then Coleridge adds: '*And man became a living soul.* Materialism will never explain those last words.'" Wilson's comments here are posted online as part of the article "Why I Believe Again"; see: http://www.newstatesman.com/religion/2009/04/conversion-experience-atheism.

7. Gardiner, *Prophets, Priests, and Kings*, 326–27.

8. Ibid., 328–29.

9. Gardiner, *Prophets, Priests, & Kings*, 339–40. Quote is from G. K. Chesterton, *The Defendant* (New York: Dodd, Mead & Company, 1904), 125–26 and 130–31.

   Historian David McCullough, speaking of President Harry Truman—a pioneering advocate of civil rights in integrating America's armed forces by executive order—once observed that coarse habits of the mouth prevalent in the time of Truman's youth marked his speech. The same was also the case with Chesterton. Even though he was passionately denouncing his country's treatment of Africans, Chesterton still originally used the "n-word" here when referring to people of African descent. It was an ugly and hurtful habit—speaking out though he was against Britain's oppression of Africans in her colonies. David McCullough's discussion of Truman's use of racial slurs appears in his audio lecture "Character Above All: Harry S. Truman," published on cassette by Simon & Schuster Audio in April 1996.

   It should also be said here that though Chesterton had close, cordial, lifelong friendships with many people of Jewish ethnicity, and denounced Hitler's treatment of Jews in Germany before his death in 1936, some things that he said and wrote have been called anti-Semitic. For full discussions of this subject, see Michael Coren's biography, *Gilbert: The Man Who Was G. K. Chesterton* (New York: Paragon House, 1990), 195–217. See also Pearce, *Wisdom and Innocence*, 436–51. Lastly, see William Oddie's article "The Philosemitism of G. K. Chesterton," which originally appeared in the November-December issue of *Faith* magazine (a UK publication). The entire text of this article appears online at: http://www.faith.org.uk/publications/Magazines/Nov08/Nov08CommentOnTheComments.html.

10. As quoted in Robert Isaac and Samuel Wilberforce, *The Life of William Wilberforce*, ed. Caspar Morris (Philadelphia: Henry Perkins, 1839), 507.

11. Gardiner, *Prophets, Priests, and Kings*, 331.
12. Ibid., 332.

Chapter 19: A Near Closing of the Curtain

1. G. K. Chesterton, as quoted in Maisie Ward, *Gilbert Keith Chesterton* (New York: Sheed & Ward, 1943), 385.
2. Special Cable to the *New York Times*, "G. K. Chesterton Dying," a 94-word news flash published on Sunday, 3 January 1915, page 1.
3. "Cecil Chesterton Here," the *New York Times* 13 January 1915, 7.
4. The information in this paragraph, and the quote therein, are taken from Joseph Pearce, *Wisdom and Innocence: A Life of G. K. Chesterton* (San Francisco: Ignatius Press, 1996), 213–14.
5. The information in this paragraph, and the quote therein, and the information in the paragraph preceding, are taken from Pearce, *Wisdom and Innocence*, 216–17.
6. Frances Chesterton, as quoted in Ward, *Gilbert Keith Chesterton*, 387.
7. Ibid., 389.
8. Ibid., 389.
9. George Bernard Shaw to G. K. Chesterton, as quoted in Ward, *Gilbert Keith Chesterton*, 390.
10. Ibid., 392.

Chapter 20: *What I Saw in America*

1. "G. K. Chesterton, 62, Noted Author, Dies," a 1,996-word obituary in the *New York Times*, Monday, 15 June 1936, page 1.
2. All of the information supplied in this paragraph, as well as the quotes therein, is taken from Joseph Pearce, *Wisdom and Innocence: A Life of G. K. Chesterton* (San Francisco: Ignatius Press, 1996), 254.
3. See Maisie Ward, *Gilbert Keith Chesterton* (New York: Sheed & Ward, 1943), 158. Here Shaw's description of Chesterton is as follows: "Chesterton is our 'Quinbus Flestrin,' the young Man Mountain, a large abounding gigantically cherubic person who is not only large in body and mind beyond all decency, but seems to be growing larger as you look at him."
4. As quoted in Ward, *Gilbert Keith Chesterton*, 563.
5. Ward, *Gilbert Keith Chesterton*, 563.
6. A description of G. K. and Frances Chesterton in Pearce, *Wisdom and Innocence*, 254.
7. All of the information supplied in this paragraph, as well as the quotes therein, is taken from Pearce, *Wisdom and Innocence*, 255.
8. "Mr. Chesterton," the *New York Times*, 12 January 1921, 14.
9. G. K. Chesterton, *What I Saw In America* (London: Hodder and Stoughton, 1922), 7.
10. Ibid., 14–15.
11. Ibid., 17–18.
12. Ibid., 33.
13. Ibid., 307–8.
14. All of the information supplied in this paragraph is taken from Pearce, *Wisdom and Innocence*, 255.
15. Ada Chesterton, *The Chestertons* (London: Chapman and Hall, 1941), 255–57.

Chapter 21: Saint Francis

1. G. K. Chesterton, *Varied Types* (New York: Dodd, Mead and Company, 1903), 63.
2. G. K. Chesterton, *St. Francis of Assisi* (London: Hodder & Stoughton 1923), 16.
3. The first American edition appeared in 1924, published in New York by the firm of George H. Doran Co.
4. G. K. Chesterton, *Orthodoxy* (New York: John Lane, 1909), 107.
5. G. K. Chesterton, *The Autobiography of G.K. Chesterton* (London: Hutchinson & Co., 1936), 94–95.
6. Chesterton, *St. Francis of Assisi*, 17.
7. Chesterton, *Varied Types*, 65.
8. Ibid., 66.
9. Ibid, 68. Here, Chesterton wrote: "The clear and tranquil life of the Three Vows had a fine and delicate effect on the genius of Francis. He was primarily a poet."
10. Ibid., 67.
11. Ibid., 67–68.
12. Maisie Ward, *Gilbert Keith Chesterton* (New York: Sheed & Ward, 1943), 477.
13. This quote and information supplied by Ward in *Gilbert Keith Chesterton*, 477.
14. This portion of the poem, "The Convert," appears in Ward, *Gilbert Keith Chesterton*, 477.
15. A quote given in Ward, *Gilbert Keith Chesterton*, 481.
16. Frederick Buechner, *Speak What We Feel* (New York: HarperCollins, 2001), 119.
17. Chesterton, *St. Francis of Assisi*, 90–91.
18. Ibid, 62–63.
19. Ibid., 98–99.
20. Ibid., 111.
21. Ibid., 101.
22. Chesterton, *Orthodoxy* (London: John Lane, 1909), 94–95.
23. Ibid., 96.
24. Chesterton, *St. Francis of Assisi*, 101–2.
25. Ward, *Gilbert Keith Chesterton*, 483.
26. G. K. Chesterton, *St. Francis of Assisi*, 87.
27. This sentence and the quote immediately preceding it are taken from Chesterton, *Varied Types*, 67–68.
28. Joseph Pearce, *Wisdom and Innocence: A Life of G. K. Chesterton* (San Francisco: Ignatius Press, 1996), 293.
29. Ward, *Gilbert Keith Chesterton*, 219.
30. Ibid.

Chapter 22: Over to You, Mr. Wells

1. A quote from Charles Gilmore, commandant of the Chaplain's School of the RAF during World War II, as cited in Joseph Pearce, *Wisdom and Innocence: A Life of G. K. Chesterton* (San Francisco: Ignatius Press, 1996), 311. See also Roger Lancelyn Green and Walter Hooper, *C. S. Lewis: A Biography* (London: Souvenir Press, 1987), 208.
2. Gilmore, as cited in Pearce, *Wisdom and Innocence*, 303.
3. H. G. Wells, *The Outline of History: Being a Plain History of Life and Mankind* (London: George Newnes Limited, 1919–1920), 24 vols. "Written with the advice and editorial help of Mr. Ernest Barker, Sir H. H. Johnston, Sir E. Ray Lankester,

and Professor Gilbert Murray." Complete in the scarce original 24 "Fortnightly Parts," bound in the original color pictorial paper wraps. Each part comprises 32 pages and is profusely illustrated throughout with black-and-white photographs and drawings, charts and maps, and 2 color plates (save for part 13, which has one color plate, as issued). Part 24 comprises pages 737–780 and includes an index, table of contents, and list of color plates.

4. Wells, *Outline of History*. The British edition was published in London by George Newnes Ltd in 1920.

5. See Pearce, *Wisdom and Innocence*, 304. Here Pearce states: "Wells's book had been published in separate sections, each of which had been attacked vehemently and vociferously by Belloc."

6. See Pearce, *Wisdom and Innocence*, 305.

7. As Maisie Ward wrote in *Gilbert Keith Chesterton* (New York: Sheed & Ward, 1943), 182: "Gilbert was not really concerned in this book [*Heretics*] to bang his contemporaries about so much as to study their mistakes and so discover what was wrong with modern thought." And on page 606 of the same work, Ward wrote: "Gilbert loved to praise his fellows in the field of letters even when their philosophy differed from his own."

8. Prefatory note to G. K. Chesterton, *The Everlasting Man*, fourth printing (New York: Dodd, Mead and Company, 1925).

9. Ward, *Gilbert Keith Chesterton*, 392, 604.

10. H. G. Wells, as quoted in Ward, *Gilbert Keith Chesterton*, 435. It should be stated here that there were occasional strains on the friendship between Wells and Chesterton. Wells could be prickly and hot-tempered at times, as Maisie Ward documents in her authoritative study. But she also demonstrates that Chesterton's capacity for the "soft answer that turns away wrath" always ensured that any irritability on Wells's part was mollified. Within an exchange of letters, their old intimacy was always quickly restored.

11. Chesterton, *The Everlasting Man*, xi.

12. Ibid., xxii–xxiii.

13. Ibid., 16–17.

14. Garry Wills, *Chesterton* (New York: Image/Doubleday Books, 2001), 228.

15. Chesterton, *The Everlasting Man*, 201.

16. Ibid., 201–2.

17. Ibid., 207–9.

18. William Lyon Phelps (1865–1943) attended Yale University (B.A., 1887; Ph.D., 1891) and Harvard University (M.A., 1891), taught at Harvard for a year, and then returned to Yale, where he was for forty-one years a member of the English department and Lampson professor from 1901 until his retirement in 1933. For years his students voted him Yale's most inspiring professor. This biographical information is taken from an *Encyclopedia Britannica* essay posted at: http://www .britannica.com/EBchecked/topic/455456/William-Lyon-Phelps.

19. William Lyon Phelps, as quoted in *The Collected Works of G. K. Chesterton, volume 2* (San Francisco: Ignatius Press, 1986), 7.

20. G. K. Chesterton, *Orthodoxy* (New York: John Lane, 1909), 13–14.

21. G. K. Chesterton, *William Blake* (London: Duckworth & Co., 1910), 210.

22. C. S. Lewis, *Surprised by Joy* (New York: Harcourt, Brace Jovanovich, 1955), 213–15.

23. Ibid., 191.
24. From C. S. Lewis, *The Essential C. S. Lewis*, ed. Lyle W. Dorsett (New York: Touchstone Books, 1996), 47.
25. *The Everlasting Man* became Lewis's favorite literary prescription for seekers interested in the truth-claims of Christianity. Sometimes he recommended Chesterton twice on the same day (as he did to Rhonda Bodle and Walden Howard 31 December 1947). In all, he referenced Chesterton eighteen times in his published correspondence, and *The Everlasting Man* nine times in his published correspondence.
26. C. S. Lewis to Charles Williams, 11 March 1936, in *The Collected Letters of C. S. Lewis*, volume 2 (San Francisco: HarperSanFrancisco, 2004), 183.
27. Lewis to N. Fridama, 15 February 1946, in *Collected Letters*, vol. 2, 702–703.
28. Lewis to Rhonda Bodle, 31 December 1947, in *Collected Letters*, vol. 2, 823.
29. Lewis to Corbin Scott Carnell, 10 December 1958, in *The Collected Letters of C. S. Lewis*, volume 3 (San Francisco: HarperOne, 2007), 995.
30. Lewis to Margaret Gray, written from Magdalene College, Cambridge, 9 May 1961. *Collected Letters*, volume 3, 1264.
31. Lewis to Walden Howard, 31 December 1947, in *Collected Letters* volume 2, 824.
32. C. S. Lewis to Sheldon Vanauken, 14 December 1950—a letter in the public domain and posted online at: http://www.catholiceducation.org/articles/arts/al0176.html.
33. C. S. Lewis to Sheldon Vanauken, 23 December 1950—a letter in the public domain and posted online at: http://www.catholiceducation.org/articles/arts/al0176.html. See chapter 14 of C. S. Lewis, *Surprised by Joy* (London: Geoffrey Bles, 1955). Lewis's comments here about the influence of George MacDonald and Chesterton toward his embrace of Christianity deserve to be quoted in full: "George MacDonald had done more to me than any other writer; of course it was a pity he had that bee in his bonnet about Christianity. He was good *in spite of it*. Chesterton had more sense than all the other moderns put together; bating, of course, his Christianity."
34. H. G. Wells, as quoted in Ward, *Gilbert Keith Chesterton*, 604–5.

Chapter 23: Chaucer

1. G. K. Chesterton, *Chaucer* (London: Faber & Faber Ltd., 1932). See also *The Collected Works of G. K. Chesterton*, volume 18 (San Francisco: Ignatius Press, 1991), 172.
2. Introduction to Harold Bloom, ed., *Geoffrey Chaucer's The Canterbury Tales*, part of Bloom's Modern Critical Views series (New York: Infobase Publishing, 2008), 1.
3. Peter Ackroyd, *Chaucer* (New York: Nan A. Talese, 2005), 83–84.
4. G. K. Chesterton, "The Little Birds Who Won't Sing," which first appeared in *Tremendous Trifles* (London: Methuen & Co., 1909), 195–201. Interestingly, from the standpoint of Chesterton's place in popular culture and literary circles, this essay was later included in E. V. Knox, ed., *On Running After One's Hat and Other Whimsies*, by G. K. Chesterton (New York: Robert M. McBride & Company, 1935). Knox selected the contents of this collection and was at this time the editor of the celebrated British magazine *Punch*.
5. Introduction, Harold Bloom, ed., *Geoffrey Chaucer's Canterbury Tales*, 1.
6. Ibid.
7. *Collected Works of G. K. Chesterton*, vol. 18, Carlyle, Tolstoy, Stevenson, Chaucer, 156.
8. Corinne Saunders, ed., *Chaucer*, part of the Blackwell Guides to Criticism series

(Oxford: Blackwell Publishers, Ltd., 2001), 11. Corinne Saunders is a professor in the Department of English Studies at the University of Durham in England. She specializes in medieval literature and has edited *The Blackwell Companion to Medieval Poetry.*

9. Jodi-Anne George, ed., *Geoffrey Chaucer: The General Prologue to the Canterbury Tales,* part of The Columbia Critical Guides series of scholarly monographs (New York: Columbia Univ. Press, 2000), 37–38.

10. *Collected Works of G. K. Chesterton,* vol. 18, 273–74.

11. G. K. Chesterton, *The Autobiography of G.K. Chesterton* (London: Hutchinson, 1936), 99–100. The other information presented here, which deals with Chesterton's time of study under W. P. Ker, has been gleaned from Jacqueline Banerjee's brief but excellent article on the Victorian Web, "G. K. Chesterton." This article, accessed 27 May 2010, is posted online at: http://www.victorianweb.org/authors/chesterton/bio.html.

12. *Collected Works of G. K. Chesterton,* vol. 18, 160–70.

13. Introduction, Harold Bloom, ed., *Geoffrey Chaucer's Canterbury Tales,* 1.

14. *Collected Works of G. K. Chesterton,* vol. 18, 172.

15. Ibid., 310.

16. Ibid., 173.

Chapter 24: The Pillar of the Apennines

1. Maisie Ward, *Gilbert Keith Chesterton* (New York: Sheed & Ward, 1943), 166.

2. Ibid., 367. Here, T. H. Lawrence is quoted as saying, "I have not met G. K. C.: Shaw always calls him a man of colossal genius."

3. These quotes regarding St. Thomas Aquinas appear in Brian Davies, ed., *Thomas Aquinas: Contemporary Philosophical Perspectives* (New York: Oxford Univ. Press, 2002), 3–4.

4. Such distinguished Thomist scholars as Étienne Gilson, Jacques Maritain, and Anton C. Pegis have all expressed their admiration for Chesterton's study of St. Thomas Aquinas. To this list might be added James A. Weisheipl, who wrote an appreciative review of Chesterton's book for the *Archives Internationales d'Histoire des Sciences.* Christopher Hollis has also written of Chesterton's unique contribution to Thomist studies through his book. For more, see Joseph Pearce, *Wisdom and Innocence: A Life of G. K. Chesterton* (San Francisco: Ignatius Press, 1996), 433–35.

5. This story is recounted in Ward, *Gilbert Keith Chesterton,* 619.

6. At the web site for *The Oxford Dictionary of National Biography,* see Bernard Bergonzi, "Chesterton, Gilbert Keith (1874–1936)," first published September 2004, http://dx.doi.org/10.1093/ref:odnb/32392.

7. Ward, *Gilbert Keith Chesterton,* 620.

8. Ibid. Maisie Ward wrote that Gilson's considered assessment first appeared in Cyril Clemens, *Chesterton as Seen by His Contemporaries* (Webster Groves, MO: Mark Twain Society, 1939), 150–51.

9. G. K. Chesterton, *St. Thomas Aquinas* (New York: Sheed & Ward, Inc., 1933), ix.

10. Ibid.

11. Ibid., x–xi.

12. Ibid., 19–20.

13. Ibid., 31–32.

14. Ibid., 55–58.
15. See D. J. Conlon, ed., *G. K. Chesterton: The Critical Judgments 1900–1937* (Antwerp: Antwerp Studies in Literature, 1976), 510–11. The full text of the TLS review of *Saint Thomas Aquinas* appears there.
16. Ibid.
17. Chesterton, *St. Thomas Aquinas*, 9.
18. Anton Charles Pegis (1905–78) completed his doctoral dissertation under Étienne Gilson at the University of Toronto. His was a distinguished academic career, during which he taught at Marquette University, Fordham University, and the University of Toronto. In 1950, Pegis was received into the prestigious Royal Society of Canada.
19. From Anton C. Pegis, "Appreciation" of Chesterton G. K. Chesterton, *St. Thomas: The Dumb Ox*" (New York: Image/Doubleday Books, 1956), xi–xii.

Chapter 25: Men Must Endure Their Going Hence

1. Maisie Ward, *Gilbert Keith Chesterton* (New York: Sheed & Ward, 1943), 646.
2. Ibid.
3. As reported in John Gross's review of Michael Ffinch, *G. K. Chesterton* (San Francisco: Harper & Row Publishers, 1986), which was published in "Books of the Times," in the 10 February 1987 edition of the *New York Times*.
4. Ward, *Gilbert Keith Chesterton*, 646.
5. Edward M. Kingsbury, "The Rewarding Autobiography of G. K. Chesterton," a 2,278-word review in the *New York Times*, Sunday, 8 November 1936, BR3.
6. Ibid.
7. Ibid.
8. G. K. Chesterton, *Autobiography*, fifth impression (London: Hutchinson & Co., 1936), 36.
9. Ibid., 31–34. Italics added.
10. Kingsbury, "Rewarding Autobiography."
11. Ibid.
12. Ibid.
13. This quote and all the information contained in this paragraph are taken from Joseph Pearce, *Wisdom and Innocence: A Life of G. K. Chesterton* (San Francisco: Ignatius Press, 1996), 473.
14. Maisie Ward, *Return to Chesterton* (London: Sheed & Ward, 1952), 268.
15. All the information contained in this paragraph has been gleaned from Pearce, *Wisdom and Innocence*, 477–78.
16. All the information regarding the circumstance of Chesterton's final illness has been gleaned from Pearce, *Wisdom and Innocence*, 478–79.
17. From an article published by Chesterton in the *Illustrated London News* on June 13, 1936.

Epilogue: A Near View of the Man as He Was

1. Historian and biographer Sir Arthur Bryant on Chesterton, as quoted in D. J. Conlon, ed., *G. K. Chesterton: The Critical Judgments 1900–1937* (Antwerp, Belgium: Antwerp Studies in Literature, 1976), 535. Bryant's tribute originally appeared in the *Illustrated London News*, 31 October 1936, 764.

2. John B. Kennedy, "The Ebullient Genius of G. K. Chesterton," in the *New York Times Book Review*, 28 June 1936, BR2 and BR22.

3. Much of the information for this story about Shaw was gleaned from St. John Irvine, *Bernard Shaw: His Life, Work and Friends* (New York: William Morrow and Company, 1956), 365.

4. T. S. Eliot's assessment of Chesterton in the *Criterion* is quoted in M. D. Aeschliman, "Chesterton's Marvelous Year," *National Review*, 14 July 2008. Aeschliman is a professor of education at Boston University.

5. Eliot's comments here originally appeared in "In Memory of Henry James," *Egoist*, vol.1, 1918. Eliot's jibe at Chesterton is quoted in Kristian Smidt, "T. S. Eliot's Criticism of Modern Prose Fiction," in *English Studies*, vol. 75, no. 1, January 1995, pp. 64–80.

6. Eliot's critique of Chesterton's book on Robert Louis Stevenson was published in the *Nation and Athenaeum*, 31 December 1927. See also Pearce, *Wisdom and Innocence*, 356.

7. Ibid.

8. This praise of Chesterton by Eliot was originally published in the *New English Weekly* (VII. 18, 1935). This quote from Eliot appears in Smidt, "T. S. Eliot's Criticism."

9. G. K. Chesterton, *The Thing: A Collection of Ephemeral Papers*, chapter 2, "The Sceptic as Critic" (London: Sheed & Ward, 1929). In this essay Chesterton is referring to T. S. Eliot's article "The Humanism of Irving Babbitt," the *Forum*, July 1928.

10. Eliot's obituary appears in the *Tablet*, 20 June 1936, p. 785. The text of this obituary is given in full in D. J. Conlon, ed., *G. K. Chesterton: The Critical Judgments (1900–1937)* (Antwerp, Belgium: Antwerp Studies in English Literature, 1976), 531–32.

11. This praise of Chesterton by Eliot was originally published in the *New English Weekly* (VII. 18, 1935). This quote from Eliot appears in the article Smidt, "T. S. Eliot's Criticism."

12. The *Tablet*, 20 June 1936, 785.

13. Ibid.

14. Ibid.

15. Ibid.

16. Ibid.

17. Ibid.

18. Ibid.

19. Ibid.

20. Eliot's assessment of Chesterton in the *Criterion* is quoted in M. D. Aeschliman, "Chesterton's Marvelous Year," *National Review*, 14 July 2008.

21. The line "with halting steps and slow" is taken from "The Messenger," a poem by Mary Bassett Clarke (Ida Fairfield), published in *Autumn Leaves* (Buffalo, NY: Charles Wells Moulton, 1895), 100. The quote applied here to Chesterton is taken from G. K. Chesterton, *George Bernard Shaw* (New York: John Lane Company, 1909), 101–2.

A Chesterton Timeline

1. The publication dates given here are for the British editions of Chesterton's books.

Bibliography

Nearly all of the books listed here are cited in the book. However, the bibliography is not a complete record of all the works and sources listed in the notes.

Bergonzi, Bernard. "G. K. Chesterton," *The Oxford Dictionary of National Biography* (2004).

Chesterton, G. K. *The Autobiography of G. K. Chesterton*. fifth impression. London: Hutchinson & Co., 1936.

——, *Orthodoxy*. New York: Doubleday, 2001. Introduction by Philip Yancey.

Conlon, D. J., ed. *G. K. Chesterton: The Critical Judgments*. Antwerp: Universitaire Faculteiten, 1976.

——, ed. *G. K. Chesterton: A Half Century of Views*. Oxford: Oxford University Press, 1987.

Coren, Michael. *Gilbert: The Man Who Was G. K. Chesterton*. New York: Paragon House, 1990.

Dale, Alzina Stone. *The Outline of Sanity: A Life of G. K. Chesterton*. Grand Rapids, Michigan: William B. Eerdmans, 1982.

Ffinch, Michael. *G. K. Chesterton: A Biography*. San Francisco: Harper and Row, 1986.

Hollis, C. *The Mind of Chesterton*. London: Hollis & Carter, 1970.

Kenner, Hugh. *Paradox in Chesterton*. London: Sheed & Ward, 1948.

Oddie, William. *Chesterton and the Romance of Orthodoxy: The Making of G. K. C. 1874–1908*. New York: Oxford University Press, 2009.

Sullivan, John *G. K. Chesterton: A Bibliography*. London: University of London, 1958.

——, *Chesterton Continued: A Bibliographical Supplement*. London: University of London, 1968.

Ward, Maisie. *Gilbert Keith Chesterton*. New York and London: Sheed & Ward, 1943.

——, "Gilbert Keith Chesterton," the original essay for *The Dictionary of National Biography* (1949).

West, Julius. *G. K. Chesterton: A Critical Study*. London: Martin Secker, 1915.

Wills, Garry. *Chesterton*. New York: Image/Doubleday, 2001.

About the Author

Kevin Belmonte holds a B.A. in English Literature from Gordon College, an M.A. in Church History from Gordon-Conwell Seminary, and a second master's degree in American and New England Studies from the University of Southern Maine (Portland).